HANDBOOK
on the
CONSTITUTIONS
of the
UNITED STATES
and
GEORGIA

HANDBOOK on the CONSTITUTIONS of the UNITED STATES and GEORGIA

By

MERRITT B. POUND

and

ALBERT B. SAYE

DEPARTMENT OF POLITICAL SCIENCE
UNIVERSITY OF GEORGIA

TENTH EDITION

UNIVERSITY OF GEORGIA PRESS
ATHENS 1975

Printed in the United States of America

Foreword
(to first edition)

The General Assembly of Georgia passed the following act in the year 1923:

> . . . all schools and colleges in this State that are sustained or in any manner supported by public funds shall give instruction in the essentials of the United States Constitution and the Constitution of Georgia, including the study of and devotion to American institutions and ideals, and no student in said schools and colleges shall receive a certificate of graduation without previously passing a satisfactory examination upon the provisions and principles of the United States Constitution and the Constitution of the State of Georgia.

For the benefit of students not exempted from this requirement by course credit, the University of Georgia offers examinations over the two Constitutions on the first Thursday after Washington's birthday.

In 1936 Dr. Albert B. Saye prepared a pamphlet in mimeographed form for use in connection with a series of lectures designed to aid students in preparing for these examinations. The original pamphlet entitled *Outline and Questions on the Constitutions of the United States and the State of Georgia*, of which this booklet is an outgrowth, was published in printed form in 1940 and again in 1942.

The adoption by the people of Georgia of the Constitution of 1945 necessitated a revision of the outline and questions on the Constitution of Georgia. It was decided by Dr. Saye, the original author, to expand beyond the outline stage and to include within the expanded booklet the actual texts of the Constitutions of the United States and of Georgia with discussions of the provisions of these documents. The undersigned was invited to collaborate and is responsible for the sections devoted to the Constitution of the United States. The sections applying to the Constitution of Georgia were prepared by Dr. Saye.

This handbook is offered to the students of the University System of Georgia and to the citizens of Georgia with the hope that it will aid them to an intelligent understanding of the constitutional principles under which our national and state governments operate.

MERRITT B. POUND

Athens, Georgia
November, 1945

Preface

Tenth Edition

In the revision of this *Handbook*, minor changes, including the addition of Amendments XXIV, XXV, and XXVI, have been made in Part I relating to the Constitution of the United States. Part II, dealing with the Constitution of Georgia, has been revised extensively.

Amendments to the Constitution of Georgia of statewide application have been inserted in the body of the document at the appropriate place, followed in each case by an editorial note. Local amendments (*i.e.*, amendments affecting directly only a particular political subdivision, such as a city, county, or school district, or two or more such subdivisions) are not indicated in the copy of the Constitution presented here. For citations to these local amendments, see the *Table of Amendments to the Constitution of Georgia* published in 1973 by the Institute of Government of the University of Georiga, Athens, Ga.

Suggestions for revision in this *Handbook* made by both teachers and students have been helpful. We welcome further suggestions.

A.B.S.

CONTENTS

PART I

THE CONSTITUTION OF THE UNITED STATES

PART II

THE CONSTITUTION OF GEORGIA

PART I

The Constitution of the United States

Introduction

HISTORICAL BACKGROUND

Political institutions result from an evolutionary growth. Thus most American political institutions have their origin in the constitutional history of England prior to the 18th Century. The American Revolution did not produce an immediate and drastic change in the forms of local government; it only severed the political tie that bound the colonies to the Mother Country. Separated from England by time and space the American colonists developed self reliance. Gradually social, economic, religious and political differences appeared. It was but natural that the colonies should seek independence.

From the day the Mayflower arrived in Plymouth Bay in 1620 a series of political incidents occurred which became antecedents of modern American government. Even before the Pilgrims had gone ashore they drew up an agreement known as the Mayflower Compact. This marks the beginning of cooperative political action on the part of individual English colonists in the New World. In 1639 the river towns of the Connecticut Valley drew up the Fundamental Orders of Connecticut, the first written constitution in history by which a government came into existence. In 1641 the Massachusetts Body of Liberties became the first law code drawn up on North American soil. The four New England colonies in 1643 formed a cooperative agreement among themselves called the New England Confederation for protection from the Indians. It was the first cooperative agreement between colonies. In 1754 an attempt was made at Albany to draw all of the colonies into a closer union and Benjamin Franklin presented a plan of union which was rejected. After the treaty of peace ending the French and Indian War (1763) England changed her commercial policy. A stamp tax, levied on several commodities, aroused bitter opposition in the colonies and a Stamp Act Congress was assembled to protest this tax. The stamp tax was repealed but events were rapidly leading to the break. In 1774 all of the colonies except Georgia sent representatives to the First Continental Congress. Again protests against grievances were sent to the English crown.

In 1775 there assembled in Philadelphia representatives of all the colonies in the Second Continental Congress. Though this Congress had no legal basis it became a *de facto* government and the first national government of the United States. By the Declaration of Independence (1776) it proclaimed the thirteen colonies independent of English control and proceeded to raise an army, appoint a commander-in-chief, borrow money and negotiate treaties—things only a government can do. The common stress of the times made the *de facto* system of government work, but it was realized that it could be only a temporary expedient.

ARTICLES OF CONFEDERATION

On June 7, 1776, simultaneously with his resolution of independence, Richard Henry Lee offered a resolution in the Continental Congress to form a confederation. His resolution was adopted on June 11 and a committee was appointed to prepare a plan. The Articles of Confederation were adopted by Congress on November 15, 1777, but they provided for unanimous state acceptance and were not ratified by Maryland, the last state to agree, until March 1, 1781.

The Articles of Confederation established the first *de jure* national government and became the first written constitution of the United States. This constitution served from March 2, 1781, until the present constitution was ratified and became effective in 1789. There were thirteen articles and, as the title implies, they created a confederate government. Article I stated: "The title of this Confederacy shall be 'The United States of America'." Article II left no doubt as to the nature of the new government. "Each State retains its sovereignty, freedom and independence. . . . " In the preamble the new constitution was called "Articles of Confederation and perpetual Union," but Article III weakened this definition somewhat by the statement that the states had entered "a firm league of friendship with each other...."

Article IV contained several provisions which were carried over almost verbatim into the present constitution. "Free inhabitants of each of these States . . . shall be entitled to all privileges and immunities of free citizens in the several States. . . ." It also provided for rendition of fugitives and ended with the following clause: "Full faith and credit shall be given in each of these States to the records, acts and judicial proceedings of the courts and magistrates of every other State."

Article V provided for a Congress of one chamber to be composed of from two to seven delegates from each state annually appointed. Regardless of the number of delegates a state decided to send to Congress each state had only one vote.

Article VI imposed limitations upon the states. There were to be no treaties without the consent of Congress or interference with treaties entered into by the United States. No vessels of war should be kept in time of peace except as Congress approved, nor should any state engage in war without this consent.

Article VII placed the land forces under the states with the right of each state to appoint all officers within its forces up to and including the rank of colonel. Though Article IX conferred on Congress the sole and exclusive right of determining on war and peace, Article VII definitely put the national government in the position of having to rely upon the states for its armed forces.

Article VIII placed upon the states the obligation of contributing to all national expenses in proportion to the land values in each state but gave no power to Congress to collect these obligations, saying, "The taxes for paying that proportion shall be laid and levied by the authority and direction of the Legislatures of the several States. . . ."

Article IX, the longest of the thirteen, enumerated the powers of Congress but no important power was to be exercised "unless nine States assent to the same." Under this limitation legislation was often defeated, even though unopposed, by the absence of delegates.

In Article X a committee of the states was provided for which could exercise such powers in a recess of Congress as Congress saw fit to vest in this committee. However, no powers requiring the votes of the delegates of nine states could thus be exercised.

Article XI was an invitation to Canada to membership in the Confederation.

Article XII recognized all obligations incurred by Congress before the ratification of the Articles as valid debts against the United States.

Article XIII provided that amendments to the Articles must be agreed to in Congress and confirmed by the legislatures of all the states.[1]

Certain defects of the Articles of Confederation are obvious. The absence of a strong national government reflected the jealousy of the states of their recent independence. Serving as the constitution of the United States during the period commonly known as "The critical period in American History" the Articles, nevertheless, had some definite accomplishments. The country was kept united. The peace treaty with England was negotiated and signed. The Northwest Ordinance of 1787, the basis of

1. *Documents Illustrative of the Formation of the Union of the American States.* House Doc. No. 398, 69th Congress, 1st Session (Washington, 1927), 27-37.

territorial regulation to the present day, was adopted, and the antecedents of executive departments were created.

Weaknesses were many. There was a President of the Congress of the United States, but no clearly defined executive department and no national system of courts. The states were completely sovereign and alone had jurisdiction over individuals. Requisitions for money and troops were made on the states. It was government by supplication. Congress could not regulate interstate commerce and the difficulties of amending the Articles were great.

THE FEDERAL CONVENTION

The inability of Congress under the Articles of Confederation to regulate interstate commerce resulted in controversies between the states. Maryland and Virginia were having trouble over navigation on the Potomac River. Maryland claimed that under its original charter the south bank of the river was its southern boundary and placed restrictions on the use of the river by Virginia. Virginia countered by imposing duties on goods entering the Chesapeake bound for Maryland. The two states agreed to discuss these difficulties by conference and five delegates, three from Maryland, two from Virginia, met at Alexandria in 1785. They adjourned to Mount Vernon at Washington's invitation and there reached an amicable agreement. However, it was decided by the delegates that since interstate controversies were also plaguing the other members of the Confederation all of the states should be invited to send delegates to a similar conference at Annapolis in 1786. The legislatures of Virginia and Maryland issued such an invitation. Only five states were represented when this second conference convened, but out of it came the suggestion that all states select delegates to attend a convention in Philadelphia for the purpose of discussing revision of the Articles of Confederation. Among those present at Annapolis were Alexander Hamilton of New York and James Madison of Virginia. The date of the convention was set for May 14, 1787, but it was not until May 25 that a quorum had arrived and the convention began its sessions.

Every state, with the exception of Rhode Island, selected delegates. Only fifty-five actually appeared at any of the sessions though more were designated to attend. Twenty-nine delegates were present at the opening session. The average attendance was about forty. Thirty-nine delegates, representing twelve states, signed the Constitution as it was finally adopted.

Among the prominent delegates who played leading parts in

the deliberations were George Washington, Edmund Randolph and James Madison of Virginia; Benjamin Franklin, James Wilson and Gouverneur Morris of Pennsylvania; Alexander Hamilton of New York; and William Patterson of New Jersey.

On the whole the delegates were property owners and shareholders in the defunct confederate government. Many of them had vested interests in a strong government able to protect property rights and investments. There were few representatives of the small farming and mechanic classes. Of the fifty-five delegates who attended one or more sessions, forty were holders of public securities; fourteen were speculating in lands; and fifteen were slaveholders. Most of the members were experienced in government and many had been members of the Continental Congress. It was a well educated group with at least twenty-four college graduates among its membership. Thirty-one delegates were trained in the law. The membership, on the whole, was young and vigorous, the average age of the members being about forty. There were, however, older statesmen present such as Franklin and Washington. The chaotic conditions of the years following the Revolution had convinced the majority of the members that a strong national government was a necessity.

George Washington, the best known and most highly respected American, was chosen to preside at the convention. Most delegates were instructed only to discuss revision of the Articles of Confederation, but it was early decided to present to the states for approval an entirely new constitution. Meetings of the convention were secret and voting was by states.

The Virginia delegation had prepared its plan of union prior to the opening session of the convention. It was presented by Edmund Randolph and is known as the Randolph, the Virginia, or the Large State Plan. Under this plan the national government was to be greatly strengthened and an entirely new machinery of government was to be established. It called for a national executive, a national tribunal, and a bicameral legislature with proportional representation in each chamber.

The Large State Plan, with its provision for proportional representation in Congress, met with opposition from the delegates of the small states who presented a plan known as the Patterson, the New Jersey, or the Small State Plan. It was presented by William Patterson of New Jersey. By this plan only the glaring defects of the Articles of Confederation were to be corrected. Congress was to remain a unicameral body with equal state representation.

There was a high degree of unanimity among the delegates

that the national government should be strengthened, but compromises were necessary because of the difference in size and the social and economic interests of the various states. The Connecticut delegates presented the compromise between the Large and the Small State Plans. Known at the Connecticut Compromise, or Great Compromise, it called for the present form of Congress, namely, a House of Representatives with representation proportional to population, and a Senate with equal state representation.

Sectional differences were also in evidence. A difference of opinion arose between the northern states and the southern slaveholding states as to the counting of slaves for representation in the House of Representatives. A later decision to apportion direct taxes among the states in proportion to population gave a basis for another compromise. It was decided by the Three-fifths Compromise that three-fifths of the slave population should be counted both for representation and direct taxes.

Lack of control of interstate commerce, it has been pointed out several times, was a glaring defect of the Articles of Confederation. Nevertheless, the southern states were reluctant to give Congress the power to control commerce without some assurance that the slave trade should not be interfered with under this power or southern exports penalized. A compromise gave Congress the broad power to regulate foreign and interstate commerce but denied it the right to place duties on exports or to interfere with the slave trade prior to 1808.

A single elective executive, to be known as the President, was agreed upon, and a federal court system was provided for. Ratification was to be by conventions in the states. Ratification by nine states was necessary to make the new constitution effective.

Thirty-nine delegates representing twelve states signed the completed document on September 17, 1787, each subordinating certain personal opinions to the combined wisdom of the majority of the delegates.

CAMPAIGN FOR RATIFICATION

The campaign for ratification revealed opposition in several key states, namely, Virginia, Pennsylvania, Massachusetts and New York. Among the objections raised were: there was no bill of rights or protection of the individual from the assumption of powers on the part of the nation government; the national government was too strong; or, the national government was too weak. Nevertheless, the friends of ratification proved strongest and eleven states, two more than the necessary minimum, had ratified in convention in time for the election of President Washington and his inauguration on April 30, 1789. Rhode Island and North Carolina alone held out. In New York, where opposition was great, Alexander Hamilton, James Madison and John Jay in a series of published articles signed "Publius" and known collectively as *The Federalist*, or *The Federalist Paper*, were influential in getting the document approved.

FUNDAMENTAL PRINCIPLES OF THE CONSTITUTION

Among the cardinal principles of the Constitution is that of popular sovereignty and limited government. This means that ultimately all government is subject to the will of the people and that the people, acting through their elected representatives, can amend the fundamental law. Specific limitations are placed upon the national government in Article I, Section 9, and in Articles of Amendment I-VIII, XIII, XV, and XIX. Prohibitions are placed upon the states in Article I, Section 10, and in Amendments XIII, XIV, and XIX. Article IV, Section 4, imposes the obligation upon the national government of guaranteeing republican government to the states.

By means of the Constitution a federal government was created. A government of the federal type is one in which there is a distribution of powers in the fundamental law between the national and state governments. The national government is one of delegated powers and the states have reserved and inherent powers. In the United States, in the case of a conflict of powers, the Supreme Court is the final arbiter.

In its designated field the national government is supreme. The Constitution of the United States is the supreme law of the land. Any other law in conflict, national or state, is void. Citizens of the United States are thus bound by the following laws, each of which must conform to all of those above it: the Constitution of the United States, laws and treaties of the United States made in pursuance of the Constitution, state constitutions and state laws. It is the duty of the judiciary to uphold the supreme law.

Under the Articles of Confederation there was no national judiciary and the executive and legislative branches were not separate. One of the principles of the Constitution is the separation of powers. Congress makes the laws, the executive enforces them, the courts interpret them and punish offenders for their violation. Each of these three coordinate branches of the national government is distinct in personnel and officials can hold office in only one branch. In order to prevent either of the three branches from assuming an undue proportion of powers, it is provided that there shall be checks and balances. The President can check Congress by means of his veto; the courts can check Congress by means of judicial review of legislation; Congress can check the courts by its powers of impeachment, and by the same power can check the executive branch; Congress has an additional check on the executive in that the Senate must ratify treaties and confirm appointments; Congress, also, by its right of initiating constitutional amendments, can overcome the effects of judicial decisions.

America's unique contribution to constitutional government is the doctrine of judicial review of legislation. This means that any law passed by a legislative body, either Congress or a state legislature, may be subjected to review and interpretation by the courts. When Congress oversteps its delegated or implied powers, when a state encroaches on the powers of the national government, or when either a state or the national government abrogates guaranteed civil liberties, the federal judiciary may declare the act unconstitutional, invalid and void. Other laws, not necessarily unconstitutional, are also subject to judicial interpretation and subsequently mean what the courts say they mean even if such meaning was not in the intent of the legislative body enacting the law. This power of the judiciary to review and interpret is not specifically stated in the Constitution. The practice, however, was followed in the colonial period of our history. Two early cases involving this principle were *Holmes* vs. *Walton*, decided in the New Jersey courts in 1780, and *Trevett* vs. *Weeden*, a Rhode Island decision of 1786. In the famous case of *Marbury* vs. *Madison* in 1803 the Supreme Court of the United States declared an act of Congress unconstitutional and proclaimed the doctrine of judicial review. In 1810 in the case of *Fletcher* vs. *Peck* an act of the General Assembly of Georgia was declared void, and in 1816 in *Martin* vs. *Hunter's Lessee*, a case appealed from the Virginia courts, the power of the federal courts to review and reverse the decisions of state courts was enunciated.

The Constitution of the United States is brief, simple, and was beautifully worded by the Committee on Style under the chairmanship of Gouverneur Morris of Pennsylvania. It possesses definiteness in principle, yet elasticity in details. Its framers were not primarily interested in theory; consequently there are conspicuous omissions. No bill of rights was originally attached and the question as to the residence of sovereignty in the new federal Union was avoided. A bill of rights, consisting of the first ten amendments, was added in 1791. A bloody civil war decided the

Union to be indestructible. Many Supreme Court decisions have given meaning to obscure and controversial provisions. In addition to the bill of rights, eleven amendments have been added to change the original document.

A distinction should be drawn between the "formal" Constitution and the "real" or "living" Constitution. The formal document is composed of seven articles and twenty-one articles of amendment and may be changed in accordance with the provisions of Article V. The "real" Constitution, however, is said to grow in three other ways, namely, by those acts of Congress which change the structure of our national government, by decisions of the federal courts having a similar effect, and by usage.

Illustrations of growth by statuory amplification are the ten executive departments which have been created by acts of Congress, the present membership of 435 in the House of Representatives, and the establishment of federal courts other than the Supreme Court. The real Constitution has grown by judicial interpretation in many ways. Two illustrations are the doctrine of implied powers announced in the *McCulloch* vs. *Maryland* decision in 1819 and the doctrine of judicial review proclaimed in 1803 in the case of *Marbury* vs. *Madison*. Growth by usage may be illustrated by the development of the party system and the method of nominating presidential candidates.

THE CONSTITUTION AS AN OBJECTIVE DOCUMENT

As originally adopted the Constitution of the United States is a document of a preamble and seven relatively short articles. The preamble states: "We the people of the United States, in order to form a more perfect Union, establish justice, insure domestic tranquility, provide for the common defense, promote the general welfare, and secure the blessings of liberty to ourselves and our posterity, do ordain and establish this Constitution for the United States of America." The preamble states purposes only and does not confer any powers. It is therefore not generally considered subject to judicial interpretation. However, in the preamble to the Articles of Confederation each of the states to make up the Confederacy was enumerated. As any nine states could make the Constitution operative such enumeration in it was impossible. In the period prior to the Civil War when the major political debates were as to the nature of the Union, the meaning of the words "We the people" was often examined. Was the United States a union of sovereign states, or was it a national union of "the people of the United States"? The nationalist view was ultimately triumphant.[2]

ARTICLE I. It is composed of ten sections and is more than half of the total document in length. If titles had been assigned to the articles this would have been most likely designated "The Legislative Department". Section 1 provides for a bicameral Congress consisting of the House of Representatives and the Senate. Section 2 provides for membership in the House of Representatives, how and by whom elected, term of office, qualifications, apportionment among the several states, enumeration of the number of Representatives each state should originally have, method of filling vacancies, the power of choosing officers, and the power of impeachment.

Section 3 describes the Senate, its membership, how and by whom chosen, qualifications, the President of the Senate, his right to vote, other officers and how chosen, and the power to try impeachments. It should be noted that Clause 1 states that Senators shall be chosen by the state legislatures but that direct election by the people has been substituted by Amendment XVII.

Section 4 confers on the states the right to prescribe the times, places and manner of holding elections for Congress but gives Congress the right to alter such regulations. Under this provision Congress has decreed that Congressional elections shall take place on the Tuesday following the first Monday in November of even years and that Representatives shall be elected from Congressional Districts. This section also calls for an annual meeting of Congress on the first Monday in December until a different date is set by law. Amendment XX, ratified in 1933, changed the date of the annual meeting to January 3.

Section 5 deals with the powers of each House over its membership and the rules of legislative procedure.

Section 6 discusses the compensation, privileges and disqualification of members of Congress.

Section 7 confers upon the House of Representatives the right to originate revenue bills, and contains provisions as to orders, concurrent resolutions, and the overriding of a Presidential veto.

Section 8 contains eighteen clauses. The first seventeen are the enumerated powers of Congress. Clause 18 is the "necessary and proper", or "the elastic", clause, a loose construction or liberal interpretation of which by the Supreme Court is the basis of the implied powers of Congress. This doctrine of "implied powers" was first enunciated by the Supreme Court in the

---

2. See *Texas* vs. *White* (1869), 7 Wallace 700.

famous case of *McCulloch* vs. *Maryland* in 1819. It is safe to say that if Congress today were limited to the enumerated powers it could not do a majority of the things it does.

The words "Negro" and "slave" are not to be found in the Constitution though Negro slavery was a recognized institution.

Section 9 prohibits Congress from interfering with the slave trade prior to the year 1808. It further states that the writ of *habeas corpus* shall not be suspended except in case of rebellion or invasion; that no bill of attainder nor *ex post facto* law shall be passed; that no direct taxes shall be levied unless apportioned among the states on the basis of population; that no export taxes shall be levied; that imports shall be uniform; that no money shall be withdrawn from the treasury except by legal appropriation; and that no titles of nobility shall be granted. Clause 4, prohibiting direct taxes unless apportioned on the basis of population, was modified by Amendment XVI which gave Congress the right to levy income taxes without apportionment.

Section 10 places limitations upon the states similar to those placed upon Congress in Section 9 and, in addition, denies to the states the right to enter any treaties or alliances, coin money, make anything but gold and silver coin legal tender, lay duties on imports or exports, or without the consent of Congress, keep troops and ships in time of peace.

ARTICLE II. This article might be entitled "The Executive Department". It provides in Section 1 for the office of President, his term of office, how elected, qualifications, on whom his duties devolve in case of removal or death, his compensation and oath of office. In Section 2 the President is named Commander-in-Chief. He is given the power to require opinions of the heads of executive departments. He is given powers of appointment and pardon and the right to make treaties. Section 3 confers upon him the right to communicate with Congress, call Congress into session or adjourn it in case of disagreement between the Houses, receive ambassadors, and commission officers of the United States. He is charged with the duty of seeing that the laws are faithfully executed. He shall be removed on conviction of crime.

ARTICLE III. This article might naturally be entitled "The Judicial Department". Section 1 proclaims "The judicial power of the United States shall be vested in one Supreme Court, and such inferior courts as the Congress may from time to time ordain and establish." The framers did not attempt to set up the details of our judicial system but left them to the decision of Congress. The judges, however, of whatever courts Congress has created or shall create shall hold their offices during good behavior and receive a compensation which shall not be diminished during their continuance in office. As a result of the wording of this section all members of the federal judiciary hold their positions for life unless they resign or are convicted on impeachment charges. In addition to the Supreme Court composed of nine justices Congress has established Circuit Courts of Appeal, District Courts, and other special federal courts. Section 2 confers upon the Supreme Court original jurisdiction in all cases involving ambassadors, other public ministers, and consuls, and in cases in which a state is a party. The judicial power shall extend to all cases in law and equity arising under the Constitution, the laws of the United States, or treaties. All trial of crimes, except in cases of impeachment, shall be by jury. Section 3 defines treason and gives Congress the power to declare punishment for this crime.

ARTICLE IV. This article is often called the "Full faith and credit" article, or "Relations between the states." It proclaims in Section 1 that "Full faith and credit shall be given in each state to the public acts, records, and judicial proceedings of every other State." Section 2 provides that citizens of each state shall be accorded all of the privileges and immunities of citizens in all other states and that fugitives from justice shall be delivered to the officers of the state in which the crime was allegedly committed. Section 3 makes provision for the admission of new states. Section 4 outlines some of the obligations of the United States towards the states. Each state shall be guaranteed a republican form of government and shall be protected from invasion and, upon request, from domestic violence.

ARTICLE V. This is an article of only one paragraph and is devoted to the amending process. Two methods of proposal and two methods of ratification are provided, making, in different combinations of proposal and ratification, four possible methods of constitutional amendment. Until the ratification of Amendment XXI in 1933 only one method had been used, namely, proposal by two-thirds of both Houses of Congress and ratification by the legislatures of three-fourths of the states. The Twenty-first Amendment, however, contained within itself the provision that it should be ratified by conventions in three-fourths of the states. Thus, two methods have now been used. A limitation was placed upon amendments to clause 1 and 4 of Article I, Section 9, until the year 1808, and a permanent restriction was placed on any amendment to the Constitution which would deprive any state of its equal suffrage in the Senate without its consent. The issue has not yet arisen but it is quite doubtful that any provision within a constitutional document designed to prohibit amendment could be enforced.

Article VI. This is sometimes called "The Supreme law of the land" article as the Constitution is so described in it. Debts contracted prior to the adoption of the Constitution are declared valid. This article also requires all federal and state officers to take an oath or affirmation to support the Constitution but declares there shall never be a religious test for holding federal office.

Article VII. This article, the schedule of ratification, has accomplished its purpose and is no longer operative. "The ratification of the conventions of nine states shall be sufficient for the establishment of this Constitution between the States so ratifying the same." It should be noted that ratification was by conventions in the states called for that purpose and not by either the state legislatures or the people of the states by direct vote.

AMENDMENTS TO THE CONSTITUTION OF THE UNITED STATES

Bill of Rights. It will be recalled that one of the objections raised to the Constitution was that there were not within it sufficient safeguards against the assumption by the national government of arbitrary power over the individual citizen. Some who were opposed on these grounds were persuaded to support ratification by the promise that an early attempt would be made to amend the Constitution to provide such safeguards. James Madison, who had been elected to the House of Representatives, accordingly proposed a series of amendments in that body during its first session. Seventeen were adopted by the House and twelve of these received the assent of the Senate. Two of them failed of ratification by the legislatures of three-fourths of the states but the remaining ten became effective on November 3, 1791. These first ten amendments are known as the Bill of Rights and, because of their adoption so closely following the adoption of the Constitution itself, are generally considered almost a part of the original document. The first eight of these amendments deal with specific individual rights. The last two are more general in application. The Bill of Rights as a whole guarantees such substantive rights as freedom of speech, of religion and of the press, and such procedural rights as trial by jury and speedy and public trials.

Amendment XI. The amendment was proposed as a result

of the case of *Chisholm* vs. *Georgia* in which a citizen of South Carolina secured a judgment against Georgia. It provides that a state can no longer be compelled to defend itself in the federal courts against a citizen of another state.

AMENDMENT XII. In the election of 1800 Jefferson and Burr received the same number of electoral votes for President because of the provision in Article II that each elector should cast two votes without indicating which was for President and which for Vice-President. To prevent a repetition the manner of casting electoral votes was changed so that each elector shall cast one vote for President and one for Vice-President.

AMENDMENT XIII. This, the first of the Civil War amendments, abolished slavery. It was declared ratified in 1865.

AMENDMENT XIV. This, the second of the Civil War amendments, has been the source of much litigation and interpretation. Section 1 constitutionally defines citizenship for the first time and adds that "No State shall make or enforce any law which shall abridge the privilege or immunities of citizens of the United States; nor shall any State deprive any person of life, liberty, or property, without due process of law; nor deny to any person within its jurisdiction the equal protection of the laws." Section 2 was a threat to the South in that it was an attempt to force enfranchisement of the Negroes on these states under penalty of having membership in the House of Representatives curtailed in proportion to the number of citizens not allowed to vote. Section 3 permitted Congress to remove the disabilities incurred by Southerners for participation in the Confederacy. Section 4 made invalid any debts incurred in support of the rebellion against the United States or claims for the loss of slaves.

AMENDMENT XV. The third and last Civil War amendment prohibits the denial of the suffrage on account of race, color, or previous condition of servitude.

AMENDMENT XVI. Article I, Section 9, clause 4 of the Constitution provides that "No capitation or other direct tax shall be laid, unless in proportion to the census or enumeration heretofore directed to be taken". Under this provision the Supreme Court had declared an income tax invalid. This amendment authorizes Congress to levy such a tax.

AMENDMENT XVII. Article I called for the election of Senators by the legislatures of the states. This amendment substituted direct popular vote.

AMENDMENT XVIII. Probably the most controversial amendment to the Constitution. It prohibited the manufacture and sale of intoxicating liquors. It was ratified in 1920 and repealed in 1933. It thus became the first amendment to the Constitution to be subsequently repealed.

AMENDMENT XIX. Gave suffrage to women.

AMENDMENT XX. This amendment changed the annual sessions of Congress from the first Monday in December to January 3, thus destroying the "Lame Duck" session of Congress, which, under the old date for the assembly of Congress, brought back to that body for another session those who had been defeated at the polls. It also shortened the second term of President Roosevelt by the difference between March 4, the old date for the inauguration, and January 20, the new date.

AMENDMENT XXI. Repeal of the XVIII Amendment.

AMENDMENT XXII. Limits President to two elective terms.

AMENDMENT XXIII. Gives three electoral votes to the District of Columbia.

AMENDMENT XXIV. Prohibits the use of a poll tax in federal elections.

AMENDMENT XXV. Provides line of succession in case of disability of the President.

AMENDMENT XXVI. Prohibits either the United States or a State from abridging the right of citizens who are 18 years of age to vote because of age.

The Constitution of the United States

We, the people of the United States, in order to form a more perfect union, establish justice, insure domestic tranquility, provide for the common defense, promote the general welfare, and secure the blessings of liberty to ourselves and our posterity, do ordain and establish this Constitution for the United States of America.

ARTICLE I

SECTION I

All legislative powers herein granted shall be vested in a Congress of the United States, which shall consist of a Senate and House of Representatives.

SECTION II

The House of Representatives shall be composed of members chosen every second year by the people of the several States, and the electors in each State shall have the qualifications requisite for electors of the most numerous branch of the State legislature.

No person shall be a Representative who shall not have attained to the age of twenty-five years, and been seven years a citizen of the United States, and who shall not, when elected, be an inhabitant of that State in which he shall be chosen.

Representatives and direct taxes shall be apportioned among the several States which may be included within this Union, according to their respective numbers, *which shall be determined by adding to the whole number of free persons, including those bound to service for a term of years,*[1] and excluding Indians not taxed, *three-fifths of all other persons.*[2] The actual enumeration shall be made within three years after the first meeting of the Congress of the United States, and within every subsequent term of ten years, in such manner as they shall by law direct. The number of Representatives shall not exceed one for every thirty thousand, but each State shall have at last one Representative; *and until such enumeration shall be made, the State of New Hampshire shall be entitled to choose three, Massachusetts eight,*

1. Altered by the Fourteenth Amendment.
2. Rescinded by the Fourteenth Amendment.

Rhode Island and Providence Plantations one, Connecticut five, New York six, New Jersey four, Pennsylvania eight, Deleware one, Maryland six, Virginia ten, North Carolina five, South Carolina five, and Georgia three.[3]

When vacancies happen in the representation from any State, the executive authority thereof shall issue writs of election to fill such vacancies.

The House of Representatives shall choose their Speaker and other officers, and shall have the sole power of impeachment.

SECTION III

The Senate of the United States shall be composed of two Senators from each State, *chosen by the legislature thereof,*[4] for six years; and each Senator shall have one vote.

Immediately after they shall be assembled in consequence of the first election, they shall be divided as equally as may be into three classes. The seats of the Senators of the first class shall be vacated at the expiration of the second year, of the second class at the expiration of the fourth year, and of the third class at the expiration of the sixth year, so that one third may be chosen every second year; *and if vacancies happen by resignation or otherwise during the recess of the legislature of any State the executive thereof may make temporary appointments until the next meeting of the legislature, which shall then fill such vacancies.*[5]

No person shall be a Senator who shall not have attained to the age of thirty years, and been nine years a citizen of the United States, and who shall not, when elected, be an inhabitant of that State for which he shall be chosen.

The Vice-President of the United States shall be President of the Senate, but shall have no vote, unless they be equally divided.

The Senate shall choose their other officers, and also a President *pro tempore* in the absence of the Vice-President or when he shall exercise the office of the President of the United States.

The Senate shall have the sole power to try all impeachments. When sitting for that purpose, they shall be on oath or affirmation. When the President of the United States is tried, the Chief Justice shall preside; and no person shall be convicted without the concurrence of two thirds of the members present.

Judgment in cases of impeachment shall not extend further than to removal from office, and disqualification to hold and en-

3. Temporary provision.
4. Modified by the Seventeenth Amendment.
5. Modified by the Seventeenth Amendment.

joy any office of honor, trust, or profit under the United States; but the party convicted shall, nevertheless, be liable and subject to indictment, trial, judgment, and punishment, according to law.

SECTION IV

The times, places, and manner of holding elections for Senators and Representatives shall be prescribed in each State by the legislature thereof; but the Congress may at any time by law make or alter such regulations, except as to the places of choosing Senators.

The Congress shall assemble at least once in every year, and such meeting shall be on the first Monday in December, unless they shall by law appoint a different day.[6]

SECTION V

Each house shall be the judge of the elections, returns, and qualifications of its own members, and a majority of each shall constitute a quorum to do business; but a smaller number may adjourn from day to day, and may be authorized to compel the attendance of absent members, in such manner, and under such penalties, as each house may provide.

Each house may determine the rules of its proceedings, punish its members for disorderly behavior, and with the concurrence of two thirds, expel a member.

Each house shall keep a journal of its proceedings, and from time to time publish the same, excepting such parts as may in their judgment require secrecy, and the yeas and nays of the members of either house on any question shall, at the desire of one fifth of those present, be entered on the journal.

Neither house, during the session of Congress, shall, without the consent of the other, adjourn for more than three days, nor to any other place than that in which the two houses shall be sitting.

SECTION VI

The Senators and Representatives shall receive a compensation for their services, to be ascertained by law and paid out of the Treasury of the United States. They shall, in all cases except treason, felony, and breach of the peace, be privileged from arrest during their attendance at the sesson of their respective houses, and in going to and returning from the same; and for any speech or debate in either house they shall not be questioned in any other place.

No Senator or Representative shall, during the time for which

---

6. Superseded by the Twentieth Amendment.

he was elected, be appointed to any civil office under the authority of the United States, which shall have been created, or the emoluments whereof shall have been increased, during such time; and no person holding any office under the United States shall be a member of either house during his continuance in office.

SECTION VII

All bills for raising revenue shall originate in the House of Representatives; but the Senate may propose or concur with amendments as on other bills.

Every bill which shall have passed the House of Representatives and the Senate shall, before it become a law, be presented to to the President of the United States; if he approves he shall sign it, but if not he shall return it, with his objections, to that house in which it shall have originated, who shall enter the objections at large on their journal and proceed to reconsider it. If after such reconsideration two thirds of that house shall agree to pass the bill, it shall be sent, together with the objections, to the other house, by which it shall likewise be reconsidered, and if approved by two thirds of that house it shall become a law. But in all such cases the votes of both houses shall be determined by yeas and nays, and the names of the persons voting for and against the bill shall be entered on the journal of each house respectively. If any bill shall not be returned by the President within ten days (Sundays excepted) after it shall have been presented to him, the same shall be a law, in like manner as if he had signed it, unless the Congress by their adjournment prevent its return, in which case it shall not be a law.

Every order, resolution, or vote to which the concurrence of the Senate and House of Representatives may be necessary (except on a question of adjournment) shall be presented to the President of the United States; and before the same shall take effect, shall be approved by him, or being disapproved by him, shall be repassed by two thirds of the Senate and House of Representatives, according to the rules and limitations prescribed in the case of a bill.

SECTION VIII

The Congress shall have power to lay and collect taxes, duties, imposts, and excises, to pay the debts and provide for the common defense and general welfare of the United States; but all duties, imposts, and excises shall be uniform throughout the United States.

To borrow money on the credit of the United States.

To regulate commerce with foreign nations and among the several States, and with the Indian tribes;

To establish a uniform rule of naturalization, and uniform laws on the subject of bankruptcies throughout the United States;

To coin money, regulate the value thereof, and of foreign coin, and fix the standard of weights and measures;

To provide for the punishment of counterfeiting the securities and current coin of the United States;

To establish post-offices and post-roads;

To promote the progress of science and useful arts by securing for limited times to authors and inventors the exclusive rights to their respective writings and discoveries.

To constitute tribunals inferior to the Supreme Court;

To define and punish piracies and felonies committed on the high seas and offenses against the law of nations;

To declare war, grant letters of marque and reprisal, and make rules concerning captures on land and water;

To raise and support armies, but no appropriation of money to that use shall be for a longer term than two years;

To provide and maintain a navy;

To make rules for the government and regulation of the land and naval forces.

To provide for calling forth the militia to execute the laws of the Union, suppress insurrections, and repel invasions;

To provide for organizing, arming, and disciplining the militia, and for governing such part of them as may be employed in the service of the United States, reserving to the States respectively the appointment of the officers, and the authority of training the militia according to the discipline prescribed by Congress;

To exercise exclusive legislation in all cases whatsoever over such district (not exceeding ten miles square) as may, by cession of particular States and the acceptance of Congress, become the seat of the Government of the United States, and to exercise like authority over all places purchased by the consent of the legislature of the State in which the same shall be, for the erection of forts, magazines, arsenals, dockyards, and other needful buildings; and

To make all laws which shall be necessary and proper for carrying into execution the foregoing powers, and all other powers vested by this Constitution in the Government of the United States, or in any department or officer thereof.

SECTION IX

The migration or importation of such persons as any of the States now existing shall think proper to admit shall not be pro-

hibited by the Congress prior to the year one thousand eight hundred and eight, but a tax or duty may be imposed on such importation, not exceeding ten dollars for each person.[7]

The privilege of the writ of *habeas corpus* shall not be suspended, unless when in case of rebellion or invasion the public safety may require it.

No bill of attainder or *ex post facto* law shall be passed.

No capitation or other direct tax shall be laid, unless in proportion to the census or enumeration hereinbefore directed to be taken.

No tax or duty shall be laid on articles exported from any State.

No preference shall be given by any regulation of commerce or revenue to the ports of one State over those of another; nor shall vessels bound to or from one State be obliged to enter, clear, or pay duties in another.

No money shall be drawn from the Treasury but in consequence of appropriations made by law; and a regular statement and account of the receipts and expenditures of all public money shall be published from time to time.

No title of nobility shall be granted by the United States; and no person holding any office of profit or trust under them shall, without the consent of the Congress, accept of any present, emolument, office, or title, of any kind whatever, from any king, prince, or foreign State.

SECTION X

No State shall enter into any treaty, alliance, or confederation; grant letters of marque and reprisal; coin money; emit bills of credit; make anything but gold and silver coin a tender in payment of debts; pass any bill of attainder, *ex post facto* law, or law impairing the obligation of contracts, or grant any title of nobility.

No State shall, without the consent of Congress, lay any imposts or duties on imports or exports, except what may be absolutely necessary for executing its inspection laws; and the net produce of all duties and imposts, laid by any State on imports or exports, shall be for the use of the Treasury of the United States; and all such laws shall be subject to the revision and control of the Congress.

No State shall, without the consent of Congress, lay any duty of tonnage, keep troops or ships of war in time of peace, enter

7. Temporary provision.

into any agreement or compact with another State or with a foreign power, or engage in war, unless actually invaded or in such imminent danger as will not admit of delay.

ARTICLE II

SECTION I

The executive power shall be vested in a President of the United States of America. He shall hold his office during the term of four years, and together with the Vice-President, chosen for the same term, be elected as follows:

Each State shall appoint, in such manner as the legislature thereof may direct, a number of electors, equal to the whole number of Senators and Representatives to which the State may be entitled in the Congress; but no Senator or Representative, or person holding an office of trust or profit under the United States, shall be appointed an elector.

The electors shall meet in their respective States and vote by ballot for two persons, of whom one at least shall not be an inhabitant of the same State with themselves. And they shall make a list of all the persons voted for, and of the number of votes for each; which list they shall sign and certify, and transmit sealed to the seat of government of the United States, directed to the President of the Senate. The President of the Senate shall, in the presence of the Senate and House of Representatives, open all the certificates, and the votes shall then be counted. The person having the greatest number of votes shall be the President, if such number be a majority of the whole number of electors appointed; and if there be more than one who have such a majority, and have an equal number of votes, then the House of Representatives shall immediately choose by ballot one of them for President; and if no person have a majority, then from the five highest on the list the said House shall in like manner choose the President. But in choosing the President the votes shall be taken by States, the representation from each State having one vote; a quorum for this purpose shall consist of a member or members from two thirds of the States, and a majority of all the States shall be necessary to a choice. In every case, after the choice of the President, the person having the greatest number of votes of the electors shall be the Vice-President. But if there should remain two or more who have equal votes, the Senate shall choose from them by ballot the Vice-President[8]

8. Superseded by the Twelfth Amendment.

The Congress may determine the time of choosing the electors and the day on which they shall give their votes, which day shall be the same throughout the United States.

No person except a natural-born citizen, or a citizen of the United States at the time of the adoption of this Constitution, shall be eligible to the office of President; neither shall any person be eligible to that office who shall not have attained to the age of thirty-five years, and been fourteen years a resident within the United States.

In case of the removal of the President from office, or of his death, resignation, or inability to discharge the powers and duties of the said office, the same shall devolve on the Vice-President, and the Congress may by law provide for the case of removal, death, resignation, or inability, both of the President and Vice-President, declaring what officer shall then act as President, and such officer shall act accordingly until the disability be removed or a President shall be elected.

The President shall, at stated times, receive for his services a compensation which shall neither be increased nor diminished during the period for which he may have been elected, and he shall not receive within that period any other emolument from the United States or any of them.

Before he enter on the execution of his office he shall take the following oath or affirmation:

"I do solemnly swear (or affirm) that I will faithfully execute the office of President of the United States, and will to the best of my ability preserve, protect, and defend the Constitution of the United States."

SECTION II

The President shall be commander-in-chief of the army and navy of the United States, and of the militia of the several States when called into the actual service of the United States; he may require the opinion, in writing, of the principal officer in each of the executive departments, upon any subject relating to the duties of their respective offices, and he shall have power to grant reprieves and pardons for offenses against the United States, except in cases of impeachment.

He shall have power, by and with the advice and consent of the Senate, to make treaties, provided two thirds of the Senators present concur; and he shall nominate, and, by and with the advice and consent of the Senate, shall appoint ambassadors, other public ministers and consuls, judges of the Supreme Court, and all other officers of the United States, whose appointments are not herein otherwise provided for, and which shall be established by law; but the Congress may by law vest the appointment of such inferior officers, as they think proper, in the President alone, in the courts of law, or in the heads of departments.

The President shall have power to fill up all vacancies that may happen during the recess of the Senate, by granting commissions which shall expire at the end of their next session.

SECTION III

He shall from time to time give to the Congress information of the state of the Union, and recommend to their consideration such measures as he shall judge necessary and expedient; he may, on extraordinary occasions, convene both houses, or either of them, and in case of disagreement between them with respect to the time of adjournment, he may adjourn them to such time as he shall think proper; he shall receive ambassadors and other public ministers; he shall take care that the laws be faithfully executed, and shall commission all the officers of the United States.

SECTION IV

The President, Vice-President, and all civil officers of the United States shall be removed from office on impeachment for and conviction of treason, bribery, or other high crimes and misdemeanors.

ARTICLE III

SECTION I

The judicial power of the United States shall be vested in one Supreme Court, and in such inferior courts as the Congress may from time to time ordain and establish. The judges, both of the supreme and inferior courts, shall hold their offices during good behavior, and shall, at stated times, receive for their services a compensation which shall not be diminished during their continuance in office.

SECTION II

The judicial power shall extend to all cases, in law and equity, arising under this Constitution, the laws of the United States, and the treaties made, or which shall be made, under their authority; to all cases affecting ambassadors, other public ministers, and consuls; to all cases of admiralty and maritime jurisdiction; to controversies to which the United States shall be a party; to controversies between two or more States; *between a State and citizens of another State;*[9] between citizens of different States; be-

9. Restricted by the Eleventh Amendment.

tween citizens of the same State claiming lands under grants of different States, and between a State, or the citizens thereof, and foreign States, citizens, or subjects.

In all cases affecting ambassadors, other public ministers, and consuls, and those in which a State shall be a party, the Supreme Court shall have original jurisdiction. In all the other cases before mentioned the Supreme Court shall have appellate jurisdiction, both as to law and fact, with such exceptions and under such regulations as the Congress shall make.

The trial of all crimes, except in cases of impeachment, shall be by jury; and such trial shall be held in the State where the said crimes shall have been committed, but when not committed within any State, the trial shall be at such place or places as the Congress may by law have directed.

SECTION III

Treason against the United States shall consist only in levying war against them, or in adhering to their enemies, giving them aid and comfort. No person shall be convicted of treason unless on the testimony of two witnesses to the same overt act, or on confession in open court.

The Congress shall have power to declare the punishment of treason, but no attainder of treason shall work corruption of blood or forfeiture except during the life of the person attainted.

ARTICLE IV

SECTION I

Full faith and credit shall be given in each State to the public acts, records, and judicial proceedings of every other State. And the Congress may by general laws prescribe the manner in which such acts, records, and proceedings shall be proved, and the effect thereof.

SECTION II

The citizens of each State shall be entitled to all privileges and immunities of citizens in the several States.[10]

A person charged in any State with treason, felony, or other crime, who shall flee from justice, and be found in another State, shall, on demand of the executive authority of the State from which he fled, be delivered up, to be removed to the State having jurisdiction of the crime.

10. Extended by the Fourteenth Amendment.

No person held to service or labor in one State, under the laws thereof, escaping into another, shall, in consequence of any law or regulation therein, be discharged from such service or labor, but shall be delivered up on claim of the party to whom such service or labor may be due.[11]

SECTION III

New States may be admitted by the Congress into this Union; but no new State shall be formed or erected within the jurisdiction of any other State; nor any State be formed by the junction of two more States or parts of States, without the consent of the legislatures of the States concerned as well as of the Congress.

The Congress shall have power to dispose of and make all needful rules and regulations respecting the territory or other property belonging to the United States; and nothing in this Constitution shall be so construed as to prejudice any claims of the United States or any particular State.

SECTION IV

The United States shall guarantee to every State in this Union a republican form of government, and shall protect each of them against invasion, and on application of the legislature, or of the executive (when the legislature cannot be convened), against domestic violence.

ARTICLE V

The Congress, whenever two thirds of both houses shall deem it necessary, shall propose amendments to this Constitution, or, on the application of the legislatures of two thirds of the several States, shall call a convention for proposing amendments, which in either case shall be valid to all intents and purposes as part of this Constitution, when ratified by the legislatures of three fourths of the several States, or by conventions in three fourths thereof, as the one or the other mode of ratification may be proposed by the Congress, *provided that no amendments which may be made prior to the year one thousand eight hundred and eight shall in any manner affect the first and fourth clauses in the ninth section of the first article*,[12] and that no State, without its consent, shall be deprived of its equal suffrage in the Senate.

---

11. Superseded by the Thirteenth Amendment in so far as pertaining to slaves.

12. Temporary clause.

ARTICLE VI

All debt contracted and engagements entered into, before the adoption of this Constitution, shall be as valid against the United States under this Constitution as under the confederation.[13]

This Constitution, and the laws of the United States, which shall be made in pursuance thereof, and all treaties made, or which shall be made, under the authority of the United States, shall be the supreme law of the land; and the judges in every State shall be bound thereby, anything in the Constitution or laws of any State to the contrary notwithstanding.

The Senators and Representatives before mentioned, and the members of the several State legislatures, and all executive and judicial officers both of the United States and of the several States, shall be bound by oath or affirmation to support this Constitution; but no religious test shall ever be required as a qualification to any office or public trust under the United States.

ARTICLE VII

The ratification of the conventions of nine States shall be sufficient for the establishment of this Constitution between the States so ratifying the same.

Done in convention by the unanimous consent of the States present, the seventeenth day of September, in the year of our Lord one thousand seven hundred and eighty-seven, and of the independence of the United States of America the twelfth. In witness whereof, we have hereunto subscribed our names.

[Signed by][14]

AMENDMENTS

I. Congress shall make no law respecting an establishment of religion, or prohibiting the free exercise thereof; or abridging the freedom of speech or of the press; or the right of the people peaceably to assemble, and to petition the government for a redress of grievances.

II. A well-regulated militia being necessary to the security of a free state, the right of the people to keep and bear arms shall not be infringed.

III. No soldier shall, in time of peace, be quartered in any

---

13. Extended by the Fourteenth Amendment.

14. The signatures are omitted here.

house without the consent of the owner, nor in time of war, but in a manner to be prescribed by law.

IV. The right of the people to be secure in their persons, houses, papers, and effects, against unreasonable searches and seizures, shall not be violated, and no warrants shall issue but upon probable cause, supported by oath or affirmation, and particularly describing the place to be searched, and the person or things to be seized.

V. No person shall be held to answer for a capital or otherwise infamous crime, unless on a presentment or indictment of a grand jury, except in cases arising in the land or naval forces, or in the militia, when in actual service in time of war or public danger; nor shall any person be subject for the same offense to be twice put in jeopardy of life or limb; nor shall be compelled in any criminal case to be a witness against himself, nor be deprived of life, liberty, or property, without due process of law; nor shall private property be taken for public use without just compensation.

VI. In all criminal prosecutions the accused shall enjoy the right to a speedy and public trial, by an impartial jury of the State and district wherein the crime shall have been committed, which district shall have been previously ascertained by law, and to be informed of the nature and cause of the accusation; to be confronted with the witnesses against him; to have compulsory process for obtaining witnesses in his favor, and to have the assistance of counsel for his defense.

VII. In suits at common law, where the value in controversy shall exceed twenty dollars, the right of trial by jury shall be preserved, and no fact tried by a jury shall be otherwise re-examined in any court of the United States, than according to the rules of the common law.

VIII. Excessive bail shall not be required, nor excessive fines imposed, nor cruel and unusual punishments inflicted.

IX. The enumeration in the Constitution of certain rights shall not be construed to deny or disparage others retained by the people.

X[15] The powers not delegated to the United States by the Constitution, nor prohibited by it to the States, are reserved to the States respectively, or to the people.

XI[16] The judicial power of the United States shall not be construed to extend to any suit in law or equity, commenced or

---

15. The first ten amendments took effect December 15, 1791.
16. Proclaimed January 8, 1798.

prosecuted against one of the United States by citizens of another State, or by citizens or subjects of any foreign State.

XII.[17] The electors shall meet in their respective States and vote by ballot for President and Vice-President, one of whom, at least, shall not be an inhabitant of the same State with themselves; they shall name in their ballots the person voted for as President, and in distinct ballots the person voted for as Vice-President, and they shall make distinct lists of all persons voted for as President and of all persons voted for as Vice-President, and of the number of votes for each; which lists they shall sign and certify, and transmit sealed to the seat of the government of the United States, directed to the President of the Senate. The President of the Senate shall, in the presence of the Senate and House of Representatives, open all the certificates and the votes shall then be counted. The person having the greatest number of votes for President shall be the President, if such number be a majority of the whole number of electors appointed; and if no person have such a majority, then from the person having the highest numbers not exceeding three on the list of those voted for as President, the House of Representatives shall choose immediately, by ballot, the President. But in choosing the President the votes shall be taken by States, the representation from each State having one vote; a quorum for this purpose shall consist of a member or members from two thirds of the States, and a majority of all States shall be necessary to a choice. And if the House of Representatives shall not choose a President whenever the right of choice shall devolve upon them, before the *fourth day of March*[18] next following, then the Vice-President shall act as President, as in the case of the death or other constitutional disability of the President.

The person having the greatest number of votes as Vice-President shall be the Vice-President, if such number be a majority of the whole number of electors appointed; and if no person have a majority, then from the two highest numbers on the list the Senate shall choose the Vice-President: a quorum for the purpose shall consist of two thirds of the whole number of Senators, and a majority of the whole number shall be necessary to a choice. But no person constitutionally ineligible to the office of President shall be eligible to that of Vice-President of the United States.

---

17. Proclaimed September 25, 1804.
18. Superseded by the Twentieth Amendment.

XIII.[19] *Section* 1. Neither slavery nor involuntary servitude, except as a punishment for crime whereof the party shall have been duly convicted, shall exist within the United States or any place subject to their jurisdiction.

XIV.[20] *Section* 1. All persons born or naturalized in the United States, and subject to the jurisdiction thereof, are citizens of the United States and of the State wherein they reside. No State shall make or enforce any law which shall abridge the privileges or immunities of citizens of the United States; nor shall any State deprive any person of life, liberty, or property, without due process of law; nor deny to any person within its jurisdiction the equal protection of the laws.

Section 2. Representatives shall be apportioned among the several States according to their respective numbers, counting the whole number of persons in each State, excluding Indians not taxed. But when the right to vote at any election for the choice of electors for President and Vice-President of the United States, Representatives in Congress, the executive and judicial officers of a State, or the members of the legislature thereof, is denied to any of the male inhabitants of such State, being twenty-one years of age, and citizens of the United States, or in any way abridged, except for participation in rebellion, or other crime, the basis of representation therein shall be reduced in the proportion which the number of such male citizens shall bear to the whole number of male citizens twenty-one years of age in such State.

Section 3. No person shall be a Senator or Representative in Congress, or elector of President and Vice-President, or hold any office, civil or military, under the United States or under any State, who, having previously taken an oath as a member of Congress, or as an officer of the United States, or as a member of any State legislature, or as an executive or judicial officer of any State, to support the Constitution of the United States, shall have engaged in insurrection or rebellion against the same, or given aid or comfort to the enemies thereof. But Congress may, by a vote of two thirds of each house, remove such disability

Section 4. The validity of the public debt of the United States, authorized by law, including debts incurred for payment of pensions and bounties for services in suppressing insurrection or re-

---

19. Proclaimed December 18, 1865.
20. Proclaimed July 28, 1868.

bellion, shall not be questioned. But neither the United States nor any State shall assume or pay any debt or obligation incurred in aid of insurrection or rebellion against the United States, or any claim for the loss or emancipation of any slave; but all such debts, obligations, and claims shall be held illegal and void.

Section 5. The Congress shall have power to enforce, by appropriate legislation, the provisions of this article.

XV[21] *Section* 1. The right of citizens of the United States to vote shall not be denied or abridged by the United States or by any State on account of race, color, or previous condition of servitude.

Section 2. The Congress shall have power to enforce this article by appropriate legislation.

XVI.[22] The Congress shall have power to lay and collect taxes on incomes, from whatever source derived, without apportionment among the several States, and without regard to any census or enumeration.

XVII[23] The Senate of the United States shall be composed of two Senators from each State, elected by the people thereof, for six years; and each Senator shall have one vote. The electors in each State shall have the qualifications requisite for electors of the most numerous branch of the State legislature.

When vacancies happen in the representation of any State in the Senate, the executive authority of such State shall issue writs of election to fill such vacancies: *Provided*, That the legislature of any State may empower the executive thereof to make temporary appointments until the people fill the vacancies by election as the legislature may direct.

This amendment shall not be so construed as to affect the election or term of any Senator chosen before it becomes valid as part of the Constitution.

XVIII[24] SECTION 1. *After one year from the ratification of this article the manufacture, sale, or transportation of intoxicating liquors within, the importation thereof into, or the exportation thereof from the United States and all territory subject to the jurisdiction thereof for beverage purposes is hereby prohibited.*

SECTION 2. *The Congress and the several States shall have concurrent power to enforce this article by appropriate legislation.*

---

21. Proclaimed March 30, 1870
22. Proclaimed February 25, 1913
23 Proclaimed May 31, 1913.
24. Proclaimed January 29, 1919.

SECTION 3. *This article shall be inoperative unless it shall have ratified as an amendment to the Constitution by the legislatures of the several States, as provided in the Constitution, within seven years from the date of the submission hereof to the States by the Congress.*[25]

XIX.[26] *Section* 1. The right of citizens of the United States to vote shall not be denied or abridged by the United States or by any State on account of sex.

Section 2. Congress shall have power to enforce this article by appropriate legislation.

XX.[27] *Section* 1. The terms of the President and Vice-President shall end at noon on the 20th day of January, and the terms of Senators and Representatives at noon on the 3rd day of January, of the years in which such terms would have ended if this article had not been ratified; and the terms of their successors shall then begin.

Section 2. The Congress shall assemble at least once in every year, and such meeting shall begin at noon on the 3rd day of January, unless they shall by law appoint a different day.

Section 3. If at the time fixed for the beginning of the term of the President, the President-elect shall have died, the Vice-President-elect shall become President. If a President shall not have been chosen before the time fixed for the beginning of his term, or if the President-elect shall have failed to qualify, then the Vice-President-elect shall act as President until a President shall have qualified, and the Congress may by law provide for the case wherein neither a President-elect nor a Vice-President-elect shall have qualified, declaring who shall then act as President, or the manner in which one who is to act shall be selected, and such person shall act accordingly until a President or Vice-President shall have qualified.

Section 4. The Congress may by law provide for the case of the death of any of the persons from whom the House of Representatives may choose a President whenever the right of choice shall have devolved upon them, and for the case of the death of any of the persons from whom the Senate may choose a Vice-President whenever the right of choice shall have devolved upon them.

---

25. Rescinded by the Twenty-first Amendment.
26. Proclaimed August 26, 1920.
27. Proclaimed February 6, 1933.

Section 5. Sections 1 and 2 shall take effect on the 15th day of October following the ratification of this article.

Section 6. This article shall be inoperative unless it shall have been ratified as an amendment to the Constitution by the legislatures of three-fourths of the several States within seven years from the date of its submission .

XXI.[28] *Section* 1. The Eighteenth article of amendment to the Constitution of the United States is hereby repealed.

Section 2. The transportation or importation into any State, territory, or possession of the United States for delivery or use therein of intoxicating liquors, in violation of the laws thereof, is hereby prohibited.

Section 3. This article shall be inoperative unless it shall have been ratified as an amendment to the Constitution by conventions in the several States, as provided in the Constitution, within seven years from the date of the submission hereof to the States by the Congress.

XXII.[29] *Section* 1. No person shall be elected to the office of the President more than twice, and no person who has held the office of President, or acted as President, for more than two years of a term to which some other person was elected President shall be elected to the office of President more than once. But this Article shall not apply to any person holding the office of President when this Article was proposed by the Congress, and shall not prevent any person who may be holding the office of President, or acting as President, during the term within which this Article becomes operative from holding the office of President or acting as President during the remainder of such term.

XXIII.[30] *Section* 1. The District constituting the seat of Government of the United States shall appoint in such manner as the Congress may direct:

A number of electors of President and Vice President equal to the whole number of Senators and Representatives in Congress to which the District would be entitled if it were a State, but in no event more than the least populous State; they shall be in addition to those appointed by the States, but they shall be considered, for the purposes of the election of President and Vice President, to be electors appointed by a State; and they

28. Proclaimed December 5, 1933.
29. Proclaimed March 3, 1951.
30. Ratified May 29, 1961.

shall meet in the District and perform such duties as provided by the twelfth article of amendment.

Section 2. The Congress shall have power to enforce this article by appropriate legislation.

XXIV.[31] *Section* 1. The right of citizens of the United States to vote in any primary or other election for President or Vice-President, or for Senators or Representatives in Congress, shall not be denied or abridged by the United States or any State by reason of failure to pay any poll tax or other tax.

Section 2. The Congress shall have power to enforce this article by appropriate legislation.

XXV.[32] *Section* 1. In case of the removal of the President from office or of his death or resignation, the Vice President shall become President.

Section 2. Whenever there is a vacancy in the office of the Vice President, the President shall nominate a Vice President who shall take office upon confirmation by a majority vote of both Houses of Congress.

Section 3. Whenever the President transmits to the President pro tempore of the Senate and the Speaker of the House of Representatives his written declaration that he is unable to discharge the powers and duties of his office, and until he transmits to them a written declaration to the contrary, such powers and duties shall be discharged by the Vice President as Acting President.

Section 4 Whenever the Vice President and a majority of either the principal officers of the executive departments or of such other body as Congress may by law provide, transmit to the President pro tempore of the Senate and the Speaker of the House of Representatives their written declaration that the President is unable to discharge the powers and duties of his office, the Vice President shall immediately assume the powers and duties of the office as Acting President.

Thereafter, when the President transmit to the President pro tempore of the Senate and the Speaker of the House of Representatives his written declaration that no inability exists, he shall resume the powers and duties of his office unless the Vice President and a majority of either the principal officers of the executive departments or of such other body as Congress may by law provide, transmit within four days to the President pro tempore of the Senate and the Speaker of the House of Repre-

31. Certified February 5, 1964.
32. Certified February 23, 1967.

sentatives their written declaration that the President is unable to discharge the powers and duties of his office. Thereupon Congress shall decide the issue, assembling within forty-eight hours for that purpose if not in session. If the Congress, within twenty-one days after receipt of the latter written declaration, or, if Congress is not in session, within twenty-one days after Congress is required to assemble, determines by a two-thirds vote of both Houses that the President is unable to discharge the powers and duties of his office, the Vice President shall continue to discharge the same as Acting President; otherwise, the President shall resume the powers and duties of his office.

XXVI. Section 1. The right of citizens of the United States, who are 18 years of age or older, to vote shall not be denied or abridged by the United States or by any State on account of age.

Section 2. The Congress shall have power to enforce this article by appropriate legislation.[33]

33. Certified July 7, 1971.

Questions on the Constitution of the United States

PART I

History and Fundamental Principles

1. Explain fully the meaning of "constitutional government."
2. What was the first national government of the United States? What powers did it exercise? How long did it last?
3. What was the first written constitution of the United States? Just when and how long was it in effect? Was it satisfactory? What were its defects?
4. When and where was the Federal Convention held? How many delegates attended? How many signed the Constitution? Was Thomas Jefferson present? Who were the most prominent delegates? What class of people did the delegates represent?
5. Describe the organization and procedure of the Federal Convention. What were the two great plans of union? Give the provisions of each?
6. Explain why the Constitution is often referred to as "a bundle of compromises." Give the provision of the principal compromises.
7. What are the provisions of Article VII? What objections were raised against the Constitution? When did it go into effect? Had all of the states ratified at this time?
8. How does a federal government differ from a unitary government? Explain the terms "delegated," "implied," "reserved," "inherent," and "enumerated" powers.
9. Explain what is meant by "the separation of powers," and "checks and balances."
10. Give an example of judicial review and explain fully the fundamental principles of government involved.

PART II

The Constitution as an Objective Document

I. *General.*

1. Compare the length of the Constitution of the United States to that of Georgia.

2. Describe the arrangement of the Constitution. How many articles are there?
3. Describe the wording. Are there any repetitions? Criticise the use of broad terms.

II. *Preamble.*

1. What is the meaning of the opening words, "We, the People of the United States. . . ."?
2. What were the objects of establishing the Constitution?

III. *Article I.*

1. With what subject does Article I deal? Is there any significance to this arrangement?
2. How many members are there in the House of Representatives? How is this number determined? How apportioned?
3. Who can vote for representatives?
4. How are vacancies in the House filled?
5. What are the qualifications of representatives?
6. Who presides over the House? How is he chosen? What power does he exercise?
7. How can you explain the equal representation of the States in the Senate?
8. What was the original method of choosing senators?
9. What is meant by describing the Senate as a continuous body? What is the term of a Senator?
10. What are the qualifications for a Senator?
11. Who presides over the Senate? How is he chosen? Compare his powers to those of the Speaker of the House.
12. Describe the process of impeachment.
13. What action has Congress taken under Article I, Section 4, Clause I, in regard to the time, places, and manner of holding elections?
14. What is the term of "a Congress"? How often does it have to meet? May it meet oftener? How did Amendment XX affect the time of meeting? Do we still have "long" and "short" sessions?
15. Give the powers and duties of each house, and the privileges of members prescribed in Sections 5 and 6.
16. Would the adoption of the cabinet system of government necessitate an amending of the Constitution?
17. What provision is made in regard to revenue measures? How is the spirit of this violated in practice?

18. Explain how a bill is introduced and passed.
19. Summarize the powers of Congress found in Section 8. Why is the 18th paragraph of this section especially important?
20. What distinct prohibitions are imposed upon the Central Government in Section 9? Can you suggest reasons for these?
21. What distinct prohibitions are imposed upon the State Governments in Section 10?
22. Explain the following terms: "bill of attainder," "writ of habeas corpus," "ex post facto laws," "export taxes."
23. Can a state enter into any treaty? Can a state enter into any "agreement" with another state or a foreign state?
24. How does Article I compare in length with the other articles? How many sections does it contain?

IV. *Article II.*

1. Does the Constitution provide for a plural or single executive? Is there any provision relating to a cabinet? Heads of departments? Is there any distinction between the "cabinet" and the "heads of the executive departments"?
2. What is the term of a president? Can he serve more than two terms?
3. What are the qualifications of the president and vice-president?
4. Describe the original method of electing the president. What changes were made by the 12th Amendment? The 20th?
5. How has the development of political parties affected the method of election? Describe the present method of election.
6. How can a president be removed from office? Discuss the succession to the presidency. How is this determined?
7. What oath is required of the president? Who administers it?
8. Summarize the following powers of the president: (a) military, (b) executive, (c) legislative.
9. What is the address on the "state of the union"?

V. *Article III.*

1. To what extent does the Constitution entrust the organization of the federal judicial system to Congress? What definite provisions are stated to insure a relative independence of the judiciary?

2. Describe the Supreme Court and discuss its importance.
3. Outline the structure of the federal courts as they exist today and summarize the function of each.
4. What is the jurisdiction of the Federal Courts as described by the Constitution?
5. What is meant by "equity"? By "cases of admiralty and maritime jurisdiction"? By "original jurisdiction"? By "appellate jurisdiction"?
6. How is trial by jury safeguarded in the Constitution?
7. How is treason defined? What is meant by "attainder of treason"? By "corruption of blood"?

VI. *Article IV.*

1. What inter-state duties and obligations are specifically laid down in Article IV? Are these of much value?
2. What is the meaning of the "full faith and credit" clause?
3. What is the meaning of the first sentence in Section 2?
4. Describe the process of rendition.
5. Does the word "slave" appear in the body of the Constitution? Are any references made to slave? Does the word appear in the amendments?
6. How may new States be admitted into the Union? Does the territory have to be contiguous?
7. What authority has power over property and land belonging to the U. S.?
8. What is meant by a "republican form of government"? What branch of the national government decides whether a State's government is republican?

VII. *Article V.*

1. In what four ways may the Constitution be amended? How many of these ways have been used?
2. Could the Constitution be so amended as to deprive the smaller states of their "equal suffrage in the Senate"?

VIII. *Article VI.*

1. What is the "supreme law of the land"?
2. In case of a conflict between a State law and a National law, which prevails? Always?
3. What officials are bound by oath to support the Constitution?

IX. *Article VII.*

1. How was the Constitution ratified, by the States or by the people?

X. *Amendments to the Constitution.*

1. Which of the amendments are referred to as the "Bill of Rights"? Why so called? When were they adopted? Summarize the provisions of these amendments.
2. What are some of the rights referred to in the ninth amendment as being retained by the people?
3. Identify the tenth amendment. Was it necessary?
4. Can a State be sued? What led to the eleventh amendment?
5. What led to the twelfth amendment? What are its chief provisions?
6. The thirteenth, fourteenth, and fifteenth amendments were Reconstruction or Civil War amendments. What was each and why was it proposed?
7. Which amendment is longest? Which do you consider most important? Why?
8. Quote section one of the fourteenth amendment and explain the meaning of each of the three clauses in the second sentence. Does the word "person" include corporations? Is the clause ". . . nor shall any State deprive any person of life, liberty or property, without due process of law" a repetition of the statement in the fifth amendment that "No person shall . . . be deprived of life, liberty, or property without due process of law"?
9. Why has section two of the fourteenth amendment never been enforced?
10. Identify the sixteenth amendment and explain the odd wording.
11. In what sense did the seventeenth amendment impair the design of the framers of the Constitution? Was it a wise step?
12. Can one amendment repeal another? What provision does the twenty-first amendment make for the protection of "dry" states?
13. Which three amendments deal with the suffrage? Who can vote for members of Congress? Do we have a uniform electorate?
14. Why is the twentieth amendment called the "lame duck" amendment?
15. On what date will future presidents take office? Members of Congress? How often must Congress meet? Could it change the date of its meetings?

16. What provisions are made for succession to the presidency?
17. What significance is there to the provisions found in the eighteenth, twentieth, and twenty-first amendments limiting the period of ratification to seven years?
18. How did the ratification of the twenty-first amendment differ from the method previously used?
19. Under the twenty-second amendment what are the minimum and maximum limits to Presidential tenure?
20. Do residents of the District of Columbia have any voice in the election of the President?
21. How is a vacancy in the office of Vice President filled?
22. What is the procedure for determining whether the President "is unable to discharge the powers and duties of his office"?

Bibliography

Any good textbook on American government will aid in interpreting the Constitution. Saye, Pound and Allums, *Principles of American Government* (Prentice-Hall, Inc., publishers; frequent revisions) is a text often used at the University. The Department of State has published a *Documentary History of the Constitution of the United States of America, 1786-1870* (3 vols., Washington, 1894-1900). *The Constitution of the United States of America, Analysis and Interpretation* edited by E. S. Corwin (Sen. Doc. 170, 82nd Congress, 2nd Sess.) is a helpful reference. For an extensive and detailed study of the Constitution there can be no substitute for the actual decisions of the Supreme Court. Among the most helpful summaries of these decisions are Gerald Gunther, *Constitutional Law* (Mineola, N.Y.: Foundation Press, 1975). Martin Shapiro and R. T. Tresolini, *American Constitutional Law* (New York: Macmillan Co., 1975), and Albert B. Saye, *American Constitutional Law, Text and Cases* (Columbus, Ohio: Charles E. Merrill Co., 1975). An excellent short history of the Court is Robert G. McCloskey's *The American Supreme Court* (University of Chicago Press, 1960).

PART II

The Constitution of Georgia

Introduction

Since the Declaration of Independence, the State of Georgia has had eight constitutions. On April 15, 1776, the Third Provincial Congress of Georgia, in session at Augusta because of the commencement of hostilities at Savannah, drew up "Rules and Regulations of Government," but they were brief, incomplete and of an avowedly temporary character. A few days after the receipt of the Declaration of Independence, Archibald Bulloch, President of the Council of Safety in Georgia, called a constitutional convention which framed Georgia's Constitution of 1777, a brief document vesting most governmental authority in the legislature. Following her entrance into the Federal Union, Georgia adopted a new constitution in 1789, modeled extensively on the Constitution of the United States. A new constitution with more detailed provisions was adopted by a convention in 1798. The Civil War and Reconstruction gave Georgia four new constitutions, adopted in 1861, 1865, 1868, and 1877. The present constitution was adopted in 1945. The constitution of 1777, 1789, 1798, and 1865 were framed and adopted by constitutional conventions; the constitutions of 1861, 1868 and 1877 were drawn up by constitutional conventions and ratified by popular vote; the constitution of 1945 was written by a commission and ratified by popular vote.

Because of the abuse of power during the Reconstruction period, the framers of the Constitution of 1877, led by Robert Toombs, placed numerous restrictions upon the powers of government, particularly in the field of finance. As a result of the inclusion of numerous provisions statutory in nature, the document was amended 301 times in a period of sixty-eight years. Article VII alone, entitled "Finance, Taxation and Public Debt," was amended 188 times, but not more than fifteen per cent of these amendments were of general interest, the greater number of them being applicable to a single city or county. Recognizing the need for a new constitution, in 1931 the Institute of Public Affairs of the University of Georgia published *A Proposed Constitution for Georgia* drawn up by a committee of prominent citizens. This document proposed a thorough revision of the structure of government, including such radical changes as the substitution of 30 districts for the existing 161 counties as the basis of representation in the General Assembly. The publicity given the document served to stimulate interest in constitutional revision, and most of the press of the state actively supported the movement.

Under the leadership of Governor Arnall, an appointed commission wrote a new Constitution, and it was ratified by popular vote in 1945. While a definite improvement, this document continued most of the limitations on governmental power found in the Constitution of 1877. As a result, amendments were added to the Constitution of 1945 at every general election. By 1970, the total number of amendments to the Constitution stood at 691. Of these amendments, 116 were of statewide application and 575 were local amendments affecting only a particular city, county, or other political subdivision. Some sections of the Constitution had become a hodgepodge of amendments.

Commissions to revise the Constitutions were appointed in 1963 and 1969. Both of these commissions wrote a new constitution, but neither of the documents was adopted. The federal district court in Atlanta enjoined the Secretary of State from submitting to the people the question of ratification of the Constitution written in 1964. The court held that a malapportioned legislature could not submit a new constitution to the people. The constitution written by the Commission of 1969 died in committee in the legislature.

The Constitution of 1945

The traditional method used by the States in the American Union to get a new constitution is the convention method. The State legislature authorizes a convention, the people elect delegates, the delegates assembled in a convention write a constitution, and the document is submitted to popular vote for ratification or rejection. Georgia did not use this method to get her new constitution in 1945. She used the commission method.

Under the commission method, the legislature authorizes a commission to write a constitution. A commission is smaller than a convention, and its members are appointed. Several States had used commissions to write amendments to their constitutions, but Georgia was the first State to adopt a new constitution by the commission method.

CONSTITUTIONAL COMMISSION OF 1943-1944

In March, 1943, the General Assembly passed a resolution, sponsored by Governor Ellis Arnall, providing for a commission of twenty-three members to revise the Constitution. The commission was to be composed of the Governor, the President of the Senate, the Speaker of the House of Representatives, three members of the Senate appointed by the President, five members of the House appointed by the Speaker, a justice of the Supreme Court designated by the Court, a judge of the Court of Appeals designated by the Court, the Attorney General, the State Auditor, two judges of the Superior Courts, three practicing attorneys-at-law and three laymen appointed by the Governor. The resolution provided that the report of this commission should be submitted to the General Assembly either in the form of proposed amendments to the Constitution or as a proposed new constitution, to be acted upon by the General Assembly and submitted to the people for ratification or rejection.

PROS AND CONS

There were two principal arguments in favor of the use of an appointed commission instead of an elected convention to revise the Constitution of Georgia. In the first place, the existing Constitution required a two-thirds vote of the total membership of both houses of the General Assembly to call a constitutional convention, and previous attempts to call a convention had failed. Since the work of the proposed commission would be submitted directly to the General Assembly and subjected to revision before submission to the people, the resolution creating it met with approval whereas a resolution calling a convention would probably have failed. Secondly, the preamble of the resolution authorizing the commission expressed the view that a revision of the Constitution could be accomplished "more satisfactorily by a small commission . . . than through a constitutional convention."[1] A criticism advanced against the use of the appointed commission was that this method gave the incumbent administration too great an influence in shaping the fundamental law. Governor Arnall himself served as chairman of the commission and appointed eight of the other members; yet it should be noted that none of the *ex officio* members (the Attorney General, State Auditor, etc.) were appointed to their office by the Governor.

WORK OF THE COMMISSION

As chairman, Governor Arnall divided the members of the commission into seven subcommittees, composed of seven members each, to make preliminary studies of designated articles of the Constitution. He also designated the chairman of these subcommittees. Most of the subcommittees did a considerable amount of work, involving public hearings in some cases, before the first meeting of the full commission in the Supreme Court room of the State Capitol on January 6, 1944. Prior to the second meeting of the full commission, April 10-13, all of the subcommittees filed written reports with the Governor, and these served as the basis of discussion as the commission proceeded to a consideration of the Constitution, article by article.

A portion of the time of the April meeting was devoted to public hearings. Most of the members of the commission were businessmen who made a personal sacrifice to be present at the State Capitol, and the total number of days that the commission was in session was only fifteen. At its last meeting, on December 9, the commission appointed the Governor, the President of the Senate, and the Speaker of the House as a committee on final revisions. As revised by this committee, the Constitution was printed and submitted to the General Assembly in January, 1945.

Fully ninety per cent of the provisions of the Constitution of 1945 are taken from the amended Constitution of 1877. The

1. *Georgia Law*, 1943, p. 1680.

work of the commission on revision was confined primarily to a revision of the form and organization of the document, albeit some of the changes in substance were of significance.

ADOPTION OF CONSTITUTION

After extensive study and a number of revisions, the General Assembly approved the proposed new Constitution and submitted it to the people for ratification or rejection. The commission itself had been equally divided on the question of eliminating the constitutional ban against a successive term for the Governor. As chairman Governor Arnall broke the tie by voting to eliminate the ban, but the General Assembly reversed the commission's action on this controversial issue. At a special election held on August 7, 1945, the new Constitution was approved by a vote of 60,065 to 34,417.

ANALYSIS OF THE CONSTITUTION OF 1945

The following statements, made without regard to the technicalities of legal phraseology and subject to the error inherent in all generalizations, point out the main provisions of the Constitution of 1945. Students will profit from reading in full the articles from the Constitution printed below before attempting to read the summary statements given here.

ARTICLE I
The Bill of Rights

The Bill of Rights of the Constitution of Georgia includes all the guarantees of personal liberty found in the first eight amendments of the Constitution of the United States (freedom of religion, speech, press, etc.) and many others, among them a prohibition against banishment beyond the limits of the state or whipping as a punishment for crime. This long Bill of Rights dates from 1861. The earlier constitutions of Georgia had enumerated only four or five personal liberties. Thomas R. R. Cobb presented to the Convention of 1861 a *Declaration of Fundamental Principles* embodying in twenty-eight paragraphs his conservative philosophy of government This was adopted as Article I of the Constitution of 1861, and has been continued with minor alterations in subsequent constitutions.

Of the provisions of the Bill of Rights, the due process clause providing that "No person shall be deprived of life, liberty or property, except by due process of law," is most extensive in scope. In application it means that no person can be deprived of life, liberty, or property by any process which the judiciary considers unfair, arbitrary, or unreasonable.

The most satisfactory approach to understanding the meaning of any clause in the Bill of Rights is to study the decisions of the Supreme Court wherein the clause has been the subject of litigation. These decisions are published by the state under the title *Georgia Reports*, of which there were two hundred and thirty volumes in 1975. Volume two of the *Georgia Code Annotated*, published by the Harrison Company of Atlanta, contains citations to the leading cases. Another helpful tool in locating citations to the court decisions is the *Georiga Digest*, published in twenty-three volumes by the West Publishing Company of St. Paul, Minnesota.

ARTICLE II
The Elective Franchise

The Constitution provides that "Elections by the people shall be by ballot, and only those persons shall be allowed to vote who have first registered in accordance with the requirements of law." It sets up the following specific qualifications for electors: (1) citizenship of the United States and of Georgia, (2) age eighteen or upward, and (3) residence in the state at least thirty days immediately preceding the election. A person does not have to possess the age and residence qualifications of a voter at the time he registers. The Constitution provides that he may register if he either possesses these qualifications or "will possess them at the date of the election occuring next after his registration."

The Georgia Constitution provides a literacy test for voters, but this was superceded by the federal Voting Rights Act of 1965, applicable to seven Southern States, including Georgia. A State or political subdivision subject to the 1965 act must secure federal approval before any change is made in its election laws, for example, a change in election districts. This approval must be secured from either the District Court of the District of Columbia or from the Attorney General.

REGISTRATION

In each county the Judge of the Superior Court appoints three registrars from a list of six persons submitted by the Grand Jury. One of the registrars is designated "chief registrar." All three are appointed for terms of four years. The county tax collector is a deputy to the board of registrars, and the registrars may appoint additional deputy registrars. The registrars may maintain one or more offices.

A person must apply in person to register. Exception is made for persons in the military services and certain others, to whom an "absentee applicant" form may be mailed upon request.

The registrars revise the registration lists biennially. A person's name is removed from the list if he has not voted in a general or primary election within a three year period.

Detailed provisions covering registration and voting procedure are contained in the *Georgia Election Code*, revised frequently and distributed by the Secretary of State. Among other things, this Code provides that an application to register to vote is not effective for any general election or primary occurring within a period of 50 days after it is filed. The United States Supreme Court has sustained this provision.

VOTING BY MAIL

Voting by mail is permitted for an elector who is required to be away from his residence on election day, or who because of physical disability will be unable to be present at the polls. Application in writing for an absentee ballot should be filed with the county board of registrars not more than ninety days prior to the primary or election involved. Upon receipt of his ballot, the elector marks it and returns it to the board of registrars. Absentee ballots not returned and received by the registrars before the day and hour for the closing of the polls are not counted.

WRITE-IN VOTES

A constitutional amendment of 1966 provides that "No person elected on a write-in vote shall be eligible to hold office unless notice of his intention of candidacy was given twenty or more days prior to the election," and sets forth the procedure to be used in giving this notice.

ARTICLE III
The Legislative Department

Legislative power is vested in a General Assembly, composed of a Senate and House of Representatives. The General Assembly is given power to make all laws deemed necessary and proper for the welfare of the state, provided they are not repugnant to the Constitutions of Georgia or the United States.

THE SENATE

As amended in 1968, the Constitution provides that the Senate shall consist of not less than 54 members and not more than 56. "Each Senator shall be elected from and represent one Senatorial District. The General Assembly may create, rearrange and change Senatorial Districts as it deems proper, except that each Senatorial District shall be composed of one or more counties, or may be composed of a portion of one county, but not otherwise. The apportionment of the Senate shall be changed by the General Assembly, if necessary, after each United States decennial census becomes official."

THE HOUSE OF REPRESENTATIVES

The written Constitution of 1945 provides that the 8 largest counties in the State shall have three members each in the House of Representatives, the 30 next largest counties shall have 2 representatives each, and the remaining 121 counties shall have 1 representative each. These provisions, however, are no longer followed. The federal courts ruled in 1964 that representation in both houses of all state legislatures had to be based on population. Under statutes passed to comply with federal court orders, in 1975 the Georgia House of Representatives was composed of 180 members elected from 154 districts. Most of the districts were composed of a county or a group of counties.

QUALIFICATIONS OF MEMBERS

"The Senators shall be citizens of the United States who have attained the age of twenty-five years, and who shall have been citizens of this State for four years, and for one year residents of the district from which elected."

"The Representatives shall be citizens of the United States who have attained the age of twenty-one years, and who shall have been citizens of the State for two years, and for one year residents of the counties from which elected."

"The seat of a member of either house shall be vacated on his removal from the district or county from which he was elected."

Members of the General Assembly are ineligible for appointment to any office having an emolument unless they first resign as members of the General Assembly.

TERMS

Both Senators and Representatives are elected for terms of two years.

SESSIONS

In odd numbered years (1975, 1977, etc.) the General Assembly convenes in regular sessions on the 2nd Monday in January for not more than 12 days, to organize and receive the General Appropriation Bill; it reconvenes on the 2nd Monday in February for not more than 33 days. In even numbered years the General Assembly convenes on the 2nd Monday in January for not more than 40 days.

"All business pending in the Senate or House at the adjournment of any regular session may be considered at any later regular session of the same General Assembly as if there had been no adjournment."

Special sessions. The Governor is authorized to call special sessions of the General Assembly. Such called sessions are limited to seventy days, unless at the end of that period an impeachment trial is pending. No laws can be enacted at a called session except such as relate to the objects in the Governor's proclamation convening it.

The General Assembly may also be convened in special sessions upon the initiative of its own members. When three-fifths of the members of each house certify to the Governor that in their opinion an emergency exists in the affairs of the state, it is mandatory upon him, within five days of the receipt of such certificates, to convene the General Assembly in extraordinary session for all purposes. Should the Governor fail to act, the General Assembly may convene itself "as if convened in regular session, for all purposes, provided that such extraordinary, self-convened session shall be limited to a period of thirty days, unless at the expiration of said period there shall be pending an impeachment trial. . . ."

SALARIES

The salaries of many state officials are set forth in the Constitution. The General Assembly is authorized to increase, but not to decrease, the salaries of elected officials stated in the Constitution.

An act of 1973 provides that members of the General Assembly shall receive an annual salary of $7,200, plus $36 per day while attending sessions or serving on committees between sessions.

PRIVILEGES OF MEMBERS

"The members of both Houses shall be free from arrest during their attendance on the General Assembly, and in going thereto, or returning therefrom, except for treason, felony, larcency, or breach of the peace; and no member shall be liable to answer in any other place for anything spoken in debate in either House."

POWERS OF EACH HOUSE

"Each house shall be the judge of the elections, returns, and qualifications of its members, and shall have power to punish them for disorderly behavior or mis-conduct, by censure, fine, imprisonment, or explusion; but no members shall be expelled, except by a vote of two-thirds of the House to which he belongs."

"Each house may punish by imprisonment, not extending beyond the session, any person, not a member, who shall be guilty of a contempt, by any disorderly behavior in its presence, or who shall rescue or attempt to rescue, any person arrested by order of either House."

"A majority of each house shall constitute a quorum to transact business; but a smaller number may adjourn from day to day and compel the presence of its absent members, as each house may provide."

The Constitution makes the Lieutenant Governor the President of the Senate; otherwise each house elects its own officers. Those named in the Constitution are the President, the President Pro Tempore, and the Secretary of the Senate, and the Speaker, the Speaker Pro Tempore, and the Clerk of the House of Representatives.

PROCEDURE IN LEGISLATION

The procedure in enacting laws by the General Assembly of Georgia is in general similar to the procedure used in the Congress of the United States. In both cases, before becoming a law a bill must be passed by both houses of the legislature and approved by the chief executive, or passed over the executive veto by a two-thirds vote in both houses. As in Congress, each house of the General Assembly in Georgia has a number of standing committees to which bills are referred for study before being considered on the floor. In 1974 there were 25 standing committees in the Senate and 27 in the House of Representatives. A convenient source for the composition of these committees, as well as for the personnel of the General Assembly and the rules of each house, is the *Legislative Manual* published periodically by the Secretary of State.

But while the procedure in enacting legislation in Georgia is in general similar to that in Congress, there are a number of significant differences. For example, in Georgia the vote of a majority of all members *elected* to each house is necessary to pass a bill, whereas in Congress the requisite vote is a majority of the members *present;* the Governor of Georgia is given only five days after a bill is presented to him within which he may veto it,[1] whereas the President has ten days; the Governor of Georgia may approve portions of an appropriation bill and disapprove other portions, whereas the President must accept or reject a bill in its entirety.

LOCAL LEGISLATION

As a general rule, the courts will not sustain an attack upon a law based upon the ground that the General Assembly did not comply with technical procedural rules in enacting it. As stated in a recent case, "A duly enrolled act, authenticated by the presiding officer of both houses of the General Assembly, approved by the Governor, and deposited with the Secretary of State as an existing law, is conclusively presumed to have been enacted in accordance with constitutional requirements, and it is not permissible to show the contrary by extrinsic evidence."[2] There is, however, an important exception to this rule. The Constitutional requirement that local bills be advertised in the political subdivision affected before introduction in the General Assembly was strengthened by the addition of the following clause in the Constitution of 1945: "No local or special bill shall become law unless there is attached to and made a part of said bill a copy of said notice certified by the publisher, or accompanied by an affidavit of the author, to the effect that said notice has been published as provided by law." In Smith v. McMichael[3] the Supreme Court held that local bills were void

1. The period is extended to 30 days if the General Assembly has adjourned.
2. Williams v. MacFeeley, 186 Ga. 145 (1938).
3. 203 Ga. 74 (1947).

unless the duly authenticated notice of publication was enrolled as an integral part of the bill.

SPECIAL AND GENERAL LAWS

Of the several limitations on the form and content of legislation, the one that serves most frequently as the basis of unconstitutionality (except, of course, the due process clause) is the clause in the Bill of Rights providing that "Laws of a general nature shall have uniform operation throughout the State, and no special law shall be enacted in any case for which provision has been made by an existing general law." The objective of this clause is "manifestly to prevent the confusion and uncertainty that would necessarily result if there existed at the same time a general law and a special law dealing with or regulating the same subject-matter." The limitation is frequently circumvented by passing a special law in the form of a general law, e.g., a law providing that in all counties having a population of not less than 26,750 nor more than 27,500 according to the census of 1970 or any future census the clerk of the superior court shall receive a salary in lieu of fees as provided by existing general law. The *Georgia Laws* are full of such statutes, and no one knows which of them are valid and which are void. Such a statute may be enforced for years without being tested before the courts, and the line of division between void and valid statutes in this area is not clearly defined by the court decisions.

IMPEACHMENT

The House of Representatives is vested with "the sole power to vote impeachment charges against all persons who shall have been or may be in office." The Senate is given the sole power to try impeachments. "When sitting for that purpose, the members shall be on oath, or affirmation, and shall be presided over by the Chief Justice or the presiding Justice of the Supreme Court. Should the Chief Justice be disqualified, the Senate shall select a Justice of the Supreme Court to preside. No person shall be convicted without the concurrence of two-thirds of the members present."

"Judgments in cases of impeachment shall not extend further than removal from office and disqualification to hold and enjoy any office of honor, trust, or profit within this State; but the party convicted shall, nevertheless, be liable, and subject, to indictment, trial, judgment, and punishment according to law."

LEGISLATIVE POWER

The legislative power of the General Assembly is very broad. The General Assembly is not limited to powers expressed in the Constitution. It can pass all laws that it deems advisable that are not in conflict with the Constitution of the United States or the Constitution of Georgia. In theory the national government is limited to powers granted to it by the United States Constitution. This theory of "delegated powers" is not applicable to the government of the States of the American union. Thus it is meaningless to state in the Georgia Constitution that the General Assembly is authorized to tax to support public schools. The courts will assume that the General Assembly has such power unless there is a denial of it in the Constitution. Hence the most meaningful statements of State constitutions are negative statements (e.g., freedom of speech shall not be abridged), or positive statements that have negative implications (e.g., the Supreme Court shall have seven justices).

ARTICLE IV

Public Utilities and Miscellaneous Provisions

A Public Service Commission composed of five members elected by the people for six-year terms is established to enforce the laws regulating public utilities. The General Assembly is prohibited from regulating utilities owned or operated by a county or municipality. Public utilities are forbidden to give rebates or to do anything to deceive the public as to the real rates charged.

CONTRACTS

The Federal Constitution prohibits any state from impairing the obligation of contracts, and this is construed by the Supreme Court of the United States to apply to contracts to which a state is a party as well as to private contracts. As a safe-guard against the perpetuity of contracts against the public interest, the Constitution of Georgia provides that no corporation shall receive a renewal or amendment of its charter or benefit from any law in its favor except upon the condition that its character be held thereafter subject to the provisions of the Constitution. The significance of this provision becomes clearer when considered in connection with the provision of Article VII that no department of the government shall have authority "to irrevocably give, grant, limit, or restrain" the right of taxation. Any contract aimed at encouraging monopoly is declared void.

INSURANCE COMPANIES

Resident life insurance companies are required to deposit $100,000 subject to the order of the Comptroller General of Georgia as a guaranty for the security of policy holders, and non-resident life insurance companies are required to show the Comptroller General that they have a like sum deposited with a responsible officer of the state where they are chartered. The General Assembly is directed to compel fire insurance companies to deposit reasonable securities with the Treasurer of Georgia, to make annual reports to the Comptroller General, and to publish the same at their own expense for the information and protection of the people.

PROPERTY OF WIFE

The property of a wife is not liable for the debts of her husband.

ARTICLE V

THE EXECUTIVE

The Constitution vests "the executive power" in the Governor, and it is well to emphasize the importance of this office. The election of the Governor is the state's chief political event. Candidates for the office are chosen by political parties, and some understanding of this process is essential even though parties and primaries are not mentioned in the written Constitution.

POLITICAL PARTIES

Following the Civil War of the 1860's, the Democratic party became the dominant party in Georgia as in all of the other Southern States. The harsh measures of the reconstruction years were associated with the Republican party.

Continuing a trend started during the presidency of Franklin D. Roosevelt, by the 1950's the Democratic party had become the liberal party and the Republican party the conservative party of the nation, and there was a marked increase in the number of Republican votes in Georgia. Whereas the Republicans had won less than 20% of Georgia's vote in any previous presidential election in the twentieth century, in 1952 with Eisenhower as their candidate they won 30% of the votes cast in Georgia. In 1964, the Republican candidate Barry Goldwater won 54% of Georgia's vote, and the state's electoral vote went Republican for the first time in history. In the gubernatorial election of 1966, the Republican candidate Howard H. (Bo) Callaway received more popular votes than did the Democratic candidate (Lester Maddox), but neither received a majority vote. The contest went to the General Assembly under existing law (since changed), and the Assembly elected the Democratic nominee. In the elections of 1970 and 1974 Democratic nominees for most state offices were successful.

PARTY ORGANIZATION

Both the Democratic and Republican parties have a state committee, congressional district committees, county committees, and in some cities, precinct committees. In other words, there is a party committee at every level of government at which elections are held. The parties also hold periodic conventions at most of these levels. Members of party committees at the county level are elected by the local members of the party. In general, members of committees and conventions at higher levels are appointed.

NOMINATION OF CANDIDATES

The nomination of candidates is a highly important step in the electoral process. Under present conditions, after the Democratic and Republican parties have selected their nominees for an office, the choice open to the public is a choice between two men.

In the 19th century candidates for Governor were nominated at state conventions of political parties. Early in the 20th century the Democratic party began to hold a primary election in which the people voted directly for the Democratic nominee. Men got their name on the primary ballot by paying a fee to the Democratic State Executive Committee, and the voters chose between the men listed on the primary ballot. The outcome of the election was governed, however, by a county unit rule. The candidate who received the largest popular vote carried a county and received its unit vote (2, 4, or 6 unit votes, according to the county population). This plan was outlawed by the federal courts in 1962, and since then the Democratic nominee has been chosen by a majority of the popular votes in the Democratic primary.

Prior to 1970 the Republican party chose its candidate for Governor at a state convention. The use of a primary election, however, is almost required by recent Georgia laws. A party nominating a candidate by any method other than a primary has to meet difficult technicalities, including the presentation of a petition signed by 5% of the electors, in order to get the name of its candidate on the ballot for the general election.

Under Georgia law, party primaries are conducted in each county by the Ordinary on the 2nd Wednesday in September. The Secretary of State sends to each Ordinary the names of candidates for state offices certified to him by party officials. A person wishing to get his name on his party's primary ballot must qualify with the appropriate party committee three months before the primary election.

If no candidate wins a majority vote in a primary, a runoff election is held between the two highest candidates.

OFFICIAL ELECTION OF GOVERNOR

The Governor and other officers chosen on a state-wide basis are elected by a majority of the popular vote cast in an election held quadrennially, (1974, 1978, etc.) on Tuesday after the first Monday in November. This date was chosen to coincide with the date of the election of members of Congress, who are elected every two years. Every four years presidential electors are also elected on this same day of the year, but, since presidential elections come in years divisible by four, it should be noted that Governors of Georgia and Presidents of the United States are not elected at the same time but at alternating two-year periods.

A constitutional amendment of 1968 provides that if no candidate for Governor receives a majority vote in the election, a run-off election shall be held between the two highest candidates. The same majority election rule applies to all state offices.

Term. The term of the Governor is four years "and until his successor shall be chosen and qualified." In Thompson v. Talmadge[1] the Supreme Court ruled that the Governor-elect having died between the date of the November general election and the publication of the returns by the General Assembly, the General Assembly was without authority to elect a Governor and the incumbent Governor continued in office until he voluntarily resigned in order to permit the Lieutenant Governor to exercise the executive power.

A Governor elected for a four year term is ineligible to succeed himself or to hold again the office of Governor until the expiration of four years. While no court decision has been rendered on the point, in 1950 the Attorney General ruled that this provision of Article V, Section I, Paragraph I applied only to full four-year terms and not to unexpired terms. Thus Governor Herman Talmadge, who was elected in 1948 to serve two years of his father's unexpired term, was reelected in 1950 for a full term of four years. In Henderson v. Maddox[2] the Supreme Court held that it was not persuaded "by the argument that the primary purpose of the Lieutenant Governor is to succeed to the office of Governor in the event of a vacancy and, therefore, the Constitution in barring a Governor from succeeding himself, by implication, disqualifies him from holding the office of Lieutenant Governor."

---

[1]201 Ga. 867 (1947).
[2]227 Ga. 195 (1970).

QUALIFICATIONS AND SALARY

The constitutional qualifications for the Governor are thirty years of age, citizenship of the United States for fifteen years and of Georgia for six years. The annual salary of the Governor, as stated in the Constitution, is $12,000, but by statutory law he receives additional compensation. In 1974 he received an annual salary of $50,000 plus an allowance of $25,000 for the operation of the Governor's mansion.

SUCCESSION TO GOVERNOR

The Constitution of 1954 provides for a Lieutenant Governor for the first time in the history of Georgia. He is elected at the same time and in the same manner as the Governor and must have the same qualifications. The Lieutenant Governor is President of the Senate. In the event of the death, resignation, or disability of the Governor, the Lieutenant Governor "shall exercise the executive power" until the next general election for members of the General Assembly, when a Governor will be elected for the unexpired term. However, should the next general election come within 30 days from the time the Lieutenant Governor succeeds, the Lieutenant Governor will fill the remainder of the unexpired term.

In case of the death, resignation, or disability of both the Governor and the Lieutenant Governor, succession passes to the Speaker of the House of Representatives. He shall exercise the executive power until a Governor, to be elected in a special election held within 60 days, shall qualify.

POWERS OF THE GOVERNOR

The Governor of Georgia has constitutional powers comparable to those of the governors of the other states in the American union. The Constitution vests "the executive power" in a Governor but does not define the term. A number of powers are stated specifically: "The Governor shall be commander-in-chief of the army and navy of this State, and of the militia thereof"; he "shall take care that the laws are faithfully executed, and shall be a conservator of the peace throughout the State"; he shall issue writs of election to fill all vacancies in the General Assembly;

he may call special sessions of the General Assembly; he may veto legislative acts; and he may require information in writing from all state employees "on any subject relating to the duties of their respective offices or employment." In practice the Governor, holding a dominant position in party organization, exercises a weighty influence in legislation. The campaign pledges of a successful candidate for Governor are likely to be enacted into law by the first session of the General Assembly convening after his inauguration. Under the statutory law, the Governor is named Director of the Budget and vested with extensive control over the finances of the state.

Appointments and removals. The Governor's powers of appointment are important but, as is true in most of the states, those constitutional executive officers who are comparable to members of the President's cabinet in our national government are elected by popular vote. Such appointive powers as he possesses are largely confined to statutory officials and to the filling of vacancies caused by death, resignation, or disabilities. Most of the major appointments require Senatorial confirmation. The Governor's removal power is not nearly so extensive by comparison as that of the President of the United States. The Supreme Court of Georgia has repeatedly ruled that the Governor has no inherent power of removal. Hence in order to determine whether a particular officer is subject to removal by the Governor, and under what circumstances, it is necessary to consult the statutory law governing the office. In general, officials elected or appointed for a definite term are not subject to removal, but officials appointed for an indefinite term hold office at the pleasure of the Governor. In some instances the Governor is authorized to suspend an officer until the next meeting of the General Assembly, which may order the suspended official to be either removed or reinstated.

Suspension of death sentence. By an amendment of 1943, continued in the Constitution of 1945, the broad pardoning power formerly vested in the Governor was vested in a Board of Pardons and Paroles. "The State Board of Pardons and Paroles," stated the amendment, "shall have power to grant reprieves, pardons, and paroles, to commute penalties, remove disabilities imposed by law, and may remit any part of a sentence for any offense against the State, after conviction, except in cases of treason or impeachment, and except in cases in which the Governor refuses to suspend a sentence of death." The power of the Governor is now limited to a suspension of execution in death sentences until the Board has had time to hear an application of relief, and in cases of conviction of treason until the General Assembly has pardoned, commuted, or ordered execution of the sentence. However, upon satisfactory evidence that a person convicted of a capital offense is insane, the Governor may commit him to the insane asylum until his sanity is restored.

OTHER CONSTITUTIONAL EXECUTIVE OFFICERS

Other executive officers named in the Constitution and elected at the same time and in the same manner as the Governor are the (1) Lieutenant Governor, (2) Attorney General, (3) Comptroller General, (4) Commissioner of Agriculture, (5) Commissioner of Labor, (6) Secretary of State, and (7) State School Superintendent.

CONSTITUTIONAL BOARDS

A department headed by an individual has the advantage of concentrating power and responsibility, but some government agencies having the responsibility both to formulate and to execute policy are headed by a group of people. Numerous boards exist under the statutory law of Georgia, and fifteen state boards are provided for in the Constitution, as follows:

(1) Board of Regents of the University System (15 members; terms of 7 years)
(2) State Board of Education (10 members; terms of 7 years)
(3) Public Service Commission (5 members; terms of 6 years)
(4) Board of Pardons and Paroles (5 to 7 members; terms of 7 years)
(5) Board of Corrections (5 members; terms of 5 years)
(6) Board of Natural Resources (15 members; terms of 7 years)
(7) Personnel Board (3 members; terms of 7 years)
(8) Veterans Service Board (7 members; terms of 7 years)
(9) State Medical Education Board (5 members; terms of 4 years)
(10) Board of Community Development (20 members; terms of 6 years)
(11) State Transportation Board (10 members; terms of 5 years)
(12) State Dental Education Board (composition by statute)
(13) State Scholarship Commission (composition by statute)
(14) Constitutional Officers Election Board (ex officio membership)
(15) Judicial Qualifications Commission (7 members, terms of 4 years)

The members of most of these boards are appointed by the Governor with confirmation by the Senate, and their terms are staggered in such a way as to give continuity to their personnel. The members of the Public Service Commission are popularly elected; members of the State Transportation Board are elected by the General Assembly; and members of the Judicial Qualifications Commission are appointed as follows: two by the Supreme Court, three by the Board of Governors of the State Bar, and two by the Governor. The powers of the several boards are subject to varying degrees of control by the General Assembly. The powers of the Board of Pardons and Paroles and the State Medical Education Board are set forth in the Constitution, and the powers of the Board of Regents and the State Board of Education are "frozen" by the constitutional provision that they "shall have such powers and duties as provided by law and existing at the time of the adoption of this Constitution, together with such further powers and duties as may be hereafter provided by law." The powers of the Teacher Retirement System and the Employees Retirement System were similarly frozen by a constitutional amendment of 1952, although those two bodies are statutory, not constitutional boards. The Board of Corrections and the Veterans Service Board are specifically authorized to appoint a director as their executive officer. While the State School Superintendent is elected by popular vote, he is named in the Constitution as the executive officer of the State Board of Education.

ARTICLE VI
The Judiciary

The Supreme Court and the Court of Appeals are courts of appellate jurisdiction only. The Superior Courts, which meet in every county, are the principal trial courts. There are, however, a number of other trial courts, some of which have specialized jurisdiction. The courts of Georgia are as follows:

SUPREME COURT

The Supreme Court is composed of seven justices elected by popular vote for terms of six years. The Supreme Court has no original jurisdiction, but is a court for the correction of errors made by the Superior Courts and City Courts in cases involving: (a) the constitutionality of a law of the State of Georgia or of the United States, (b) title to land, (c) equity, (d) the construction of wills, (e) conviction of a capital felony, (f) *habeas corpus*, (g) extraordinary remedies, and (h) divorce and alimony. The Supreme Court also has authority to bring up by *certiorari* any case from the Court of Appeals.

COURT OF APPEALS

The Court of Appeals is composed of nine judges,[1] elected by popular vote for terms of six years. This court has appellate jurisdiction over the Superior and City Courts in all cases other than those in which the Supreme Court has jurisdiction. It may certify questions to the Supreme Court, and decisions of the Supreme Court are binding upon it as precedents. The judges of the Court of Appeals select one of their members as Chief Judge, and he divides the members into three divisions of three judges each for hearing cases. If there is a dissent among the three judges in a division on a case, the case is then heard by a full bench of nine judges.

COURT OF CLAIMS

The State of Georgia, like other members of the United States, is "sovereign" in the sense of being immune to most suits for damages commenced by individuals, except to the extent that the State waives this immunity.

The traditional method used by citizens to gain compensation for claims against the State of Georgia has been special acts of the General Assembly awarding damages to named individuals. A constitutional amendment of 1974 authorizes the General Assembly to establish a Court of Claims to dispose of cases involving claims against the State. The extent of the State's immunity to be waived and details concerning the Court of Claims are left to the discretion of the General Assembly.

SUPERIOR COURTS

The state is divided by statute into 42 superior court judicial circuits, with one or more judges in each. Judges of the Superior Courts are elected by the people for terms of four years. The judge of a Superior Court must hold court in every county within his circuit at least twice a year. The Superior Courts are the principal state courts of original jurisdiction for both criminal and civil cases, and have exclusive jurisdiction in (a) cases of divorce, (b) criminal cases where the offender is subject to loss of life or confinment in the penitentiary (except in the case of juvenile offenders as provided by law), (c) cases respecting titles to land, and (d) equity cases.

---

1. This number is fixed by statute.

There is a District Attorney for each judiciary circuit, elected in the same manner and for the same term as the judges of the Superior Courts, to represent the state in cases before the Superior Court. In each county a sheriff enforces orders of the Superior court and a clerk keeps its records.

PROBATE COURTS

The Constitution establishes a Probate Court for each county, and provides that the judge of this court shall be elected for a term of four years. The jurisdiction of the Probate Court, fixed by statute, covers the probation of wills, administration of estates, appointment of guardians, and the issuance of lunacy commissions. The Constitution vests jurisdiction in the Probate Court in counties not having a City or County Court in misdemeanor cases arising under the Highway Patrol Act of 1937 and other traffic laws, and in all cases arising under the Compulsory School Attendance Law. Appeals from decisions of the Probate Court are taken to the Superior Court of the county.

STATE COUNTY COURTS

The Constitution enumerates certain courts and authorizes "such other courts as have been or may be established by law." The Superior Courts are made the principal trial courts and vested also with power "to correct errors in inferior judicatories"; hence most appeals from lower courts are to the Superior Court, and not to the State Supreme Court or State Court of Appeals. However, the Constitution makes an exception by allowing a direct appeal to the Supreme Court or Court of Appeals from "city courts" meeting certain specifications. Through the years 50-odd city courts with the designated specifications were created by special acts. The name "city court" was misleading since a court of this type had county-wide jurisdiction, for example, the City Court of Athens in and for Clarke County.

An act of 1970 changed the name of these courts to the "State Court of (whichever county in which the court is located) County." The act applies to "all courts in this State that are below the level of superior courts and have concurrent jurisdiction with superior courts to try misdemeanor cases by a jury trial or have civil jurisdiction unlimited in amount and concurrent with the superior courts in all matters, except those matters which are vested exclusively in the superior courts or have both of the above jurisdictions." In 1975 there were 59 such courts.

JUSTICES OF THE PEACE

The smallest political subdivision of the state is the militia district, of which there are today approximately 1,650, used primarily as voting precincts. The Constitution provides for one justice of the peace, elected by the people of the district for a term of four years, for each militia district, but authorizes the General Assembly in its discretion to replace justices of the peace by any system of courts deemed advisable in cities having a population above 20,000 or in any county having such a city within its borders. Justices of the peace have jurisdiction in all civil cases arising from contracts or from damage to personal property where the principal sum does not exceed $200. By statute justices of the peace are authorized to issue warrants for a number of purposes, including the dispossession of a tenant holding over after the expiration of his lease and the attachment of property. Those warrants are enforced by the sheriff unless the person against whom they are directed posts bond and has the matter at issue litigated in the Superior Court. The Justice of the Peace also aids in conserving the public peace by issuing warrants for the apprehension of any person charged on oath with crime, and by examining the accused and either committing him to jail to await trial or discharging him.

In addition to justices of the peace, the Constitution provides that upon the recommendation of the grand jury of any county the judge of the Superior Court may appoint one commissioned notary public for each militia district, who shall be commissioned by the governor for the term of four years. These commissioned notaries public are *ex officio* justices of the peace, and except in the method of selection, there is no difference between the office of a commissioned notary public and that of a justice of the peace. These judicial commissioned notaries public are not to be confused with notaries public of the state at large whose principal authority is to witness signatures and to administer oaths.

JUVENILE COURTS

Since 1915 a number of special acts and several general laws have provided for juvenile courts. The Juvenile Court Act of 1951 created juvenile courts for counties having a population of 50,000 or more, continued existing juvenile courts in smaller counties, and authorized the creation of a juvenile court in any county upon the recommendation of two successive grand juries.

In counties not having a juvenile court, the judge of the Superior Court was authorized to act as a juvenile court judge. Juvenile courts have jurisdiction over children under 17 years of age charged with crime.

The judge of a juvenile court for any county is appointed by the judge or judges of the Superior Court of the circuit in which the county is located. He in turn appoints probation officers, employees of detention homes, and other needed personnel.

ARTICLE VII
Taxation and Public Debt

The purposes for which the state may levy taxes are enumerated in the Constitution, and the amount of the state tax on property is limited to one-fourth mill on each dollar of the value of the taxable property. The state thus leaves the taxation of property largely to cities and counties, and relies for state revenue upon a general sales tax, an income tax, and a number of other taxes—such as taxes on the sales of motor fuel, tobacco, and alcoholic beverages.

An amendment of 1952 provides for the allocation of all motor fuel taxes to the Highway Department.

PURPOSES OF TAXATION

Article VII is the longest article in the Constitution. One reason for its excessive length is the inclusion of too many details on the purposes of taxation. As written in 1945, the list of enumerated purposes of taxation included "For educational purposes." Despite this broad authorization, during the past two decades more than a dozen amendments have been added authorizing taxation for specific educational purposes, including medical scholarships, dental scholarships, Regents' scholarships, scholarships "to students desiring to study courses in paramedical, professional or educational fields," tuition grants to children of servicemen missing in action, etc. Clearly this mass of detailed provisions should be placed in statutes, not in the Constitution.

EXEMPTIONS FROM TAXATION

For a complete list of the provisions on exemptions from taxation, the reader should turn to Section I, Paragraph IV, of Article VII. Among the many subjects included are places of religious worship or burial; building erected for and used as a college, academy or other seminary of learning; institutions of purely public characity; up to $2,000 of the value of a homestead used by the owner as his residence; up to $12,500 of the value of a homestead owned and occupied by a disable veteran; up to $4,000 of the value of a homestead owned and occupied by a person 65 years of age or over, provided the combined annual income of such aged person and his spouse does not exceed $4,000; and "The homestead of each resident of each independent school district who is 62 years of age or over and who does not have an income from all sources, including the income from all sources of all members of the family residing within said homestead, exceeding $6,000 per annum, may be exempt from all ad valorem taxation for educational purposes levied for and in behalf of such school system."

The subject is a complex one. Note that some of the paragraphs involved begin with the phrase, "The General Assembly may, by law, exempt from taxation" designated types of property, while other paragraphs begin with phrases granting positively certain exemptions, for example, "Each disabled veteran . . . is hereby granted an exemption. . . ." Moreover, some of the exemptions do not apply to all levels of government. For example, the $2,000 homestead exemption does not apply to taxes levied by municipalities.

DEBT LIMITATIONS

Other than loans to supply temporary deficits, State debts are classified as (a) general obligation debts and (b) guaranteed revenue debts. Guaranteed revenue debts are debts incurred by the State in guaranteeing payment of the revenue obligations of State instrumentalities issued to finance transportation facilities, water or sewage systems, or loans for educational purposes. The total of the general obligation debt plus the guaranteed revenue debt is limited to an amount on which the annual debt service (payment) will not exceed 15% of the total State revenue receipts of the previous fiscal year.

LIMITATIONS ON COUNTIES AND MUNICIPALITIES

Certain purposes for which counties may levy taxes are enumerated, but the General Assembly may authorize any county to levy taxes for any public purpose. The only limit on the amount of tax is a 20 mill limit on school taxes. This limitation may be removed in any county by a recommendation of the County Board of Education approved in a popular referendum.

The debt that may be incurred by a county or municipality is limited to 10% of the assessed value of the taxable property therein, and has to be approved in a referendum by a majority of the qualified voters voting therein.

ARTICLE VIII
Education

The State Board of Education, State School Superintendent, and the Board of Regents of the University System were described above in the discussion of executive officers. In addition to the officials, Article VIII provides for a county board of education and a county school superintendent for each county. The county board of education consists of five members appointed by the grand jury for terms of five years. The county school superintendent is elected by popular vote for a term of four years. These provisions, however, are not uniform throughout the state. Constitutional amendments of local application only have altered the school system in many counties, and an amendment of 1966 authorizes such changes by statute. Cities are authorized to maintain independent school systems, but no new independent system may be established.

ARTICLE IX
Homestead and Exemptions

This article provides that the property of the head of a family, and certain others, to the amount of $1,600 shall be exempt from levy and sale by any process whatsoever. The debtor may waive his right to such exemption. As a result of the economic dislocation resulting from the Civil War, a homestead and exemption clause to protect the debtor against the sale of all his property was included in the Constitution of 1868, and Article IX of the present Constitution is an outgrowth of this clause.

ARTICLE X
The Militia

This article authorizes the General Assembly to provide by law how the militia of the state shall be organized and equipped. The Officers and men are not to receive compensation except when in active service.

ARTICLE XI
Counties

Georgia is divided into 159 counties which are, on the one hand, administrative divisions of the state, and, on the other, corporate bodies vested by law with certain powers of their own. No additional counties can be created. The General Assembly may provide for the consolidation of two or more counties, provided a majority of the qualified voters of each of the counties affected give their approval in an election held for that purpose. The Constitution requires uniformity in county government, with the following exceptions: In any county the General Assembly may establish Commissioners of Roads and Revenue, abolish the office of Treasurer, and consolidate the offices of Tax Receiver and Tax Collector into the office of Tax Commissioner.

COUNTY COMMISSIONERS

The principal governing authority in 156 counties is the Board of Commissioners, which has control of taxation, roads, public buildings, paupers, and other county matters. In Towns and Union counties these powers are exercised by the Probate Court, and in Muscogee County there is a council for the consolidated Muscogee-City of Columbus government. The County Commissioners for the several counties vary in number from one to nine, but most counties have either three or five Commissioners. Most of them are elected, but in a few counties they are appointed by the grand jury.

OTHER COUNTY OFFICERS

Other officers usually found in Georgia counties include the ordinary, sheriff, clerk of the Superior Court, board of education, superintendent of schools, tax collector, tax receiver, treasurer, coroner, justices of the peace, commissioned notaries public, agricultural agent, home demonstration agent, county police, welfare board, welfare director, board of tax assessors, registrars, jury commissioners, and constables. Most of these officials are elected by popular vote for a term of four years. The first fourteen listed are mentioned in the Constitution.[1]

ARTICLE XII

The Laws of General Operation

The laws of general operation in this state are (1) the Constitution of the United States and the laws and treaties of the United States, (2) the Constitution of Georgia, and (3) the statutory laws of Georgia.

ARTICLE XIII

Amendments

Amendments to the Constitution may be proposed by a two-thirds vote of the members elected to each branch of the General Assembly. To become effective, they must be ratified by popular vote. The method of ratification differs for a "general" amendment (*i.e.*, an amendment of state-wide application) and for a "local" amendment (*i.e.*, one that affects directly only a particular political subdivision such as a city, county, or school district, or two or more subdivisions.) The Governor, Attorney General, and Secretary of State meeting together are authorized to determine which proposed amendments are general and which are local in application.

GENERAL AMENDMENTS

After passing each house of the General Assembly by a two-thirds vote, an amendment of statewide application is published in full once each week for three consecutive weeks immediately preceding the date of the next general election for members of the General Assembly, in one newspaper of general circulation in each of the state's ten congressional districts. It is submitted to a vote of the people at this election. To be ratified, it must receive an affirmative vote of a majority of the voters *voting thereon.*

LOCAL AMENDMENTS

Amendments of local application are proposed by the General Assembly in the same manner as general amendments, but the procedure for ratification is different. A local amendment is

1. Articles VI, VII, VIII, and XI, *passim.*

published in a newspaper only in the county affected, or the county wherein the political subdivision or subdivisions affected are located. To become effective, it must be approved by a majority vote of the voters voting thereon. If two or more subdivisions are affected, the votes in each shall be counted separately, and the amendment must receive the affirmative vote of a majority of the votes cast thereon in each of the subdivisions to become effective.

CRITICISM OF LOCAL AMENDMENTS

That the Constitution should be confined to basic law is a matter of general agreement among students of constitutional government. To clutter it up with numerous amendments confined in application to particular localities tends to destroy its value. If there is a provision in the Constitution that is too restrictive in application and does not meet the approval of the people, then, rather than adopting dozens of "local amendments" making exceptions to the general rule, the general rule itself should be changed. Article VIII, Section V, Paragraph I, dealing with county Boards of Education, had been amended more than 80 times by local amendments before it was altered by a general amendment in 1966. When an exception to a constitutional rule is proposed for a particular city or county or school district, the General Assembly should consider with care the advisability of modifying the general rule as applied to all political subdivisions. If the decision is against modifying the general rule, it should take a strong case to justify an exception for a particular subdivision. For example, the Constitution of 1877 was amended seven times to authorize particular cities to pass zoning laws. Then a general amendment was passed authorizing the General Assembly to grant power for zoning to any city or county having a population of one thousand or more. Was there any justification for eight amendments on this subject?

In the period from 1945 to 1974, the Constitution of 1945 was amended 831 times! One hundred and forty-seven of these amendments were of statewide application and 684 of local application. Commenting upon the trend, in *Robert v. Suttles* (1956), Justice Wyatt of the Georgia Supreme Court stated: "We are not unmindful of the argument that this is a very dangerous way in which to deal with the fundamental law of our State and that the Constitution is rapidly becoming a hodgepodge of so-called general provisions with local application. . . . We agree that the fundamental law of our State, the Constitution, by this method is being undermined and destroyed."

ARTICLE XIV
Merit System

This article provides for a State Personnel Board of three members appointed by the Governor for terms of seven years, to "administer a State Merit System under which State personnel shall be selected on a basis of merit, fitness, and efficiency according to law." The Board is non-salaried, and no State employee can be a member.

ARTICLE XV
Home Rule

Municipal corporations are created by the state in order to permit a degree of self government in densely populated areas. The General Assembly of Georgia passes acts creating municipalities and setting forth the terms of their charters. The charter of each city is a separate act of the state legislature, but Georgia also has many laws applicable to all cities, or municipal corporations. Georgia has no provision, as do some states, for the courts to incorporate municipalities, nor does Georgia have any system of optional charters.

Each municipality enjoys some degree of self government, the amount depending on the terms of its charter or other provisions of state law. The term "home rule" is ill-defined, but in general it means a large amount of self government when applied to concepts of municipal government. Some persons use the term home rule to relate specifically to the power of municipalities to change the provisions of their charters without action by the state legislature. Members of the state legislature have little knowledge or interest in the affairs of particular municipalities, and a strong case can be made for giving a large amount of self government to municipalities.

The home rule article of the Constitution of Georgia was a new provision added in 1945. The article authorized the General Assembly to establish home rule, with specified conditions. In 1951 the General Assembly passed a Municipal Home Rule Law, but the courts held it void because it did not conform to the constitutional provision of Article XV for uniform systems with optional plans, and because it amounted to a delegation of legislative authority.[1] As a result of this decision, in 1954 Article XV was amended to give the General Assembly broad authority to

1. Phillips v. City of Atlanta, 210 Ga. 72 (1953).

delegate power to municipalities. An amendment of 1966 authorizes home rule for counties.

ARTICLE XVI

Slum Clearance and Development

This article was added to the Constitution in 1954 as the result of a decision of the Supreme Court of Georgia in 1953.[2] The Court held that the Housing Authority of the City of Atlanta could not be authorized to acquire, by eminent domain, land in "blighted or slum areas" for the purpose of selling it to persons who would clear and develop it for industrial sites according to the redevelopment plan. This was held not to be a public use. The constitutional amendment provides that "such work shall constitute a governmental function undertaken for public purposes."

ARTICLE XVII

Public Transportation in Atlanta

This article declares transportation of passengers in the Atlanta metropolitan area to be a public function. It authorizes the General Assembly to create a corporation or authority to deal with the subject.

---

2. Housing Authority v. Johnson, 209 Ga. 560.

Constitution of the State of Georgia

PREAMBLE

To perpetuate the principles of free government, insure justice to all, preserve peace, promote the interest and happiness of the citizen, and transmit to posterity the enjoyment of liberty, we, the people of Georgia, relying upon the protection and guidance of Almighty God, do ordain and establish this Constitution.

ARTICLE I
BILL OF RIGHTS

SECTON I

PARAGRAPH I. *Origin and Foundation of Government.* All government, of right, originates with the people, is founded upon their will only, and is instituted solely for the good of the whole. Public officers are the trustees and servants of the people, and at all times, amenable to them.

PARAGRAPH II. *Protection the Duty of Government.* Protection to person and property is the paramount duty of government, and shall be impartial and complete.

PARAGRAPH III. *Life, Liberty, and Property.* No person shall be deprived of life, liberty, or property, except by due process of law.

PARAGRAPH IV. *Right to the Courts.* No person shall be deprived of the right to prosecute or defend his own cause in any of the courts of this State, in person, by attorney, or both.

PARAGRAPH V. *Benefit of Counsel; Accusation; List of Witnesses; Compulsory Process; Trial by Jury.* Every person charged with an offense against the laws of this State shall have the privilege and benefit of counsel; shall be furnished, on demand, with a copy of the accusation, and a list of the witnesses on whose testimony the charge against him is founded; shall have compulsory process to obtain the testimony of his own witnesses; shall be confronted with the witnesses testifying against him; and shall have a public and speedy trial by an impartial jury.

PARAGRAPH VI. *Crimination of Self Not Compelled.* No person shall be compelled to give testimony tending in any manner to criminate himself.

PARAGRAPH VII. *Banishment and Whipping as Punishment for Crime.* Neither banishment beyond the limits of the State, nor whipping, as a punishment for crime, shall be allowed.

PARAGRAPH VIII. *Jeopardy of Life or Liberty More Than Once Forbidden.* No person shall be put in jeopardy of life or liberty more than once for the same offense, save on his, or her own motion for a new trial after conviction, or in case of mistrial.

PARAGRAPH IX. *Bail; Fines; Punishment; Arrest, Abuse of Prisoners.* Excessive bail shall not be required, nor excessive fines imposed, nor cruel and unusual punishments inflicted; nor shall any person be abused in being arrested, while under arrest, or in prison.

PARAGRAPH X. *Costs.* No person shall be compelled to pay costs except after conviction on final trial.

PARAGRAPH XI. *Habeas Corpus.* The writ of Habeas Corpus shall not be suspended.

PARAGRAPH XII. *Freedom of Conscience.* All men have the natural and inalienable right to worship God, each according to the dictates of his own conscience, and no human authority should, in any case, control or interfere with such right of conscience.

PARAGRAPH XIII. *Religious Opinions; Liberty of Conscience.* No inhabitant of this State shall be molested in person or property, or prohibited from holding any public office, or trust, on account of his religious opinions; but the right of liberty of conscience shall not be so construed as to excuse acts of licentiousness, or justify practices inconsistent with the peace and safety of the State.

PARAGRAPH XIV. *Appropriations to Churches, Sects, Etc., Forbidden.* No money shall ever be taken from the public Treasury, directly or indirectly, in aid of any church, sect, or denomination of religionists, or of any sectarian institution.

PARAGRAPH XV. *Liberty of Speech or of the Press Guaranteed.* No law shall ever be passed to curtail, or restrain the liberty of speech, or of the press; any person may speak, write and publish his sentiments, on all subjects, being responsible for the abuse of that liberty.

PARAGRAPH XVI. *Searches, Seizures, and Warrants.* The right of the people to be secure in their persons, houses, papers, and effects, against unreasonable searches and seizures, shall not be violated; and no warrant shall issue except upon probable cause, supported by oath, or affirmation, particularly describing the place, or places, to be searched, and the persons or things to be seized.

PARAGRAPH XVII. *Slavery and Involuntary Servitude.* There shall be within the State of Georgia neither slavery nor involuntary servitude, save as a punishment for crime after legal conviction thereof.

PARAGRAPH XVIII. *Status of the Citizen.* The social status of the citizen shall never be the subject of legislation.

PARAGRAPH XIX. *Civil Authority Superior to Military.* The civil authority shall be superior to the military, and no soldier shall, in time of peace, be quartered in any house without the consent of the owner, nor in time of war, except by the civil magistrate, in such manner as may be provided by law.

PARAGRAPH XX. *Contempts.* The power of the Courts to punish for contempt shall be limited by legislative acts.

PARAGRAPH XXI. *Imprisonment for Debt.* There shall be no imprisonment for debt.

PARAGRAPH XXII. *Arms, Right to Keep and Bear.* The right of the people to keep and bear arms, shall not be infringed, but the General Assembly shall have power to prescribe the manner in which arms may be borne.

PARAGRAPH XXIII. *Legislative, Judicial, and Executive Powers, Separate.* The legislative, judicial, and executive powers shall forever remain separate and distinct, and no person discharging the duties of one, shall, at the same time, exercise the functions of either of the others, except as herein provided.

PARAGRAPH XXIV. *Right to Assemble and Petition.* The people have the right to assemble peaceably for their common good and to apply to those vested with the powers of government for redress of grievances by petition or remonstrance.

PARAGRAPH XXV. *Citizens, Protection of.* All citizens of the United States, resident in this State, are hereby declared citizens of this State, and it shall be the duty of the General Assembly to enact such laws as will protect them in the full enjoyment of the rights, privileges and immunities due to such citizenship.

SECTION II

PARAGRAPH I. *Libel; Jury in Criminal Cases; New Trials.* In all prosecutions or indictments for libel the truth may be given in evidence; and the jury in all criminal cases, shall be the judges of the law and the facts. The power of the judges to grant new trials in case of conviction is preserved.

PARAGRAPH II. *Treason.* Treason against the State of Georgia, shall consist in levying war against her; adhering to her enemies; giving them aid and comfort. No person shall be convicted of treason, except on the testimony of two witnesses to the same overt act, or confession in open court.

PARAGRAPH III. *Conviction, Effect of.* No conviction shall work corruption of blood, or forfeiture of estate.

PARAGRAPH IV. *Lotteries.* All lotteries, and the sale of lottery tickets, are hereby prohibited; and this prohibition shall be enforced by penal laws.

PARAGRAPH V. *Lobbying; Penalties.* Lobbying is declared to be a crime, and the General Assembly shall enforce this provision by suitable penalties.

PARAGRAPH VI. *Fraud; Concealment of Property.* The General Assembly shall have the power to provide for the punishment of fraud; and, shall provide by law, for reaching property of the debtor concealed from the creditor.

SECTION III

PARAGRAPH I. *Private ways; just compensation; relocation assistance; land acquisition policies; practices and expenses.* 1. In case of necessity, private ways may be granted upon just compensation being first paid by the applicant. Private property shall not be taken, or damaged, for public purposes, without just and adequate compensation being first paid, except that when private property is taken or damaged for public road and street purposes by the State and the counties and the municipalities of the State, just and adequate compensation therefor need not be paid until the same has been finally fixed and determined as provided by law, but such just and adequate compensation shall then be paid in preference to all other obligations except bonded indebtedness. The General Assembly may by law require the condemnor to make prepayment against adequate compensation as a condition precedent to the exercise of the right of eminent domain and provide for the disbursement of the same to the end that the rights and equities of the property owner, lien holders, and the State and its subdivisions may be protected.

2. Notwithstanding any other provisions of this Constitution, the General Assembly of the State of Georgia may by law require the State and State agencies and institutions, and counties, municipalities, school districts, political subdivisions, public authorities, public agencies, public corporatons and public instrumentalities created under this Constitution or the laws of this State: (i) to provide relocation assistance and payments to persons displaced by public projects or programs undertaken or sponsored by the foregoing public entities, including without limitation, all of those relocation assistances and payments as are, by section 210 of that certain Act of Congress of the United States of America known as the Uniform Relocation Assistance

and Real Property Acquisition Policies Act of 1970 (Public Law 91-646, 91st Congress, approved January 2, 1971), required to be made or furnished to such displaced persons by such public entities in order that federal financial assistance can be made available to such public entities with respect to the public projects or programs causing such displacements, and (ii) to establish and implement acquisition policies and practices and provide for the payment or reimbursement of necessary expenses of persons whose properties are acquired in connection with the acquisition of real property for public projects or programs, such policies, practices, payments and reimbursements to include, without limitation, those real property acquisition policies, practices, payments and reimbursements which section 305 of said Uniform Relocation Assistance and Real Property Acquisition Policies Act of 1970 requires that the foregoing public entities establish and implement or pay and reimburse, as the case may be, in acquiring real property for a public project or program in order that federal financial assistance can be made available to such public entities with respect to such projects or programs. The providing of all of such relocation assistances and payments and, in connection with the acquisition of real property for public projects or programs, the establishing of all of such policies and practices and the paying or reimbursing of all of such necessary expenses, are declared to be necessary, among other reasons, in order to avoid the loss of large sums of money which will otherwise be made available to the foregoing public entities as financial assistance by the United States of America and shall constitute governmental functions undertaken for public purposes, and the powers of taxation may be exercised and public funds expended in furtherance thereof.

[Editorial note: Paragraph I was amended in 1960 and in 1972.]

Paragraph II. *Attainder; Ex Post Facto and Retroactive Laws, Etc.* No bill of attainder, ex post facto law, retroactive law, or law impairing the obligation of contracts, or making irrevocable grant of special privileges or immunities, shall be passed.

Paragraph III. *Revocation of Tax Exemptions.* All exemptions from taxation heretofore granted in corporate charters are declared to be henceforth null and void.

Section IV

Paragraph I. *General Laws; Uniform Operation; How Varied.* Laws of a general nature shall have uniform operation throughout the State, and no special law shall be enacted in any case for which provision has been made by an existing general law. No general law affecting private rights, shall be varied in any particular case, by special legislation, except with the free consent, in writing, of all persons to be affected thereby; and no person under legal disability to contract, is capable of such consent.

[Editorial note: That portion of Paragraph I beginning with the word "except" and continuing to the end of the paragraph was added by an amendment ratified on November 8, 1960.]

PARAGRAPH II. *What Acts Void.* Legislative acts in violation of this Constitution, or the Constitution of the United States, are void, and the Judiciary shall so declare them.

SECTION V

PARAGRAPH I. *State Rights.* The people of this State have the inherent, sole and exclusive right to regulating their internal government, and the police thereof, and of altering and abolishing their Constitution whenever it may be necessary to their safety and happiness.

PARAGRAPH II. *Enumeration of Rights Not Denial of Others.* The enumeration of rights herein contained as a part of this Constitution shall not be construed to deny to the people any inherent rights which they may have hitherto enjoyed.

SECTION VI

PARAGRAPH I. *Tidewater Titles Confirmed.* The Act of the General Assembly approved December 16, 1902, which extends the title of ownership of lands abutting on tidal water to low water mark is hereby ratified and confirmed.

ARTICLE II
ELECTIVE FRANCHISE

SECTION I

PARAGRAPH I. *Elections by Ballot; Registration of Voters.* Elections by the people shall be by ballot, and only those persons shall be allowed to vote who have been first registered in accordance with the requirements of law.

PARAGRAPH II. *Who Shall Be An Elector Entitled to Register and Vote.* Every citizen of this State who is a citizen of the United States, eighteen years old or upwards, not laboring under any of the disabilities named in this Article, and possessing the qualifications provided by it, shall be an elector and entitled to register and vote at any election by the people: Provided, that no soldier, sailor or marine in the military or naval services of the United States shall acquire the rights of an elector by reason of being stationed on duty in this State.

PARAGRAPH III. *Residence Requirements to Register and Vote.* The General Assembly shall provide by law for the durational residence requirements necessary to register and vote at any election by the people except that no person shall be entitled to register and vote unless he shall have resided in the State at least thirty (30) days immediately preceding the election at which he seeks to vote.

[Editorial note: Paragraph III was amended in 1966 and in 1972.]

PARAGRAPH IV. *Qualifications of Electors.* Every citizen of this State shall be entitled to register as an elector, and to vote in all elections in said State, who is not disqualified under the provisions of Section II of Article II of this Constitution, and who possesses the qualifications prescribed in Paragraphs II and III of this Section or who will possess them at the date of the election occurring next after his registration, and who in addition thereto comes within either of the classes provided for in the two following subdivisions of this paragraph.

1. All persons who are of good character and understand the duties and obligations of citizenship under a republican form of government; or,

2. All persons who can correctly read in the English language any paragraph of the Constitution of the United States or of this State and correctly write the same in the English language when read to them by any of the registrars, and all persons who solely because of physical disability are unable to comply with the above requirements but who can understand and give a reasonable interpretation of any paragraph of the Constitution of the United States or of this State that may be read to them by any one of the registrars.

PARAGRAPH V. *Appeal From Decision of Registrars.* Any person to whom the right of registration is denied by the registars upon the ground that he lacks the qualifications set forth in the two subdivisions of Paragraph IV shall have the right to take an appeal, and any citizen may enter an appeal from the decision of the registrars allowing any person to register under said subdivisions. All appeals must be filed in writing with the registrars within ten days from the date of the decision complained of and shall be returned by the registrars to the office of the clerk of the superior court to be tried as other appeals.

PARAGRAPH VI. *Judgment of Force Pending Appeal.* Pending an appeal and until the final decision of the case, the judgment of the registrars shall remain in full force.

SECTION II

PARAGRAPH I. *Registration of Electors; Who Disfranchised.* The General Assembly may provide, from time to time, for the registration of all electors, but the following classes of persons shall not be permitted to register, vote or hold any office, or appointment of honor, or trust in this State, to-wit: 1st. Those who shall have been convicted in any court of competent jurisdiction of treason against the State, of embezzlement of public funds, malfeasance in office, bribery or larcency, or of any crime involving moral turpitude, punishable by the laws of this State with imprisonment in the penitentiary, unless such persons shall have been pardoned. 2nd. Idiots and insane persons.

SECTION III

PARAGRAPH I. *Privilege of Electors from Arrest.* Electors shall, in all cases, except for treason, felony, larceny, and breach of the peace, be privileged from arrest during their attendance on elections, and in going to and returning from the same.

SECTION IV

PARAGRAPH I. *Holder of Public Funds.* No person who is the holder of any public money, contrary to law, shall be eligible to any office in this State until the same is accounted for and paid into the Treasury.

SECTION V

PARAGRAPH I. *Sale of Liquors on Election Days.* The General Assembly shall by law forbid the sale of intoxicating drinks in this State or any political subdivision thereof on all days for the holding of any election in the area in which such election is held and prescribe punishment for any violation of the same.

SECTION VI

PARAGRAPH I. *Returns Made to Whom.* Returns of election for all civil officers elected by the people, who are to be commissioned by the Governor, and also for members of the General Assembly, shall be made to the Secretary of State, unless otherwise provided by law.

Section VII

Paragraph I. *Write-In Votes.* No person elected on a write-in vote shall be eligible to hold office unless notice of his intention of candidacy was given twenty or more days prior to the election by the person to be a write-in candidate, or by some other person or group of persons qualified to vote in the subject election, as follows: In a state general election, to the Secretary of State and by publication in a paper of general circulation in the state; in a general election of county officers, to the Judge of the Probate Court of the county in which he is to be a candidate and by publication in the official organ of the same county; in a municipal general election, to the mayor or similar officer thereof and by publication in the official gazette of the municipality holding the election. The General Assembly may enact other reasonable regulations and require compliance therewith as a condition of eligibility to hold office in this State.

[Editorial note: Section VII was added by an amendment ratified Nov. 8, 1966.]

ARTICLE III
LEGISLATIVE DEPARTMENT

Section I

Paragraph I. *Power Vested in General Assembly.* The legislative power of the State shall be vested in a General Assembly which shall consist of a Senate and House of Representatives.

Section II

Paragraph I. *Apportionment of Senate.* The Senate shall consist of not less than fifty-four and not more than fifty-six members. Each Senator shall be elected from and represent one Senatorial District. The General Assembly may create, rearrange and change Senatorial Districts as it deems proper, except that each Senatorial District shall be composed of one or more counties, or may be composed of a portion of one county, but not otherwise. The apportionment of the Senate shall be changed by the General Assembly, if necessary, after each United States decennial census becomes official.

[Editorial note: This paragraph was amended in 1962 and 1968.]

Section III

Paragraph I. *Number of Representatives.* The House of Representatives shall consist of representatives apportioned among the several counties of the State as follows: To the eight counties having the largest population, three representatives each; to the thirty counties having the next largest population, two representatives each; and to the remaining counties, one representative each.

[Editorial note: This paragraph was amended to read as quoted here by an amendment ratified Nov. 2, 1954.]

PARAGRAPH II. *Apportionment Changed, How.* The above apportionment shall be changed by the General Assembly at its first session after each census taken by the United States Government in accordance with the provisions of Paragraph I of Section III of this article.

SECTION IV

PARAGRAPH I. *Term of Members.* The members of the General Assembly shall be elected for two years, and shall serve until the time fixed by law for the convening of the General Assembly in the year following the second year of such member's term of office.

[Editorial note: This paragraph was changed by an amendment ratified on Nov. 6. 1962.]

PARAGRAPH II. *Election, When.* The first election for members of the General Assembly, under this Constitution shall take place on Tuesday after the first Monday in November, 1946, and subsequent elections biennially, on that day, until the day of election is changed by law.

PARAGRAPH III. *Meeting; time limit; adjournment.* The General Assembly shall meet in regular session on the second Monday in January, 1963, and every odd-numbered year thereafter, for no longer than twelve days to organize, to receive the proposed General Appropriations Bill, and to attend to other matters, and reconvene on the second Monday in February of each odd-numbered year for no longer than thirty-three days. The General Assembly shall meet in regular session on the second Monday in January, 1964, and in every even-numbered year thereafter. By concurrent resolution adopted by a majority of members elected to both Houses of the General Assembly, the General Assembly may adjourn any regular session to such later date as it may fix for reconvening in regular session, but shall remain in regular session no longer than forty-five days in the aggregate in odd-numbered years, and no longer than forty days, in the aggregate, in even-numbered years during the terms for which members were elected. All business pending in the Senate or House at the adjournment of any regular session may be considered at any regular session of the same General Assembly, as if there had been no adjournment. Nothing herein shall be construed to affect the power of the Governor to convoke the General Assembly in extraordinary session or the duty of the Governor to convene the General Assembly in extraordinary session upon the certificate of three-fifths of the members elected to the Senate and the House of Representatives as provided in Article V, Section I, Paragraph XII of this Constitution. If an impeachment trial is pending at the end of any regular or extraordinary session, the Senate may continue in session until such trial is completed.

[Editorial note: This paragraph was changed by amendments ratified on Nov. 6, 1956, and Nov. 6, 1962.]

PARAGRAPH IV. *Quorum.* A majority of each House shall constitute a quorum to transact business; but a smaller number may adjourn from day to day and compel the presence of its absent members, as each House may provide.

PARAGRAPH V. *Oath of Members.* Each Senator and Representative, before taking his seat, shall take the following oath, or affirmation, to-wit: "I will support the Constitution of this State and of the United States, and on all questions and measures which may come before me, I will so conduct myself, as will, in my judgment, be most conducive to the interests and prosperity of this State."

PARAGRAPH VI. *Eligibility; Appointments Forbidden.* No person holding a military commission, or other appointment, or office, having any emolument, or compensation annexed thereto, under this State, or the United States, or either of them except Justices of the Peace and officers of the militia, nor any defaulter for public money, or for any legal taxes required of him shall have a seat in either house; nor shall any Senator, or Representative, after his qualification as such, be elected by the General Assembly, or appointed by the Governor, either with or without the advice and consent of the Senate, to any office or appointment having any emolument annexed thereto, during the time for which he shall have been elected, unless he shall first resign his seat, provided, however, that during the term for which he was elected no Senator or Representative shall be appointed to any civil office which has been created during such term.

PARAGRAPH VII. *Removal From District or County, Effect of.* The seat of a member of either house shall be vacated on his removal from the district or county from which he was elected.

SECTION V

PARAGRAPH I. *Qualifications of Senators.* The Senators shall be citizens of the United States, who have attained the age of twenty-five years, and who shall have been citizens of this State for four years, and for one year residents of the district from which elected.

PARAGRAPH II. *President.* The presiding officer of the Senate shall be styled the President of the Senate. A President Pro Tempore shall be elected viva voce from the Senators and shall act in case of the death, resignation or disability of the President, or in the event of his succession to the executive power.

PARAGRAPH III. *Impeachments.* The Senate shall have the sole power to try impeachments.

PARAGRAPH IV. *Trial of Impeachments.* When sitting for that purpose, the members shall be on oath, or affirmation, and shall be presided over by the Chief Justice or the Presiding Justice of the Supreme Court. Should the Chief Justice be disqualified, the Senate shall select a Justice of the Supreme Court to preside. No person shall be convicted without the concurrence of two-thirds of the members present.

PARAGRAPH V. *Judgments in Impeachments.* Judgments, in cases of impeachment, shall not extend further than removal from office, and disqualification to hold and enjoy any office of honor, trust, or profit, within this State; but the party convicted shall nevertheless, be liable, and subject, to indictment, trial, judgment, and punishment, according to law.

SECTION VI

PARAGRAPH I. *Qualifications of Representatives.* The Representatives shall be citizens of the United States who have attained the age of twenty-one years, and who shall have been citizens of this State for two years, and for one year residents of the counties from which elected.

PARAGRAPH II. *Speaker.* The presiding officer of the House of Representatives shall be styled the Speaker of the House of Representatives, and shall be elected viva voce from the body.

PARAGRAPH III. *Power to Impeach.* The House of Representatives shall have the sole power to vote impeachment charges against all persons who shall have been or may be in office.

SECTION VII

PARAGRAPH I. *Election, Returns, Etc.; Disorderly Conduct.* Each House shall be the judge of the election, returns, and qualifications of its members and shall have power to punish them for disorderly behavior, or misconduct, by censure, fine, imprisonment, or expulsion; but no member shall be expelled, except by a vote of two-thirds of the House to which he belongs.

PARAGRAPH II. *Contempts, How Punished.* Each House may

punish by imprisonment, not extending beyond the session, any person, not a member, who shall be guilty of a contempt, by any disorderly behavior in its presence, or who shall rescue, or attempt to rescue, any person arrested by order of either House.

PARAGRAPH III. *Privilege of Members.* The members of both Houses shall be free from arrest during their attendance on the General Assembly, and in going thereto, or returning therefrom, except for treason, felony, larcency, or breach of the peace; and no member shall be liable to answer in any other place for anything spoken in debate in either House.

PARAGRAPH IV. *Journals and Acts.* Each House shall keep a journal of its proceedings, and publish it immediately after its adjournment. The General Assembly shall provide for the publication of the laws passed by each session.

PARAGRAPH V. *Where Journals Kept.* The original journal shall be preserved after publication, in the office of the Secretary of State, but there shall be no other record thereof.

PARAGRAPH VI. *Yeas and Nays, When Taken.* The yeas and nays on any question shall, at the desire of one-fifth of the members present, be entered on the Journal.

PARAGRAPH VII. *Bills to Be Read.* Every bill, before it shall pass, shall be read three times, and on three separate days, in each House, unless in cases of actual invasion, or insurrection, but the first and second reading of each local bill, shall consist of the reading of the title only, unless said bill is ordered to be engrossed.

PARAGRAPH VIII. *One Subject Matter Expressed.* No law shall pass which refers to more than one subject matter, or contains matter different from what is expressed in the title thereof.

PARAGRAPH IX. *General Appropriation Bill.* The General appropriation bill shall embrace nothing except appropriations fixed by previous laws, the ordinary expenses of the Executive, Legislative and Judicial Departments of the Government, payment of the public debt and interest thereon, and for support of the public institutions and educational interests of the State. All other appropriations shall be made by separate bills, each embracing but one subject.

PARAGRAPH X. *Bills For Revenue.* All bills for raising revenue, or appropriating money, shall originate in the House of Representatives, but the Senate may propose, or concur in amendments, as in other bills.

PARAGRAPH XI. *Public Money, How Drawn.* No money shall be drawn from the Treasury except by appropriation made by law.

Paragraph XII. *Bills Appropriating Money.* No bill or resolution appropriating money shall become a law unless, upon its passage, the yeas and nays, in each house, are recorded.

Paragraph XIII. *Acts Signed; Rejected Bills.* All acts shall be signed by the President of the Senate and the Speaker of the House of Representatives, and no bill or resolution, intended to have the effect of a law, which shall have been rejected by either house, shall be again proposed during the same session, under the same or any other title, without the consent of two-thirds of the House by which the same was rejected.

Paragraph XIV. *Majority of Members to Pass Bill.* No bill shall become a law unless it shall receive a majority of the votes of all the members elected to each House of the General Assembly, and it shall, in every instance, so appear on the Journal.

Paragraph XV. *Notice of Intention to Ask Local Legislation Necessary.* No local or special bill shall be passed, unless notice of the intention to apply therefor shall have been published in the newspaper in which the Sheriff's advertisements for the locality affected are published, once a week for three weeks during a period of sixty days immediately preceding its introduction into the General Assembly. No local or special bill shall become law unless there is attached to and made a part of said bill a copy of said notice certified by the publisher, or accompanied by an affidavit of the author, to the effect that said notice has been published as provided by law. No office to which a person has been elected shall be abolished, nor the term of the office shortened or lengthened by local or special bill during the term for which such person was elected unless the same be approved by the people of the jurisdiction affected in a referendum on the question. When any local law shall add any member or members to any municipal or county governing authority, the members of which are elected by the people, such local law must provide that the member or members so added must be elected by the qualified voters of the political subdivision affected under such rules as the General Assembly may in said law provide.

[Editorial note: Paragraph XV was amended in 1952.]

Paragraph XVI. *Statutes and Sections of Code, How Amended.* No law, or section of the code, shall be amended or repealed by mere reference to its title, or to the number of the section of the Code, but the amending, or repealing act, shall distinctly describe the law to be amended or repealed, as well as the alteration to be made.

Paragraph XVII. *Corporate Powers, How Granted.* The General Assembly shall have no power to grant corporate powers and privileges to private companies, to make or change election precincts, nor to establish bridges or ferries, nor to change names of legitimate children; but it shall prescribe by law the manner in which such powers shall be exercised by the courts; it may confer this authority to grant corporate powers and privileges to private companies to the judges of the superior courts of this State in vacation. All corporate powers and privileges to banking, trust, insurance, railroad, canal, navigation, express and telegraph companies shall be issued and granted by the Secretary of State in such manner as shall be prescribed by law; and if in any event the Secretary of State should be disqualified to act in any case, then in that event the legislature shall provide by general laws by what person such charter shall be granted.

PARAGRAPH XVIII. *Recognizances.* The General Assembly shall have no power to relieve principals or securities upon forfeited recognizances, from the payment thereof, either before or after judgment thereon, unless the principal in the recognizance shall have been apprehended and placed in the custody of the proper officers.

PARAGRAPH XIX. *Yeas and Nays to Be Entered, When.* Whenever the Constitution requires a vote of two-thirds of either or both houses for the passage of an act or resolution, the yeas and nays on the passage thereof shall be entered on the Journal.

PARAGRAPH XX. *Powers of the General Assembly.* The General Assembly shall have the power to make all laws consistent with this Constitution, and not repugnant to the Constitution of the United States, which they shall deem necessary and proper for the welfare of the State.

PARAGRAPH XXI. *Signature of Governor.* No provision in this Constitution for a two-thirds vote of both houses of the General Assembly shall be construed to waive the necessity for the signature of the Governor as in any other case, except in the case of the two-thirds vote required to override the veto, to submit constitutional amendments, and in case of prolongation of a session of the General Assembly.

PARAGRAPH XXII. *Adjournment.* Neither House shall adjourn for more than three days, or to any other place, without the consent of the other, and in case of disagreement between the two Houses on a question of adjournment, the Governor may adjourn either, or both of them.

PARAGRAPH XXIII. *Zoning and Planning Laws.* The General Assembly of the State shall have authority to grant the governing authorities of the municipalities and counties authority to pass zoning and planning laws whereby such cities or counties may be zoned or districted for various uses and other or different uses prohibited therein, and regulating the use for which said zones or districts may be set apart, and regulating the plans for development and improvements on real estate therein.

PARAGRAPH XXIV. *Veterans Preference.* Any veteran who has served as a member of the armed forces of the United States during the period of a war or armed conflict in which any branch of the armed forces of the United States engaged, whether under United States command or otherwise, and was honorably discharged therefrom, shall be given such veterans preference in any civil service program established in the state government or any political subdivision thereof as may be determined by appropriate action of the General Assembly.

Provided, however, notwithstanding any such action by the General Assembly, any veteran who has served as a member of the armed forces of the United States during the period of any war or the Korean Conflict and who was honorably discharged therefrom shall be entitled to and shall receive the following preference in taking a competitive examination for employment with the state government or any political subdivision thereof:

(a) Such veteran who has at least a ten per cent service connected disability as rated and certified by the Veterans Administration shall be entitled to and shall have ten points added to his passing score on such examination; and

(b) Any other such veteran shall be entitled to and shall have five points added to his passing score on such examination.

[Editor note: Paragraph XXIV was amended in 1968.]

PARAGRAPH XXV. *Street Railways.* The General Assembly shall not authorize the construction of any street passenger railway, within the limits of any incorporate town or city, without the consent of the Corporate Authorities.

PARAGRAPH XXVI. The General Assembly, in order to insure continuity of State and local governmental operations in periods of emergency resulting from disasters caused by enemy attack, shall have the power and the immediate duty:

(1) To provide for prompt and temporary succession to the powers and duties of persons holding office in the Executive, Judicial and Legislative branches of State and local government whether filled by election or appointment, the incumbents of which may become unavailable for carrying on the powers and duties of such offices during such emergency; and

(2) To adopt such other measures as may be necessary and

proper for insuring the continuity of governmental operations during such emergency, including but not limited to the suspension of any or all constitutional legislative rules.

Any legislation heretofore adopted by the General Assembly which would have been invalid except for the provisions of this Paragraph is hereby ratified as part of the statute laws of the State of Georgia.

[Editorial note: Paragraph XXVI was added by an amendment ratified on Nov. 3, 1964.]

Section VIII

Paragraph I. *Officers of the Two Houses.* The officers of the two houses, other than the President of the Senate and Speaker of the House, shall be a President Pro Tempore and Secretary of the Senate and Speaker Pro Tempore and Clerk of the House of Representatives, and such assistants as each House may provide for.

Section IX

Paragraph I. *Compensation, Expense and Mileage.* The per diem of members of the General Assembly shall be $10.00 per day plus the additional sum of $5.00 per day for maintenance expense; and the mileage shall not exceed 10 cents for each mile traveled by the nearest practical route in going to and returning from the Capitol; but the President Pro Tem of the Senate, when serving as presiding officer thereof, and the Speaker of the House of Representatives, shall each receive $15.00 per day as per diem plus the additional sum of $5.00 per day for maintenance expense.

Section X

Paragraph I. *Viva Voce Vote; Place of Meeting.* All elections by the General Assembly shall be viva voce, and the vote shall appear on the Journal of the House of Representatives. When the Senate and House of Representatives unite for the purpose of election, they shall meet in the Representative Hall, and the President of the Senate shall, in such cases, preside and declare the results.

Section XI

Paragraph I. *Salaries of Elective Officials; How Changed.* The General Assembly may, at any time, by a majority vote of both branches prescribe other and different salaries for all of the elective officers provided for in this Constitution, but no such change shall diminish the amount of any salary set forth in the Constitution.

[Editorial note: This paragraph was altered to read as quoted by an amendment ratified Nov. 6, 1956. The last clause originally read, "but no such change shall affect the officers then in commission."]

ARTICLE IV
PUBLIC UTILITIES, EMINENT DOMAIN, POLICE POWER, INSURANCE COMPANIES, CONTRACTS, ETC.

Section I

Paragraph I. *Public Utility Tariffs and Charges. The* power and authority of regulating railroad freight and passenger tariffs and of charges of public utilities for their services, of preventing unjust discriminations, and requiring reasonable and just rates of freight and passenger tariffs and of charges of public utilities, are hereby conferred upon the General Assembly, whose duty it shall be to pass laws from time to time, to regulate such tariffs and charges, to prohibit unjust discriminations by the various railroad and public utilities of this State, and to prohibit said railroads and public utilities from charging other than just and reasonable rates and to enforce the same by adequate penalties, provided, nevertheless, that such power and authority shall never be exercised in any way to regulate or fix charges of such public utilities as are or may be owned or operated by any county or municipality of this State; except as provided in this Constitution.

Paragraph II. *Rebates.* No public utility company shall give, or pay, any rebate, or bonus in the nature thereof, directly or indirectly, or do any act to mislead or deceive the public as to the real rates charged or received for freight or passage or services furnished, any such payments shall be illegal and void; and these prohibitions shall be enforced by suitable penalties.

Section II

Paragraph I. *Right of Eminent Domain.* The exercise of the right of eminent domain shall never be abridged, nor so construed as to prevent the General Assembly from taking property and franchises, and subjecting them to public use.

Paragraph II. *Police Power.* The exercise of the police power of the state shall never be abridged, nor so construed as to permit the conduct of business in such manner as to infringe the equal rights of others, or the general well-being of the State.

Section III

Paragraph I. *Charters Revived or Amended Subject to Con-*

stitution. The General Assembly shall not remit the forfeiture of the charter of any corporation now existing, nor alter or amend the same, nor pass any other general or special law, for the benefit of said corporation, except upon the condition that such corporation shall thereafter hold its charter subject to the provisions of this Constitution; and every amendment of any charter of any corporation in this State, or any special law for its benefit, accepted thereby, shall operate as a novation of said charter and shall bring the same under the provisions of this Constitution.

Section IV

Paragraph I. *Contracts to Defeat Competition.* All contracts and agreements, which may have the effect, or be intended to have the effect, to defeat or lessen competition, or to encourage monopoly shall be illegal and void. The General Assembly of this State shall have no power to authorize any such contract or agreement.

Paragraph II. *General Assembly to Enforce Article.* The General Assembly shall enforce the provisions of this Article by appropriate legislation.

Paragraph III. *Public Service Commission as Constitutional Officers.* There shall be a Public Service Commission for the regulation of utilities, vested with the jurisdiction, powers and duties now provided by law or that may hereafter be prescribed by the General Assembly, not inconsistent with other provisions of this Constitution. Such Commission shall consist of five members, who shall be elected by the people. A Chairman shall be selected by the members of the Commission from its membership. The first Commission under this amendment shall consist of the commissioners in office at the time of the adoption of this constitutional amendment and they shall serve until December 31 after the general election at which the successor of each member is elected. Thereafter all succeeding terms of members shall be for six years. The qualifications, compensations, filling of vacancies, manner and time of election, power and duties of members of the Commission, including the chairman, shall be such as are now or may hereafter be provided by the General Assembly.

Section V

Paragraph I. *Wife's Separate Estate.* All property of the wife at the time of her marriage, and all property given to, inherited or acquired by her, shall remain her separate property, and not be liable for the debts of her husband.

SECTION VI

PARAGRAPH I. *Nonresident Insurance Companies.* All life insurance companies now doing business in this State, or which may desire to establish agencies and do business in the State of Georgia, chartered by other States of the Union, or foreign States, shall show that they have deposited with the Comptroller General of the State in which they are chartered, or of this State, the Insurance Commissioner, or such other officer as may be authorized to receive it, not less than one hundred thousand dollars, in such securities as may be deemed by such officer equivalent to cash, subject to his order, as a guarantee fund for the security of policy-holders.

PARAGRAPH II. *License by Comptroller General.* When such showing is made to the Comptroller General of the State of Georgia by a proper certificate from the State officials having charge of the funds so deposited, the Comptroller General of the State of Georgia is authorized to issue to the company making such showing, a license to do business in the State, upon paying the fees required by law.

PARAGRAPH III. *Resident Insurance Companies; Guarantee Fund.* All life insurance companies chartered by the State of Georgia, or which may hereafter be chartered by the State, shall, before doing business, deposit with the Comptroller General of the State of Georgia, or with some strong corporation, which may be approved by said Comptroller General, one hundred thousand dollars, in such securities as may be deemed by him equivalent to cash, to be subject to his order as a guarantee fund for the security of the policy-holders of the company making such deposit, all interest and dividends from such securities to be paid, when due, to the company so depositing. Any such securities as may be needed or desired by the company may be taken from said department at any time by replacing them with other securities equally acceptable to the Comptroller General, whose certificate for the same shall be furnished to the company.

PARAGRAPH IV. *General Assembly to Enact Laws for People's Protection, Etc.* The General Assembly shall from time to time enact laws to compel all fire insurance companies, doing business in this State, whether chartered by this State, or otherwise, to deposit reasonable securities with the Treasurer of this State, to secure the people against loss by the operations of said companies.

PARAGRAPH V. *Reports By Insurance Companies.* The General Assembly shall compel all insurance companies in this State, or doing business therein, under proper penalties, to make annual reports to the Comptroller General, and print the same at their own expense, for the information and protection of the people.

ARTICLE V
EXECUTIVE DEPARTMENT

Section I

Paragraph I. *Governor; Term of Office; Salary, Etc.* The executive power shall be vested in a Governor, who shall hold his office during the term of four years, and until his successor shall be chosen and qualified. The Governor serving at the time of the adoption of this Constitution and future Governors shall not be eligible to suceed themselves and shall not be eligible to hold the office until after the expiration of four years from the conclusion of his term of office. He shall have a salary of seven thousand five hundred dollars per annum until January 1, 1947. The salary of the Governor for each year thereafter shall be twelve thousand dollars per annum until otherwise provided by a law passed by a majority vote of both branches of the General Assembly, which shall not be increased or diminished during the period for which he shall have been elected; nor shall he receive, within that time, any other emolument from the United States, or either of them, or from any foreign power. The State officers, required by this Constitution to be elected at the same time, for the same term, and in the same manner as the Governor shall also hold office for four years.

Paragraph II. *Election for Governor.* The first election for Governor under this Constitution, shall be held on Tuesday after the first Monday in November of 1946, and the Governor-elect shall be installed in office at the next session of the General Assembly. An election shall take place quadrennially thereafter, on said date, until another date be fixed by the General Assembly. Said election shall be held at the places of holding general elections in the several counties of this State, in the manner prescribed for the election of members of the General Assembly, and the electors shall be the same.

Paragraph III. *Transmission, Canvassing and Publishing Election Returns.* The returns of each election district in a gubernatorial election shall be sealed up by the superintendent thereof separately from other returns and shall be transmitted to the Secretary of State. On the Tuesday next following the general election, unless the date therefor shall be changed by law, the Secretary of State shall transmit said returns to a Constitutional Officers Election Board which shall be composed of the Speaker and Clerk of the House of Representatives, the President Pro Tempore and the Secretary of the Senate, and the chairman of all standing committees of the General Assembly. Such Board shall open and publish the returns, and the person having the majority of the whole number of votes shall be declared duly elected Governor of this State. Each candidate for Governor shall be entitled to designate one person to be present at the opening of the returns.

[Editorial note: This paragraph was amended in 1968.]

PARAGRAPH IV. *Run-off Election.* In the event no gubernatorial candidate receives a majority of the whole number of votes cast in the general election, the Constitutional Officers Election Board shall continue the gubernatorial election by immediately calling a run-off election and designate as candidates therein the two persons who received the highest number of votes, who continue in life and have not declined to continue as a gubernatorial candidate. This run-off election shall be held on the third Tuesday immediately following the general election unless the date thereof shall be changed by the General Assembly. The run-off election shall be a continuation of the general election and only the electors who were entitled to vote in the general election shall be entitled to vote therein; and only those votes cast for the two persons designated shall be counted in the tabulation and canvass of the votes cast. The provisions relating to the transmission of the returns in the general election, the opening of the returns, their tabulation, canvassing and publication shall apply to the run-off election. On the Tuesday next following the run-off election, the Constitutional Officers Election Board shall convene, open, canvass, tabulate and publish the returns of the run-off election. The person having the highest number of votes entitled to be counted in the run-off election shall be declared the duly elected Governor of this State.

[Editorial note: This paragraph was amended in 1968.]

PARAGRAPH V. *General Assembly May Provide Additional Procedures.* The General Assembly may provide by law for any additional procedures or requirements connected with any subject matter embraced within Paragraphs III and IV and in connection with any contested election, provided such laws are not inconsistent with the provisions therein.

[Editorial note: This paragraph was amended in 1968.]

PARAGRAPH VI. *Qualifications of Governor.* No person shall be eligible to the office of Governor, who shall not have been a citizen of the United States fifteen years, and a citizen of the State six years, and who shall not have attained the age of thirty years.

PARAGRAPH VII. *Lieutenant Governor. Succession to Executive Power.* There shall be a Lieutenant Governor, who shall be elected at the same time, for the same term, and in the same manner as the Governor. He shall be President of the Senate, and shall receive the sum of $2,000.00 per annum. In case of the death, resignation, or disability of the Governor, the Lieutenant Governor, and in case of the death or resignation of the Governor-Elect, the Lieutenant Governor-Elect, who shall be deemed to be the Governor's successor, upon becoming the Lieutenant Governor, shall exercise the executive power and receive the compensation of the Governor until the next general election for members of the General Assembly, at which a successor to the Governor shall be elected for the unexpired term; but if such death, resignation, or disability shall occur within thirty days of the next general election, or if the term will expire within ninety days after the next general election, the Lieutenant Governor shall exercise the executive power and receive the compensation of the Governor for the unexpired term. If the Lieutenant Governor shall become a candidate for the unexpired term of the Governor, he shall thereby resign his office as Lieutenant Governor, effective upon the qualification of the Governor elected for the unexpired term, and his successor for the unexpired term shall be elected at such election. In case of the death, resignation, or disability of both the Governor and the Lieutenant Governor, the Speaker of the House of Representatives shall exercise the executive power until the removal of the disability or the election and qualification of a Governor at a special election, which shall be held within sixty days from the date on which the Speaker of the House of Representatives shall assume the executive power. A Lieutenant Governor shall be elected at the general election in 1946 and shall qualify at the same time as the Governor. Until the qualification of a Lieutenant Governor the provisions of Article V, Section I, Paragraph VIII of the Constitution of Georgia of 1877 shall remain of full force and effect.

[Editorial note: Paragraph VII was amended in 1968.]

PARAGRAPH VIII. *Unexpired Terms, Filling of.* The General Assembly shall have power to provide by law, for filling unexpired terms by special elections, execpt as provided in this Constitution.

PARAGRAPH IX. *Oath of Office.* The Governor shall, before he enters on the duties of his office, take the following oath or affirmation: "I do solemnly swear (or affirm, as the case may be) that I will faithfully execute the office of Governor of the State of Georgia, and will, to the best of my ability, preserve, protect, and defend the Constitution thereof, and the Constitution of the United States of America."

PARAGRAPH X. *Commander-in-Chief.* The Governor shall be commander-in-chief of the army and navy of this State, and of the militia thereof.

PARAGRAPH XI. *Reprieves and pardons; State Board of Pardons and Paroles.* The Governor shall have power to suspend the execution of a sentence of death, after conviction, for offenses against the State, until the State Board of Pardons and Paroles, hereinafter provided, shall have an opportunity of hearing the application of the convicted person for any relief within the power of such Board, or for any other purpose which may be deemed necessary by the Governor. Upon conviction for treason the Governor may only suspend the execution of the sentence and report the case to the General Assembly at the next meeting thereof, when the General Assembly shall either pardon, commute the sentence, direct its execution or grant a further reprieve. The Governor shall, at each session of the General Assembly, communicate to that body each case of suspension of sentence, stating the name of the convict, the offense for which he was convicted, the sentence and its date, the date of the reprieve or suspension, and the reasons for granting the same. He shall take care that the laws are faithfully executed, and shall be a conservator of the peace throughout the State. There shall be a State Board of Pardons and Paroles to be composed of not less than five or more than seven members, the number to be determined by the General Assembly. Until changed by the General Assembly, the Board shall consist of three members. The additional members of the Board, if added by the General Assembly, and the successors to the present members and all members of the Board who are subsequently appointed to fill vacancies shall continue to serve on the Board for a period of seven years or until they shall be removed from office for cause by the unanimous action of the Governor, Lieutenant Governor and Attorney General or by the judgment of the Senate in a trial of impeachment. All appointments to the Board shall be made by the Governor and shall be subject to the confirmation of the Senate. The present members of the Board shall serve out the terms to which they were appointed. The Governor shall not be a member of the State Board of Pardons and Paroles. The General Assembly shall fix the compensation of the members of the Board, but until changed by the General Assembly, the members shall continue to receive that compensation which the present members are receiving. The State Board of Pardons and Paroles shall have power to grant reprieves, pardons and paroles, to commute penalties, remove disabilities imposed by law, and may remit any part of a sentence for any offense against the State, after conviction except in cases of treason or impeachment, and except in cases in which the Governor refuses to suspend a sentence of death. Provided that such board shall act on all applications within 90 days from the filing of same, and in all cases a majority shall decide the action of the Board. If any member for any cause is unable to serve in any case involving capital punishment when the Board shall consist of three members, the Governor shall act as the third member of said Board and the action so taken in such instance shall be by unanimous vote. The State Board of Pardons and Paroles shall at each session of the General Assembly communicate to that body in full detail each case of pardon, parole, commutation, removal of the convict, the offense for which he was convicted, the sentence and its date, the date of the pardon, parole, commutation, removal of disabilities or remission of sentence and the reasons for granting the same, and the State Board of Pardons and Paroles may make rules and regulations as may be authorized by law.

Each year the Board shall elect one of its members to serve as Chairman of the Board for the ensuing year. The General Assembly may enact laws in aid of, but not inconsistent with, this Paragraph.

[Editorial note: Paragraph XI was amended in 1972.]

PARAGRAPH XII. *Writs of Election; Called Sessions of the General Assembly.* The Governor shall issue writs of election to fill all vacancies that may happen in the Senate and the House of Representatives, and shall give the General Assembly, from time to time, information of the State of the Commonwealth, and recommend to their consideration such measures as he may deem necessary or expedient. The Governor shall have power to convoke the General Assembly on extraordinary occasions, but no law shall be enacted at called sessions of the General Assembly, except such as shall relate to the object stated in his proclamation convening them; providing that such called sessions of the General Assembly shall not exceed 70 days in length, unless at the expiration of said period there shall be pending an impeachment trial of some officer of the State Government in which event the General Assembly will be authorized to remain in session until such trial shall have been completed.

Provided, however, that when three-fifths of the members elected to the House of Representatives and three-fifths of the members elected to the Senate shall have certified to the Governor of the State of Georgia that in their opinion an emergency exists in the affairs of the State of Georgia, it shall thereupon be the duty of said Governor and mandatory upon him, within five days from the receipt of such certificate or certificates, to convene said General Assembly in extraordinary session for all purposes; and in the event said Governor shall, within said time, Sundays excluded, fail or refuse to convene said General Assembly as aforesaid, then and in that event said General Assembly may convene itself in extraordinary session, as if convened in regular session, for all purposes, provided that such extraordinary, self convened session shall be limited to a period of 30 days, unless at the expiration of said period, there shall be pending an impeachment trial of some officer of the State Government, in which event the General Assembly shall be authorized to remain in session until such trial shall have been completed.

The members of the General Assembly shall receive the same per diem and mileage during such extraordinary session as is now or may be hereafter provided.

PARAGRAPH XIII. *Filling Vacancies.* When any office shall become vacant, by death, resignation, or otherwise, the Governor shall have power to fill such vacancy, unless otherwise provided by law; and persons so appointed shall continue in office until a successor is commissioned, agreeably to the mode pointed out by this Constitution, or by law in pursuance thereof.

PARAGRAPH XIV. *Appointments Rejected.* A person once rejected by the Senate, shall not be reappointed by the Governor to the same office during the same session, or the recess thereafter.

PARAGRAPH XV. *Governor's Veto.* The Governor shall have the revision of all bills passed by the General Assembly before the same shall become laws, but two-thirds of each House may pass a law notwithstanding his veto; and if any bill should not be returned by the Governor within five days (Sundays excepted) after it has been presented to him, the same shall be a law; unless the General Assembly, by their adjournment, shall prevent its return, in which event the Governor shall have thirty days (Sundays excepted) from the date of adjournment in which to approve the same, and if not approved within that time, the same shall become a law. He may approve any appropriation, and veto any other appropriation, in the same bill, and the latter shall not be effectual unless passed by two-thirds of each House.

Whenever such bill has been vetoed by the Governor, it shall be the duty of the Governor to transmit such bill to the presiding officer of the Branch of the General Assembly in which it originated, together with a list of reasons, if any, for such veto. Such transmission shall be made within thirty-five days (Sundays excepted) from the date of the adjournment of the session of the General Assembly at which such bill was passed. Such bill may be considered by the Branch of the General Assembly in which it originated at any time within the first ten days of the next regular Session of the General Assembly for the purpose of overriding the action of the Governor. In the event the action of the Governor is overridden by two-thirds of the votes of such Branch of the General Assembly the same shall be immediately transmitted by the Secretary of or the Clerk of such Branch of the General Assembly to the other Branch of the General Assembly. It shall be the duty of the presiding officer of such other Branch of the General Assembly upon receiving such bill to dispense with all business that is then being considered and to then and there consider and act upon such bill for the purpose of overriding the action of the Governor. In the event the action of the Governor is overriden by two-thirds of the votes of such Branch of the General Assembly such bill shall become law. In the event either Branch of the General Assembly should fail to override the Governor's action on a bill, such bill shall not again be presented to the General Assembly of Georgia for the purpose of overriding the action of the Governor. In the event any bill is enacted into law pursuant to the terms of this paragraph the effective date of such bill shall be on the date that such bill was acted upon by the Branch of the General Assembly last acting upon such bill.

Provided, however, that any bills that are vetoed by the Governor after the adjournment of the regular session of the General Assembly immediately preceding the general election in which the Governor is elected, shall not be subject to be overridden by the next regular session of the General Assembly.

[Editorial note: This paragraph was changed by amendments ratified on Nov. 4, 1952, and Nov. 6, 1962.]

PARAGRAPH XVI. *Governor to Approve Resolutions, Etc.* Every vote, resolution, or order, to which the concurrence of both houses may be necessary, except on a question of election or adjournment, shall be presented to the Governor, and before it shall take effect be approved by him, or, being disapproved, shall be repassed by two-thirds of each house, provided, however, that nothing contained in this Article shall be construed to confer on the Governor the right to veto or enter his disapproval of any proposal made by the General Assembly to amend this Constitution.

Paragraph XVII. *Information From Officers and Employees; Suspension of Officers.* The Governor may require information in writing from Constitutional officers, department heads, and all State employees, on any subject relating to the duties of their respective offices or employment. The General Assembly shall have authority to provide by law for the suspension of any Constitutional officer or department head from the discharge of the duties of his office and also for the appointment of a suitable person to discharge the duties of the same.

Section II

Other Executive Officers

Paragraph I. *Executive Officers, How Elected.* The Secretary of State, Attorney General, State School Superintendent, Comptroller General, Commissioner of Agriculture, and the Commissioner of Labor shall be elected by the persons qualified to vote for members of the General Assembly at the same time, and in the same manner as the Governor. The provisions of the Constitution as to the transmission, tabulation and canvassing of the returns of the election, runoff elections, contested elections, and declaration of the results of the election, applicable to the election of Governor, shall apply to the election of the above-named executive officers; and they shall be commissioned by the Governor and hold their offices for the same time as the Governor. In case of the death or withdrawal of a person having received a majority of the whole number of votes cast in an election for any of the above-named offices, the Governor elected at such election, upon becoming Governor, shall have the power to fill such office by appointing, subject to the confirmation of the Senate, an individual to serve until the next general election, at which time a successor shall be elected to serve out the unexpired term of office.

[Editorial note: This paragraph was amended in 1968 and 1972.]

Paragraph II. *Duties, Authority, and Salaries of Other Executive Officers.* The General Assembly shall have power to prescribe the duties, authority, and salaries of the executive officers, and to provide help and expenses necessary for the operation of the department of each.

Paragraph III. *Profit From Use of Public Money.* No State official shall be allowed, directly or indirectly, to receive any fee, interest, or reward from any person, bank, or corporation, for the deposit, or use, in any manner, of the public funds, and the General Assembly shall enforce this provision by suitable penalties.

Paragraph IV. *Qualifications.* No person shall be eligible to the office of the Secretary of State, Attorney General, State School Superintendent, Comptroller General, Commissioner of Agriculture, and Commissioner of Labor, unless he shall have been a citizen of the United States for ten years, and shall have resided in this State for six years next preceding his election, and shall be twenty-five years of age when elected. All of said officers shall give bond and security, under regulation to be prescribed by law, for the faithful discharge of their duties.

[Paragraph IV was amended in 1972.]

PARAGRAPH V. *Fees and Perquisites Denied.* No State official named in Paragraph I of this Section shall be allowed any fee, perquisite or compensation other than their salaries as prescribed by law, except their necessary expenses when absent from the seat of government on business for the State.

SECTION III

PARAGRAPH I. *Great Seal; What Constitutes; Custody; When Affixed to Instruments.* The great seal of the State shall be deposited in the office of the Secretary of State and shall not be affixed to any instrument of writing except by order of the Governor or General Assembly, and that now in use shall be the great seal of the State until otherwise provided by law.

SECTION IV

Board of Natural Resources

PARAGRAPH I. *Creation; membership; appointment; terms of office; powers and duties; compensation.* There is hereby created a Board of Natural Resources. Said Board of Natural Resources shall consist of one member from each Congressional District in this State, and one additional member from one of the following named counties, to-wit: Chatham, Bryan, Liberty, McIntosh, Glynn, or Camden; and four members from the State at Large. The first members of the Board of Natural Resources shall consist of those members of the State Game and Fish Commission in office at the time this paragraph is adopted, with terms provided by law. The four members from the State at Large shall be appointed by the Governor and confirmed by the Senate; initially their appointments shall be for terms of one, three, five and seven years respectively, to be designated by the Governor. Thereafter, all succeeding appointments of members of the Board of Natural Resources shall be made by the Governor and confirmed by the Senate for a term of seven years from the expiration of the previous term, except in case of an unexpired term. Insofar as it is practicable, the members of the Board shall be representative of all areas and functions encompassed within the Department of Natural Resources. All members of the Board of Natural Resources shall hold office until their successors are appointed and qualified. Vacancies in office shall be filled by appointment of the Governor and submitted to the

Senate for confirmation at the next session of the General Assembly after the making of the appointment.

The Board of Natural Resources shall have such powers, authority, duties, and shall receive such compensation and expenses as may be delegated or provided for by the General Assembly.

[Editorial note: Section IV was amended in 1972.]

Section V

State Board of Corrections

Paragraph I. *State Board of Corrections; How Composed, Director.* There shall be a State Board of Corrections composed of five members in charge of the State Penal System. The Board shall have such jurisdiction, powers, duties and control of the State Penal System and the inmates thereof as shall be provided by law. The Board shall elect a Director of Corrections who shall be the executive officer of the Board. The Board of Corrections shall be appointed by the Governor with the consent of the Senate. The first appointment shall be for terms of one, two, three, four and five years and their successors shall be appointed for terms of five years each. The compensation of the Director and members of the Board shall be fixed by law.

Section VI

State Department of Veterans Service

Paragraph I. *Veterans Service Board; How Composed; Director.* There shall be a State Department of Veterans Service and Veterans Service Board composed of seven members, who shall have such control, duties, powers and jurisdiction of the State Department of Veterans Service as shall be provided by law. Said Board shall appoint a director who shall be the executive officer of the Department. Members of the Board shall be appointed by the Governor with the advice and consent of the Senate and all members of the Board and the Director shall be veterans of some war in which the United States has engaged.

The first appointments shall be for terms of one, two, three, four, five, six and seven years. Thereafter all terms and appointments, except in case of vacancy, shall be for seven years. Vacancies shall be filled by appointment of the Governor.

Sections VII, VIII, and IX

[Editorial note: These sections create industrial development authorities for Bacon, Banks, Barrow, Berrien, Candler, and 97 other counties or cities. They cover some 400 pages, and are omitted here. For citations to the *Georgia Laws* where the detailed provisions on these authorities can be found, see the *Table of Amendments to the 1945 Constitution of Georgia* published in 1973 by the Institute of Law and Government, University of Georgia, Athens, Georgia.]

SECTION X

Department of Community Development

PARAGRAPH I. There is hereby created the Department of Community Development in lieu of and as successor to the Department of Industry and Trade. Wherever the words "Department of Industry and Trade" are used in any statute, they shall be held and taken to mean the Department of Community Development. There is hereby created a Board of Community Development in lieu of and as successor to the Board of Commissioners of the Department of Industry and Trade. Wherever the words "Board of Commissioners of the Department of Industry and Trade" are used in any statute they shall be held and taken to mean the Board of Community Development. The Board shall be composed of twenty members, two from each Congressional District in the State. The Board shall be the policy determining body of the Department and shall have such duties, powers, authority and jurisdiction relating to the Department as shall be provided by law. Nothing herein shall affect the terms of office of members of the Board of Commissioners now in office, and such members shall serve out the remainder of their respective terms and until their successors are duly elected and qualified as hereunder provided. The successors to such members, except in case of an appointment to fill a vacancy, shall be for six years dating from April 1 of the beginning year of such term. The Governor shall appoint all successors. In the event a vacancy occurs on the Board, the Governor shall appoint a person to serve the unexpired term. In making appointments to the Board, the Governor shall insure that there is representation from local governments and area planning and development commissions as provided by law. The Board shall appoint a Commissioner who shall be the Executive Officer and Administrative Head of the Department.

[Editorial note: Paragraph I was added in 1962 and amended in 1972.]

PARAGRAPH II. In addition to such powers and duties as may from time to time be conferred upon the Board of Community Development and the Department of Community Development, the Board of Community Development shall be authorized to participate with any county, municipality, non-profit organization, or any combination thereof, in the operation of any of the facilities operated by such agencies for the purpose of encouraging and promoting tourism in this State, notwithstanding any other provisions of this Constitution to the contrary.

[Editorial note: Paragraph II was added in 1966 and amended in 1972.]

SECTION XI

PARAGRAPH I. *State Transportation Board created.* There shall be a State Transportation Board, composed of as many members as there are Congressional Districts in the State. The member of the Board from each Congressional District shall be elected by a majority vote of the members of the House of Representatives and Senate from the counties and Senatorial Districts embraced or partly embraced within such Congressional District, meeting in caucus. All members shall be elected for terms of five years each and until their successors are duly elected and qualified. Nothing herein shall affect the terms of office of members of the State Highway Board now in office, and such members shall serve out the remainder of their respective terms as members of the State Transportation Board, and until their successors are duly elected and qualified as hereunder provided. The successors to such members, as their respective terms expire, shall be elected by the General Assembly as provided herein and pursuant to the provisions of law enacted or as may hereafter be enacted to implement this Paragraph. The State Transportation Board shall elect a Commissioner of the Department of Transportation, who shall be the Chief Executive Officer of the Department of Transportation, except that the Director of the State Highway Department in office at the time of approval hereof shall not be affected, except that his title shall be changed from Director of the State Highway Department to Commissioner of the Department of Transportation, and such Commissioner shall serve out the remainder of his term as Director of the State Highway Department as now provided by law. The General Assembly shall define by law the powers, duties, qualifications and compensation of the Board and of the Commissioner, and shall by law prescribe the manner, time and procedure for the election of members of the Board and the manner of filling vacancies therein.

[Editorial note: Paragraph I was added in 1964 and amended in 1972.]

Paragraph II. In order to fully comply with that certain Act of the Congress of the United States, known as Public Law 89-285, 89th Congress, S. 2084, approved October 22, 1965, and which said Public Law amended Section 131 of Title 23, United States Code, and revised the same so as to provide for the "Control of Outdoor Advertising" on the Interstate or Primary Systems of Federal-Aid Highways; provided for bonus payments to the States complying with such public law, and also provided penalties for non-compliance; and which said described Public Law further amended Chapter 1 of Title 23 of said United States Code by adding thereto a new section to provide for the "Control of Junk Yards", on such Interstate and Primary Systems of Federal-Aid Highways, and provided that Federal funds available to the States for highway purposes should be reduced by 20 percent for failure to comply with such provisions; and which said Public Law further amended and revised Section 319 of Title 23 of said United States Code so as to provide for a "Landscaping and Scenic Enhancement," and which amendment and revision of said Section provided for a bonus of 3 percent of Federal funds, otherwise available to the State, as an incentive for compliance with said provision of said Public Law; and, in order to promote the reasonable, orderly, and effective display of Outdoor Advertising, in accordance with the provisions of said described Act of Congress of the United States, and consistent with the purposes of this provision of the Constitution, the State of Georgia, acting by and through the Department of Transportation, is hereby authorized to acquire, either by negotiation or through the exercise of the Power of Eminent Domain, upon the payment of just and adequate compensation, easements or other interests in private property, for the purpose of acquiring the title to and the right to remove, or require removal, of any billboards or other outdoor advertising which may exist upon such property at the time of the ratification of this amendment, and within a distance of 660 feet of the nearest edge of the right-of-way line of any State-Aid highway, which is a part of the Interstate or Primary System of Federal-Aid Highways,–provided, however, that, as to any such advertising sign, display, or device, lawfully in existence upon any of such described highways on September 1, 1965, the owner of such advertising sign, display, or device shall not be required to remove the same until July 1, 1970; and, as to such described sign, the provision of this amendment shall not become effective until said date of July 1, 1970, except that the State may acquire the right to remove the same by voluntary negotiation with the owner thereof.

The State, acting by and through the Department of Transportation, shall be further authorized to acquire, either by negotiation or through the exercise of the Power of Eminent Domain, upon payment of just and adequate compensation, easements or other interest in land within a distance of 1,000 feet of the nearest edge of the right-of-way line of any State-Aid road, which is a part of the Federal Interstate or Primary Systems of Highways, for the purpose of requiring the owners of junk yards existing upon such property to remove the same, or to screen them from public view, in accordance with regulations which the State Transportation Board is hereby authorized to make and publish in such respect, which regulations shall conform to and comply with such described Public Law;—provided, however, that any junk yard, which was in existence on the date of the approval of said described Public Law, on October 22, 1965, and which the Commissioner of the Department of Transportation finds as a practical matter cannot be screened, and which finding is approved by the Secretary of Commerce, acting by and through the United States Bureau of Public Roads, in accordance with sub-paragraph (h) of Title II of said Public Laws, the owner of such described junk yard shall not be required to remove the same until July 1, 1970; and the provisions of this amendment, under such described circumstances, shall not be applicable except that the Department of Transportation shall be authorized to acquire the right to remove said junk yard, or to screen the same in accordance with the requirements of said Public Law by voluntary negotiation; and with the further exception that where the Secretary of Commerce, acting by and through the United States Bureau of Public Roads, refuses to approve the continued maintenance of such junk yard until July 1, 1970, the provisions of this Act shall become immediately applicable upon a proper certificate being made and entered by the Commissioner of the Department of Transportation, showing the fact of such refusal.

The necessity for such acquisition, as set forth in the preceding paragraphs of this section, as a part of that portion of the State-Aid System of Public Roads, which are also a part of the Federal Interstate or Primary System, is hereby declared, in order to avoid the loss of large sums of money which would be otherwise granted to the State in the construction and maintenance of such Road System by the United States Government.

The General Assembly shall have full authority to zone property within a distance of 1,000 feet of the nearest edge of the right-of-way line of any State-Aid Road, which is also a part of the Federal Interstate System or Primary System, for commercial or industrial purposes; and in respect thereto, to also zone such property in respect to the location of advertising signs, displays, or devices; or in respect to the establishment, removal, or control of junk yards; and to provide for rules and regulations governing both advertising and junk yards; all in conformance to and in compliance with the provisions of said Public Law of the United States Congress.

The General Assembly shall have full authority to enact such legislation as will enable this State, acting by and through the Department of Transportation, to fully comply with Title

III of said described Public Law, and in respect to "Landscaping and Scenic Enhancement"; and in such manner as to enable this State to take advantage of the bonus payment to the State from the Federal Government, as provided for in said Title.

[Editorial note: Paragraph II was added in 1966 and amended in 1972.]

PARAGRAPH III. Wherever the words "State Highway Board" are used in any statute, they shall be held and taken to mean the State Transportation Board. Wherever the word "Director" is used in connection with the Department of Transportation or State Highway Department in any statute, it shall be held and taken to mean Commissioner. Wherever the words "State Highway Department" or "State Highway Department of Georgia" are used in any statute, they shall be held and taken to mean the Department of Transportation.

[Editorial note: Paragraph III was added in 1972.]

ARTICLE VI

JUDICIARY

SECTION I

PARAGRAPH I. *Courts Enumerated.* The judicial powers of this State shall be vested in a Supreme Court, a Court of Appeals, Superior Courts, Probate Courts, Justices of the Peace, Notaries Public who are ex-officio Justices of the Peace, and such other Courts as have been or may be established by law.

PARAGRAPH II. *Unified Judicial System.* For the purposes of administration, all of the courts of the State shall be a part of one unified judicial system. The administration of the unified judicial system shall be as provided by law. As used herein, administration does not include abolition or creation of courts, selection of judges, or jurisdictional provisions other than as otherwise authorized in this Constitution. The administration provided herein shall only be performed by the unified judicial system itself and shall not be administered to or controlled by any other department of Government.

[Editorial note: Paragraph II was added in 1974.]

SECTION II

PARAGRAPH I. *Supreme Court Justices; Quorum.* The Supreme Court shall consist of seven associate justices, who shall from time to time as they may deem proper, elect one of their members as Chief Justice, and one as Presiding Justice; the office of Chief Justice as it has heretofore existed under this Constitution being hereby converted into the office of an associate justice, with the same right of incumbency and the same succession as to terms, as applied to the former office. The Chief Justice so elected by the other Justices shall be the chief presiding and administrative officer of the court, and the Presiding Justice, elected in like manner, shall perform all the duties devolving upon the Chief Justice, when he is absent or disqualified. A majority of the court shall constitute a quorum.

PARAGRAPH II. *Court to Designate Judges to Preside, When.* When one or more of the Justices of the Supreme Court are disqualified from deciding any case by interest or otherwise, the qualified Justices shall designate a judge or judges of the Superior Court to preside in said case, provided, that if all the justices are disqualified, they or a majority of them shall, despite their disqualification, select seven judges of the Superior Court to preside in the cause, but they shall make such selections by lot and in open court from not less than twelve names of such Superior Court judges.

PARAGRAPH III. *Terms of Office.* The Justices aforesaid shall hold their offices for six years, and until their successors are qualified. They shall be elected by the people at the same time and in the same manner as members of the General Assembly; provided, that the successors to the two incumbents whose terms will expire on December 31, 1946, shall be elected for the succeeding terms at the time of electing members of the General Assembly during that year; successors to the two incumbents whose terms will expire on December 31, 1948, shall be elected in like manner during that year; successors to the two incumbents whose terms will expire on December 31, 1950, shall be elected in like manner during that year and provided further that an additional or seventh Justice shall be immediately appointed by the Governor, his tenure under such appointment to expire on December 31, 1946, and his successor for the ensuing regular term of six years to be elected at the time and in the manner aforesaid at such general election to be held during that year; and all terms (except unexpired terms) shall be for six years. In case of any vacancy which causes an unexpired term, the same shall be filled by executive appointment, and the person appointed by the Governor shall hold his office until the next regular election, and until his successor for the balance of the unexpired term shall have been elected and qualified. The returns of such elections shall be made to the Secretary of State, who shall certify the result to the Governor, and commission shall issue accordingly.

PARAGRAPH IV. *Jurisdiction of Supreme Court.* The Supreme

Court shall have no original jurisdiction but shall be a court alone for the trial and correction of errors of law from the superior courts and the city courts of Atlanta and Savannah, as existed on August 16, 1916, and such other like courts as have been or may hereafter be established in other cities, in all cases that involve the construction of the Constitution of the State of Georgia or of the United States, or of treaties between the United States and foreign governments; in all cases in which the constitutionality of any law of the State of Georgia or of the United States is drawn in question; and, until otherwise provided by law, in all cases respecting title to land; in all equity cases; in all cases which involve the validity of, or the construction of wills; in all cases of conviction of a capital felony; in all habeas corpus cases; in all cases involving extraordinary remedies; in all divorce and alimony cases, and in all cases certified to it by the Court of Appeals for its determination. It shall also be competent for the Supreme Court to require by certiorari or otherwise any case to be certified to the Supreme Court from the Court of Appeals for review and determination with the same power and authority as if the case had been carried by writ of error to the Supreme Court. Any case carried to the Supreme Court or to the Court of Appeals, which belongs to the class of which the other court has jurisdiction, shall, until otherwise provided by law, be transferred to the other court under such rules as the Supreme Court may prescribe, and the cases so transferred shall be heard and determined by the court which has jurisdiction thereof. The General Assembly may provide for carrying cases or certain classes of cases to the Supreme Court and the Court of Appeals from the trial courts otherwise than by writ of error, and may prescribe conditions as to the right of a party litigant to have his case reviewed by the Supreme Court or Court of Appeals. The Supreme Court shall also have jurisdiction of and shall decide cases transferred to it by the Court of Appeals because of an equal division between the judges of that Court when sitting as a body for the determination of cases.

Paragraph V. *Cases, How Disposed Of*. The Supreme Court and the court of Appeals shall dispose of every case at the term for which it is entered on the court's docket for hearing, as provided by Paragraph VIII of this Article and Section, or at the next term. If the plaintiff in error shall not be prepared to prosecute the case at the term for which it is so entered for hearing, unless prevented by providential cause, it shall be stricken from the docket and the judgment below shall stand affirmed. No writ of error shall be dismissed because of delay in transmission of the bill of exceptions and the copy of the record, or either of them, resulting from the default of the clerk or other cause, unless it shall appear that the plaintiff in error or his counsel caused such delay. Nothing herein shall be construed to excuse the clerk for any omission of duty or to relieve him of any liability resulting therefrom.

Paragraph VI. *Judgments May Be Withheld.* In any case the Court may in its discretion withhold its judgment until the next term after the same is argued.

Paragraph VII. *The Supreme Court; How Cases To Be Heard and Determined.* The Supreme Court shall have power to hear and determine cases when sitting in a body, under such regulations as may be prescribed by it.

Paragraph VIII. *Court of Appeals.* The Court of Appeals shall consist of the Judges provided therefor by law at the time of the ratification of this amendment, and of such additional Judges as the General Assembly shall from time to time prescribe. All terms of the Judges of the Court of Appeals after the expiration of the terms of the Judges provided for by law at the time of the ratification of this amendment, except unexpired terms, shall continue six years and until their successors are qualified. The times and manner of electing Judges, and the mode of filling a vacancy which causes an unexpired term, shall be the same as are or may be provided for by the laws relating to the election and appointment of Justices of the Supreme Court. The Court of Appeals shall have jurisdiction for the trial and correction of errors of law from the superior courts and from the City Courts of Atlanta and Savannah, as they existed on August 19, 1916, and such other like courts as have been or may hereafter be established in other cities, in all cases in which such jurisdiction has not been conferred by this Constitution upon the Supreme Court, and in such other cases as may hereafter be prescribed by law; except that where a case is pending in the Court of Appeals and the Court of Appeals desires instruction from the Supreme Court, it may certify the same to the Supreme Court, and thereupon a transcript of the record shall be transmitted to the Supreme Court, which, after having afforded to the parties an opportunity to be heard thereon, shall instruct the Court of Appeals on the question so certified, and the Court of Appeals shall be bound by the instruction so given. But if by reason of equal division of opinion among the Justices of the Supreme Court no such instruction is given, the Court of Appeals may decide the question. The manner of certifying questions to the Supreme Court by the Court of Appeals, and the subsequent proceedings in regard to the same in the Supreme Court, shall be as the Supreme Court shall by its rules prescribe, until otherwise provided by law. No affirmance of the judgment of the court below in cases pending in the Court of Appeals shall result from delay in disposing of questions or cases certified from the Court of Appeals to the Supreme Court, or as to which such certificate has been required by the Supreme Court as hereinbefore provided. All writs of error in the Supreme Court or the Court of Appeals, when received by its clerk during a term of the Court and before the docket of the term is by order of the Court closed, shall be entered thereon, and when received at any other time, shall be entered on the docket of the next term; and they shall stand for hearing at the term for which they are so entered, under such rules as the Court may prescribe, until otherwise provided by law. The Court of Appeals shall appoint a clerk and a sheriff of the court. The reporter of the Supreme Court shall be reporter of the Court of Appeals until otherwise provided by law. The laws relating to the Supreme Court as to qualifications and salaries of Judges, the designation of other Judges to preside when members of the Court are disqualified, the powers, duties, salaries, fees and terms of officers, the mode of carrying cases to the Court, the powers, practice, procedure, times of sitting, and costs of the Court, the publication of reports of cases decided therein, and in all other respects, except as otherwise provided in this Constitution or by the laws as to the Court of Appeals at the time of the ratification of this amendment, and until otherwise provided by law, shall apply to the Court of Appeals so far as they can be made to apply. The decisions of the Supreme Court shall bind the Court of Appeals as precedents. The Court of Appeals shall have power to hear and determine cases when sitting in a body, except as may be otherwise provided by the General Assembly.

In the event of an equal division of judges on any case when the Court is sitting as a body, the case shall be immediately transferred to the Supreme Court.

Paragraph IX. The Supreme Court and Court of Appeals shall have jurisdiction to review by direct writ of error, and without the necessity of a motion for new trial having been made, all final judgments, orders, decrees and adjudications rendered by any juvenile court created or referred to in an Act of the General Assembly approved February 19, 1951 (Ga. Laws 1951, p. 291), as amended, and any other juvenile court that may be hereafter established, and, it shall further be the duty of the District Attorney of the judicial circuit within which juvenile court or courts are located to represent the juvenile court on such appeals. The time for filing such bill of exceptions, and the procedure governing same, shall be as now provided by law for appeals, or as may hereafter be provided by law, but in any case, the Juvenile Judge may by order grant extensions of time for the filing of such bill of exceptions so as to afford opportunity for preparation of a brief or transcript of evidence, in cases where such is required.

[Editorial note: Paragraph IX was added by an amendment of 1956 and altered by an amendment of 1968.]

PARAGRAPH X. *State Court of Claims; jurisdiction; appeals.* The General Assembly is hereby authorized to create and establish a State Court of Claims with jurisdiction to try and dispose of cases involving claims for injury or damage, except the taking of private property for public purposes, against the State of Georgia, its agencies or political subdivisions, as the General Assembly may provide by law. Notwithstanding any other provision of this Constitution, the General Assembly may provide for exclusive jurisdiction over such cases in the State Court of Claims, provide for trial of such cases without a jury, and prescribe the place and manner in which such cases may be brought and tried. The Supreme Court and the Court of Appeals shall have original jurisdiction to try and correct errors of law from such State Court of Claims according to the method of appeal to said courts now provided for or as may hereafter be provided by law. Nothing contained herein shall constitute a waiver of the immunity of the State from suit, but such sovereign immunity is expressly reserved except to the extent of any waiver of immunity provided in this Constitution and such waiver or qualification of immunity as is now or may hereafter be provided by act of the General Assembly.

[Editorial note: Paragraph X was added in 1974.]

SECTION III

Superior Courts

PARAGRAPH I. *Terms, Etc., of Superior Court Judges.* There shall be a judge of the Superior Courts for each judicial circuit, whose term of office shall be for four years, and until his successor is qualified. He may act in other circuits when authorized by law. The legislature shall have authority to add one or more additional judges of the superior court for any judicial circuit in this State, and shall have authority to regulate the manner in which the judges of such circuits shall dispose of the business thereof, and shall fix the time at which the term or terms of office of such additional judge or judges shall begin, and the manner of his appointment or election, and shall have authority from time to time to add to the number of such judges in any judicial circuit; or to reduce the number of judges in any judicial circuit; provided that at all times there shall be at least one judge in every judicial circuit of this State.

PARAGRAPH II. *Elections, When to Be Held.* The successors to the present and subsequent incumbents shall be elected by the electors of the circuit wherein the superior court judge is to serve, who are entitled to vote for members of the General Assembly, at the general election held for such members, next preceding the expiration of their respective terms.

[Editorial note: Paragraph II was altered by an amendment ratified Nov. 8, 1966.]

PARAGRAPH III. *Terms Begin, When.* The terms of the judges to be elected under the Constitution, except to fill vacancies, shall begin on the first day of January after their election. Every vacancy occasioned by death, resignation, or other causes shall be filled by appointments of the Governor until the first day of January after the general election held next after the expiration of thirty days from the time such vacancy occurs, at which election a successor for the unexpired term shall be elected.

SECTION IV

PARAGRAPH I. *Exclusive Jurisdiction Except In Juvenile Cases.*— The Superior Courts shall have exclusive jurisdiction in cases of divorce; in criminal cases where the offender is subjected to loss of life or confinement in the penitentiary, except in the case of juvenile offenders as provided by law; in cases respecting titles to land; and equity cases.

[Editorial note: This paragraph was amended in 1972.]

PARAGRAPH II. *Equity May Be Merged In Common Law Courts.* The General Assembly may confer upon the Courts of Common Law all the powers heretofore exercised by Courts of Equity in this State.

PARAGRAPH III. *General Jurisdiction.* Said Courts shall have jurisdiction in all civil cases, except as hereinafter provided.

PARAGRAPH IV. *Appellate Jurisdiction.* They shall have appellate jurisdiction in all such cases as may be provided by law.

PARAGRAPH V. *Certiorari, Mandamus, Etc.* They shall have power to correct errors in inferior judicatories by writ of certiorari, which shall only issue on the sanction of the Judge, and said Courts, and the judges thereof shall have power to issue writs of mandamus, prohibition, scire facias, and all other writs that may be necessary for carrying their powers fully into effect, and shall have such other powers as are, or may be conferred on them by law.

PARAGRAPH VI. *New Trials.* The Superior and City Courts may grant new trials on legal grounds.

PARAGRAPH VII. *Judgment of the Court.* The Court shall render judgment without the verdict of a jury in all civil cases, except actions ex delicto, where no issuable defense is filed except as otherwise provided in this Constitution, and subject to the right of trial by a jury on written demand of either party.

PARAGRAPH VIII. *Sessions.* The Superior courts shall sit in each county not less than twice in each year, at such times as have been, or may be appointed by law. The judges of said courts may, on reasonable notice to the parties, at any time, in vacation, at chambers, hear and determine, by interlocutory or final judgment, any matter or issue, where a jury verdit is not required, or may be waived.

PARAGRAPH IX. *Presiding Judge Disqualified.* The General Assembly may provide by law for the appointment of some proper person to preside in cases where the presiding judge is from any cause disqualified.

SECTION V

PARAGRAPH I. *Judges of Superior and City Courts May Alternate, When.* In any county within which there is, or hereafter may be, a City Court the Judge of said Court, and of the Superior Court may preside in the Courts of each other in cases where the judge of either Court is disqualified to preside.

SECTION VI

Probate Courts

PARAGRAPH I. *Probate Court; Judge of Probate Court; Appeals.* The powers of a court of probate shall be vested in the Probate Court and the judge of the Probate Court for each county, from whose decisions there may be an appeal, or by consent of the parties, without a decision, to the Superior Court under regulations prescribed by law.

PARAGRAPH II. *Powers.* (a) The Probate Courts shall have such powers in relation to roads, bridges, ferries, public buildings, paupers, county officers, county funds, county taxes and other county matters as may be conferred on them by law.

(b) The Probate Courts shall have jurisdiction to issue warrants, try cases, and impose sentences thereon in all misdemeanor cases arising under the Act known as the Georgia State Highway Patrol Act of 1937, and other traffic laws, and in all cases arising under the Compulsory School Attendance Law in all counties of this State in which there is no State court, provided the defendant waives a jury trial. Like jurisdiction is also conferred upon the judges of the police courts of incorporated cities and municipal court judges for offenses arising under the Georgia State Highway Patrol Act of 1937, and other traffic laws of the State within their respective jurisdictions.

PARAGRAPH III. *Term of Office.* The Judge of the Probate Court shall hold his office for a term of four years and until his successor is elected and qualified.

PARAGRAPH IV. *Constitution and Statutes.* Wherever the words "Ordinary", or "Ordinaries" or the words "Court of Ordinary" or "Courts of Ordinary" appear in this Constitution or in any statutes of this State, and such words refer to the county officer heretofore known and designated as the Ordinary or the court heretofore known and designated as the Court of Ordinary, such words are hereby stricken and the words "Judge of the Probate Court" or "Judges of the Probate Courts" or the words "Probate Court" or "Probate Courts", respectively, are hereby inserted in lieu of such stricken words. The changing of the name of the Ordinary and the Court of Ordinary to Judge of the Probate Court and Probate Court, respectively, shall not affect the status of any matter pending before any such officer or any such court at the time this Paragraph becomes effective, and any such matter may be continued or disposed of by the Judge of the Probate Court or by the Probate Court, as the case may be.

[Editorial note: The wording of Section VI was changed by a 1974 amendment.]

SECTION VII

Justices of the Peace

PARAGRAPH I. *Number and Term of office.* There shall be in each militia district one justice of the peace, whose official term, except when elected to fill an unexpired term, shall be for four years: Provided, however, that the General Assembly may, in its discretion, abolish justice courts and the office of justice of the peace and of notary public ex-officio justice of the peace in any city of this State having a population of over twenty thousand, and establish in lieu thereof such court or courts or system of courts as the General Assembly may, in its discretion, deem necessary, conferring upon such new court or courts or system of courts, when so established, the jurisdiction as to subject matter now exercised by justice courts and by justices of the peace and notaries public ex-officio justices of the peace together with such additional jurisdiction, either as to amount or sub-matter, as may be provided by law, whereof some other court has not exclusive jurisdiction under this Constitution; together with such provision as to rules and procedure in such courts, and as to new trials and the correction of errors in and by said courts, and with such further provision for the correction of errors by the Superior Court, or Court of Appeals, or the Supreme Court, as the General Assembly may, from time to time, in its discretion, provide or authorize. Any court so established shall not be subject to the rules of uniformity laid down in Paragraph I of Section IX of Article VI of the Constitution of Georgia: Provided, however, that the General Assembly may, in its discretion, abolish justice courts and the office of justice of the peace and notary public ex-officio justice of the peace in any county in this State having within its borders a city having a population of over twenty thousand, and as well in the County of Glynn, and establish in lieu thereof such court or courts or system of courts as the General Assembly may, in its discretion, deem necessary; or conferring upon existing courts, by extension of their jurisdiction as to subject matter now exercised by justice courts and by justices of the peace and notaries public ex-officio justices of the peace; together with such additional jurisdiction, either as to amount or to subject-matter, as may be provided by law, whereof some other court has not exclusive jurisdiction under this Constitution; together also with such provisions as to rules and procedure in such courts and as to new trials and the correction of errors in and by said courts, and with such further provision for the correction of errors by the Superior Court or the Court of Appeals or the Supreme Court as the General Assembly may, from time to time, in its discretion, provide or authorize. The civil court of Fulton County shall have jurisdiction in Fulton County and outside the city limits of Atlanta either concurrently with, or supplemental to, or in lieu of justice courts, as may be now or hereafter provided by law. Any court so established shall not be subject to the rules of uniformity laid down in Paragraph I of Section IX of Article VI of the Constitution of Georgia.

PARAGRAPH II. *Jurisdiction.* Justices of the peace shall have jurisdiction in all civil cases arising ex contractu and in cases of injury or damage to and conversion of personal property, when the principal sum does not exceed two hundred dollars, and shall sit monthly at fixed times and places but in all cases there may be an appeal to a jury in said court, or an appeal to the Superior Court under such regulations as may be prescribed by law.

PARAGRAPH III. *Elections and Commissions.* Justices of the peace shall be elected by the legal voters in their respective districts, and shall be commissioned by the Governor. They shall be removable on conviction for malpractice in office.

SECTION VIII
Notaries Public

PARAGRAPH I. *Appointment; Number; Term; Removal.* Commissioned notaries public, not to exceed one for each militia district, may be appointed by the judges of the superior courts in their respective circuits, upon recommendation of the grand juries of the several counties. They shall be commissioned by the Governor for the term of four years and shall be ex-officio justices of the peace, and shall be removable on conviction for malpractice in office.

SECTION IX
Uniformity of Courts

PARAGRAPH I. *Uniformity Provided For.* Except as otherwise provided in this Constitution, the jurisdiction, powers, proceedings and practice of all courts or officers invested with judicial powers (except City Courts) of the same grade or class, so far as regulated by law, and the force and effect of the process, judgment and decree, by such courts, severally, shall be uniform. This uniformity must be established by the General Assembly, and in case of City Courts, may be established by the General Assembly.

SECTION X
Attorney General

PARAGRAPH I. *Election; Term of Office.* There shall be an Attorney General of this State, who shall be elected by the people at the same time, for the same term and in the same manner as the Governor.

PARAGRAPH II. *Duties.* It shall be the duty of the Attorney General to act as the legal adviser of the Executive Department, to represent the State in the Supreme Court in all capital felonies; and in all civil and criminal cases in any court when required by the Governor and to perform such other services as shall be required of him by law.

Section XI

District Attorney

Paragraph I. *Number; Term of Office; Vacancies.* There shall be a District Attorney for each judicial circuit, whose official term (except to fill a vacancy) shall be four years. The successors of present and subsequent incumbents shall be elected by the electors of the circuit wherein the District Attorney is to serve, who are qualified to vote for members of the General Assembly, at the general election held next preceding the expiration of their respective terms. Every vacancy occasioned by death, resignation, or other cause shall be filled by appointment of the Governor, until the first day of January after the general election held next after the expiration of 30 days from the time such vacancy occurs, at which election a successor for the unexpired term shall be elected.

[Editorial note: Paragraph I was altered by amendments ratified in 1966 and 1968.]

Paragraph II. It shall be the duty of the District Attorney to represent the State in all cases in the superior court of his circuit and in all cases taken up from the superior court of his circuit to the Supreme Court, and Court of Appeals and to perform such other services as shall be required of him by law.

Paragraph III. Wherever the words "solicitor general" are used in any statute they shall be held and taken to mean the District Attorney.

Section XII

Salaries of Justices, Judges and District Attorneys

Paragraph I. *Salaries of Justices, Judges and District Attorneys.* The Justices of the Supreme Court each shall have out of the treasury of the State salaries of not less than $8,000 per annum; the Judges of the Court of Appeals each shall have out of the treasury of the State salaries of not less than $8,000 per annum; the Judges of the Superior Courts each shall have out of the treasury of the State salaries of not less than $6,000 per annum and the District Attorneys shall each have out of the treasury of the State a salary of not less than $250.00 per annum with the right of the General Assembly to authorize any county to supplement the salary of a judge of the Superior Court and District Attorney of the Judicial Circuit in which such county lies out of county funds: Provided, however, where such salary is, at the time of the adoption of this Constitution, being supplemented out of county funds under existing laws, such laws shall remain in force until altered by the General Assembly: Provided, further, that the Board of County Commissioners of Richmond County, or the Ordinary, or such other board or person as may from time to time have charge of the fiscal affairs of said county, shall without further legislative action continue to supplement from said County's treasury the salary of the Judge of Superior Court of the circuit of which the said County of Richmond is a part, by the sum of Two Thousand ($2,000) Dollars per annum, which shall be in addition to the amount received by said judge out of the State treasury, and such payments are declared to be a part of the court expenses of said County, and such payment shall be made to the judge now in office during his present or subsequent terms, as well as to his successors, with the authority in the General Assembly to increase such salary from the County treasury as above provided.

PARAGRAPH II. *Power to Abolish or Reinstate Fees of District Attorney.* The General Assembly shall have power, at any time, by a majority vote of each branch, to abolish the fees at present accruing to the office of District Attorney in any particular judicial circuit, and in lieu thereof to prescribe a salary for such office, without regard to the uniformity of such salaries in the various circuits; and shall have the further power to determine what disposition shall be made of the fines, forfeitures and fees accruing to the office of district attorney in any such judicial circuit where the fees are abolished; and likewise shall have the further power, if it so desires, to abolish such salary and reestablish such fees; but in either event, when so changed, the change shall not become effective until the end of the term to which the District Attorney was elected.

SECTION XIII

Qualifications of Justices, Judges, Etc.

PARAGRAPH I. *Age; Citizenship; Practice of Law.* No person shall be Justice of the Supreme Court, Court of Appeals, Judge of Superior Courts, or Attorney General, unless, at the time of his election, he shall have attained the age of thirty years, and shall have been a citizen of the State three years, and have practiced law for seven years; and no person shall be hereafter elected District Attorney, unless at the time of his election he shall have attained twenty-five years of age, shall have been a citizen of the State for three years, and shall have practiced law for three years next preceding his election.

Paragraph II. Chief Justices Emeritus and Justices Emeritus of the Supreme Court; Judges Emeritus of the Court of Appeals; and Judges Emeritus of the Superior Courts shall be eligible to preside in or over the Supreme Court of Georgia, the Court of Appeals of Georgia and the Superior Courts of this State. The General Assembly shall prescribe the method or manner in which they may be called upon for temporary service.

[Editorial note: Paragraph II was added by an amendment ratified Nov. 6, 1956. The wording was changed to read as quoted by an amendment ratified on Nov. 4, 1958.]

Paragraph III. *Discipline, Removal, and Involuntary Retirement.* (a) Judicial Qualifications Commission. There shall be a Judicial Qualifications Commission. It shall consist of seven members, as follows: (i) two judges of any court of record, each selected by the Supreme Court for a four-year term; (ii) three members of the State Bar, who shall have practiced law in this State for at least ten years and who shall be elected by the Board of Governors of the State Bar for a four-year term; and (iii) two citizens, neither of whom shall be a member of the State Bar, who shall be appointed by the Governor for a four-year term. Of the initial membership of the Commission, one of the judges selected by the Supreme Court, two of the members elected by the Board of Governors, and one of the citizens appointed by the Governor, shall serve for terms of two years each, and all other members shall serve for terms of four years each. Thereafter, all members shall serve for terms of four years each and until their successors are elected or appointed and have qualified. Whenever any member ceases to hold the office or to possess the qualifications which entitled him to be appointed a member, his membership shall terminate, and the appointing authority shall select his successor for the unexpired term. No member of the Commission shall receive any compensation for his services but shall be allowed his necessary expenses for travel, board and lodging incurred in the performance of his duties. No member of the Commission except the Judges shall hold any other public office or be eligible for appointment to a State judicial office so long as he is a member of the Commission. No member shall hold office in any political party or organization. No act of the Commission shall be valid unless concurred in by a majority of its members. The Commission shall select one of its members to serve as chairman.

(b) Procedure and Grounds. A justice or judge of any court of this State, in accordance with the procedure prescribed in this Paragraph, may be removed or otherwise disciplined for willful misconduct in office, or willful and persistent failure to perform his duties, or habitual intemperance; or for conduct prejudicial to the administration of justice which brings the judicial office into disrepute; or he may be retired for disability seriously interfering with the performance of his duties, which is, or is likely to become, of a permanent character. The Commission may, after such investigation as it deems necessary, order a hearing to be held before it concerning the removal or retirement of a justice or a judge, or the Commission may in its discretion request the Supreme Court to appoint a special master to hear and take evidence in the matter and to report thereon to the Commission. If, after hearing, or after considering the record and report of the master, the Commission finds good cause therefor, it shall recommend to the Supreme Court the removal, other discipline, or retirement, as the case may be, of the justice or judge.

The Supreme Court shall review the record of the proceedings on the law and facts, and in its discretion may permit the introduction of additional evidence and shall order removal, other discipline, or retirement, as it finds just and proper, or wholly reject the recommendation. Upon an order for retirement, the justice or judge shall thereby be retired with the same rights and privileges as if he retired pursuant to statute. Upon an order for removal, the justice or judge shall thereby be removed from office, and his salary shall cease from the date of the order.

The Supreme Court shall prescribe rules governing privilege, confidentiality, and practice and procedure in all proceedings brought hereunder. A justice or judge who is a member of the Commission or Supreme Court shall not participate in any proceedings involving his own removal, other discipline or retirement.

[Editorial note: Paragraph III was added in 1972.]

Section XIV

Venue

Paragraph I. *Divorce Cases.* Divorce cases shall be brought in the county where the defendant resides, if a resident of this state; if the defendant be not a resident of this state, then in the county in which the plaintiff resides, provided, that any person who has been a resident of any United States Army Post or military reservation within the State of Georgia for one year next preceding the filing of the petition may bring an action for divorce in any county adjacent to said United States Army Post or military reservation.

PARAGRAPH II. *Land Titles.* Cases respecting titles to land shall be tried in the county where the land lies, except where a single tract is divided by a county line, in which case the Superior Court of either county shall have jurisdiction.

PARAGRAPH III. *Equity Cases.* Equity cases shall be tried in the county where a defendant resides against whom substantial relief is prayed.

PARAGRAPH IV. *Suits Against Joint Obligors, Co-partners, Etc.* Suits against joint obligors, joint promissors, co-partners, or joint trespassers, residing in different counties, may be tried in either county.

PARAGRAPH V. *Suits Against Maker, Endorser, Etc.* Suits against the maker and endorser of promissory notes, or drawer, acceptor and endorser of foreign or inland bills of exchange, or like instruments, residing in different counties, shall be brought in the county where the maker or acceptor resides.

PARAGRAPH VI. *All Other Cases.* All other civil cases shall be tried in the county where the defendant resides, and all criminal cases shall be tried in the county where the crime was committed, except cases in the Superior Courts where the Judge is satisfied that an impartial jury cannot be obtained in such county.

Section XV

Change of Venue

Paragraph I. *Power to Change Venue.* The power to change the venue in civil and criminal cases shall be vested in the Superior Courts to be exercised in such manner as has been, or shall be, provided by law.

Section XVI

Jury Trial

Paragraph I. *Right of Trial By Jury.* The right of trial by jury, except where it is otherwise provided in this Constitution, shall remain inviolate, but the General Assembly may prescribe any number, not less than five, to constitute a trial, or traverse jury, except in the superior court.

Paragraph II. *Selection of Jurors.* The General Assembly shall provide by law for the selection of the most experienced, intelligent and upright men to serve as grand jurors, and intelligent and upright men to serve as traverse jurors. Nevertheless, the grand jurors shall be competent to serve as traverse jurors. The General Assembly shall have the power to require jury service of women also, under such regulations as the General Assembly may prescribe.

Paragraph III. *Compensation of Jurors.* It shall be the duty of the General Assembly by general laws to prescribe the manner of fixing compensation of jurors in all counties in this State.

Section XVII

County Commissioners

Paragraph I. *Power to Create County Commissioners.* The General Assembly shall have power to provide for the creation of county commissioners in such counties as may require them, and to define their duties.

Section XVIII

What Courts May Be Abolished

Paragraph I. *Power to Abolish Courts.* All courts not specially mentioned by name in the first section of this Article may be abolished in any county at the discretion of the General Assembly.

Paragraph II. *Supreme Court Cost; Pauper Oath.* The cost in the Supreme Court and Court of Appeals shall not exceed $15.00 until otherwise provided by law. Plaintiffs in error shall not be required to pay costs in said courts when the usual pauper oath is filed in the court below.

ARTICLE VII

FINANCE, TAXATION AND PUBLIC DEBT

Section I

Power of Taxation

Paragraph I. *Taxation, a Sovereign Right.* The right of taxation is a sovereign right—inalienable, indestructible—is the life of the State, and rightfully belongs to the people in all republican governments, and neither the General Assembly, nor any, nor all other departments of the Government established by this Constitution, shall ever have the authority to irrevocably give, grant, limit, or restrain this right; and all laws, grants, contracts, and all other acts, whatsoever, by said government, or any department thereof, to affect any of these purposes, shall be, and are hereby, declared to be null and void, for every purpose whatsoever; and said right of taxation shall always be under the complete control of, and revocable by, the State, notwithstanding any gift, grant or contract, whatsoever, by the General Assembly.

The power to tax corporations and corporate property, shall not be surrendered or suspended by any contract, or grant to which the State shall be a party.

The General Assembly is hereby authorized to provide by law for the granting of funds to a county in which is located land belonging to the State consisting of at least 20,000 acres from which such county receives no taxes. The General Assembly is authorized to provide in such law the procedure for determining the amount of funds and all other matters relative to any such grant.

[Editorial note: The last paragraph in Paragraph I was added by an amendment ratified Nov. 6, 1962].

PARAGRAPH II. *Taxing Power Limited.*

1. The General Assembly shall not by vote, resolution, or order, grant any donation or gratuity in favor of any person, corporation or association.

The General Assembly is authorized to provide by law for the payment of two hundred and fifty thousand dollars ($250,000.00) to the first person, firm or corporation, or combination thereof, which puts down and brings in the first commercial oil well in this State. Such well must produce at least 100 barrels of oil per day, and the determination as to whether such well is producing this amount is hereby vested in the Director of the State Department of Mines, Mining and Geology. Said law shall provide for the distribution of said amount as the General Assembly may by statute provide between the company or individual who drills or causes to be drilled said well, the contractor who furnishes the equipment, among such workmen and employees actually engaged in the job, and to the mineral and/or property owner where the well is drilled. The General Assembly shall provide for the method of payment by the Governor.

[Editorial note: The provisions authorizing a bounty for the first commercial oil well were added by amendment ratified Nov. 6, 1956.]

Notwithstanding any other provision of this Constitution, whenever the State Board of Vocational Education may be entitled to receive Federal funds made available under the vocational Rehabilitation Act, 29 United States Code, Chapter 4, or any amendment thereto, said Board shall be authorized to receive and administer such funds in accordance with the terms of the grant, and where the grant so provides, may disburse said funds to non-profit corporations or associations which are engaged solely in the vocational rehabilitation of disabled persons, provided, however, that nothing in this paragraph shall be construed to authorize the expenditure of any State funds until the same shall have been appropriated by the General Assembly.

[Editorial note: This paragraph was added in 1966.]

2. The General Assembly shall not grant or authorize extra compensation to any public officer, agent or contractor after the service has been rendered or the contract entered into.

The General Assembly is hereby authorized to provide by law for reimbursing the employees of the Game and Fish Commission who received a retroactive pay raise in 1966 and were subsequently required to remit the amount of said raise to the State Treasurer.

[Editorial note: The last sentence above was added in 1968.]

3.The levy of taxes on property for any one year by the General Assembly for all purposes, except to provide for repelling invasions, suppressing insurrections, or defending the State in time of war, shall not exceed one-fourth (¼) mill on each dollar of the value of the property taxable in the State, provided, however, that until some other method permitted by the laws of the United States for the taxation of national banking associations or corporations is enacted by the General Assembly for the taxation of the shares of stock of banking corporations and other monied capital coming into competition with such banking corporations, such property may be taxed at a rate not exceeding five (5) mills on each dollar of the value thereof.

[Editorial note: This sub-paragraph originally read as follows: "The levy of taxes on property for any one year by the General Assembly for all purposes, except to provide for repelling invasions, suppressing insurrections, or defending the State in time of war, shall not exceed five (5) mills on each dollar of the value of the property taxable in the State."]

4. No poll tax shall be levied to exceed one dollar annually upon each poll.

5. There is hereby created a board to be known as the State Medical Education Board to consist of five members, one of whom shall be the President of the Medical Association of Georgia, one of whom shall be the immediate past President of the Medical Association of Georgia, and three members to be appointed by the Governor, who shall be qualified electors of the State of Georgia. The members of the board shall hold office for a term of four years beginning on the first day of April, 1953, and every four years thereafter the Governor shall appoint three members for a term of four years, and shall appoint the President and the immediate past President of the Medical Association of Georgia pursuant to their position and office in those respective capacities. Vacancies shall be filled by appointment of the Governor for the unexpired term.

The members of the Board shall serve without pay but shall be allowed $20.00 per day expenses and traveling expenses of ten cents (10¢) per mile for attending meetings of the board or in traveling elsewhere in the discharge of their duties requiring their absence from their respective places of abode, same to be paid upon the approval of the Chairman or Vice-Chairman of the Board, out of any funds made available to said Board.

The secretary of the Board shall be whomsoever is serving as the secretary of the Board of Regents, who shall keep the records and minutes of the proceedings of the Board and who shall also keep the books, records and accounts of the Board, and whose compensation as secretary of this board shall be fixed by the Board. The secretary shall prepare and contersign all checks, vouchers and warrants drawn upon the funds of the Board, and the same shall be signed by the Chairman of the Board. The secretary shall also be the treasurer of the Board and shall keep and account for all the funds of the Board, and shall execute and file with the Board a surety bond in the sum of $10,000.00, payable to the State of Georgia, and conditioned upon the faithful performance of his duties and that he shall properly account for all funds coming into his hands as such secretary, the premium on such bond to be paid out of the funds of the Board.

The board may employ clerical assistance as is required and needed.

The board shall elect a chairman and also a vice-chairman to serve in the absence or inability of the chairman. The board shall maintain an office at the Medical College of Georgia, and shall meet at the said office or elsewhere at least once each quarter at such time as may be fixed by the board. Special meetings shall be held upon call of the chairman. Three members of the board shall constitute a quorum for the transaction of business, and the board shall keep full, complete and permanent minutes and records of all its proceedings and actions.

It shall be the duty of the board to receive and pass upon, allow or disallow all applications for loans or scholarships made by students who are bona fide citizens and residents of the State of Georgia and who desire to become doctors of medicine and who are acceptable for enrollment in a qualified four-year medical school. The purpose of such loans shall be to enable such applicants to obtain a standard four-year medical education which will qualify them to become licensed, practicing physicians within the State of Georgia. It shall be the duty of the board to make a careful and full investigation of the ability, character and qualifications of each applicant and determine his fitness to become the recipient of such loan or scholarship, and for that purpose the board may propound such examination to each applicant which it deems proper, and the said board may prescribe such rules and regulations as it deems necessary and proper to carry out the purpose and intention of this bill. The investigation of the applicant shall include an investigation of the ability of the applicant, or of the parents of such applicant, to pay his own tuition at such a medical school and the board in granting such loans and scholarships shall give preference to qualified applicants who, or whose parents, are unable to pay the applicant's tuition at such a medical school.

The said board shall have authority to grant to each applicant deemed by the board to be qualified to receive the same, a loan or scholarship for the purpose of acquiring a medical education as herein provided for, upon such terms and conditions to be imposed by the board as provided for in this bill.

Applicants who are granted loans or scholarships by the Board shall receive a loan or scholarship not to exceed $10,000.00 to any one applicant to be paid at such time and in such manner as may be determined by the Board with which to defray the tuition and other expenses of any such applicant in any responsible, accepted and accredited four-year medical college or school in the United States. The loans and scholarship herein provided shall not exceed the sums herein stated, but they may be prorated in such manner as to pay to the medical college or school to which any applicant is admitted such funds as are required by that college or school, and the balance to be paid direct to the applicant; all of which shall be under such terms and conditions as may be provided under rules and regulations of the Board. The said loans or scholarships to be granted to each applicant shall be based upon the condition that the full amount thereof shall be repaid to the State of Georgia in cash in full with 4% interest from the date of each payment by the State on such loan or scholarship, same to be payable annually, the first annual payment to be due on or before one year from the date the applicant completes his internship, or same may be repaid to the State of Georgia in services to be rendered by the applicant by practicing his profession at some place within the State of Georgia to be approved by the board. One-fifth of the loan or scholarship, together with interest thereon, shall be credited to the applicant for each year of practicing his profession in a community of 10,000 population or less, according to the United States Dicennial Census of 1960 or any future such dicennial census, or at Milledgeville State Hospital, Gracewood State School and Hospital, or at any facility operated by or under the jurisdiction of the State Department of Public Health or at any prison or detention camp or work camp operated under the jurisdiction of the State Board of Corrections, and no annual interest on the scholarship loan shall be paid during such practice or service. Credit for practice at Milledgeville State Hospital, Gracewood State School and Hospital, or at any facility operated by or under the jurisdiction of the State Department of Public Health or at any of the above facilities of the State Board of Corrections, shall be retroactive and shall apply to any applicants engaging in such practice at any time. In the event an applicant has repaid any part of such loan or scholarship for which he would otherwise have received credit for service, he shall be repaid whatever sum is necessary to take into consideration the credit he would have received. After the third full year of practice or services within this State as herein provided, but not before, the said applicant shall be privileged, entirely at the discretion of the Board, to pay off the balance of the scholarship or loan, together with accrued interest thereon, and upon such payment shall be relieved from further obligations under his contract for loan or scholarship.

Each applicant before being granted a loan or scholarship shall enter into a contract with the State of Georgia, agreeing to the terms and conditions upon which the loan or scholarship shall be granted to him, which said contract shall include such terms and provisions as will carry out the full purpose and intent of this Act, and the form thereof shall be prepared and approved by the Attorney-General of this State, and shall be signed by the chairman of the board, countersigned by the secretary and shall be signed by the applicant. For the purposes of this Act the disabilities of minority of all applicants granted loans or scholarships hereunder shall be and the same are hereby removed and the said applicants are declared to be of full lawful age for the purpose of entering into the contract hereinabove provided for, and such contract so executed by an applicant is hereby declared to be a valid and binding contract the same as though the said applicant were of the full age of 21 years and upward. The board is hereby vested with full and complete authority and power to sue in its own name any applicant for any balance due the board on any such contract.

It shall be the duty of the board to contact and make inquiry of such of the four-year medical colleges and schools as herein provided as it deems proper, and make such arrangements and enter into such contracts, within the limitations as to cost as herein provided, for the admission of students granted loans or scholarships by the board, such contracts to be approved by the Attorney-General of this State, and the money obligations of such contract as made by the board with any such colleges shall be paid for out of funds to be provided by law for such purposes, and all students granted loans or scholarships shall attend a medical school with which the board has entered into a contract, or any accredited four-year medical school or college in which said applicant may obtain admission, and which is approved by the board.

The board shall have authority to cancel any contract made between it and any applicant for loans or scholarships upon cause deemed sufficient by the board. And the board shall have authority to cancel such contracts which it may lawfully cancel made with any of the colleges or schools as herein provided.

All payments of funds for loans or scholarships hereunder shall be made by requisition of the board signed by the chairman and the secretary directed to the auditor of public accounts, who shall thereupon issue a warrant on the treasury of the State of Georgia for the amount fixed in the requisition and payable to the person designated thereon, which said warrant upon presentation shall be paid by the treasurer out of any funds appropriated by the legislature for the purposes provided for under this Act.

All funds made available to the board by Act of the legislature for the purpose of defraying expenses of the board and the salaries of its secretary and employees shall be paid over and received by the treasurer of this board and by him deposited in some solvent bank within the State of Georgia, selected by the board, and such funds may be drawn and expended by check or warrant signed by the chairman and attested by the secretary.

The board shall make a biennial report to the legislature at each session thereof of its activities, loans or scholarships granted, names of persons to whom granted and the institutions attended by those receiving the same, the location of the applicants who have received their education and become licensed physicians and surgeons within this State as a result of the said loans and/or scholarships, and where they are practicing, and shall make a full report of all its expenditures for salaries and expenses incurred hereunder.

It is the purpose and intent of this bill to bring about an adequate supply of doctors of medicine in the more sparsely populated areas of the State of Georgia by increasing the number of medical students from Georgia in the various medical schools, and inducing a sufficient number of the graduates from medical schools to return to Georgia and practice their profession, thus affording adequate medical care to the people of Georgia.

Section 1-A. The Director of the Department of Public Health, with the approval of the State Board of Health, is hereby authorized to extend scholarships to physicians and other personnel to take post graduate courses in the various schools and clinics in the United States so as to enable them to be better qualified in the diagnosis, care and treatment of mental illness. As a prerequisite to the grant of such scholarship, the recipient thereof must agree to actively engage in the practice of his profession in a hospital operated by the State of Georgia, under the supervision of the State of Georgia, or at some place approved by the authority granting the scholarship, on the basis of one year of service for each year of training received. The remedies for the enforcing of service required shall be the same as provided for medical grants and scholarships and such other remedies as may be provided by law.

[Editorial note: Subparagraph 5 relating to the State Medical Education Board was added by an amendment ratified on November 4, 1952. This subparagraph was amended in 1960, 1962, 1964, 1966, and 1968.]

6. The Board of Regents of the University System of Georgia shall have the authority to grant to qualified students, who are citizens and bona fide residents of the State of Georgia and who would not otherwise have available the funds necessary to obtain an education, such scholarships as are necessary for them to complete programs of study offered by institutions of the the University System of Georgia, with the exception of the program leading to the degree of Doctor of Medicine. The terms and conditions thereof shall be prescribed and regulated by the Board of Regents but shall include the condition that recipients of such scholarships shall, upon the completion of their programs of study, reside in the State of Georgia and engage in activities for which they were prepared through the scholarships for a period of one year for each $1,000 received. The General Assembly shall appropriate such funds to the Board of Regents of the University System of Georgia as it sees fit in order to carry out the purposes of this provision.

It shall be the duty of the Board of Regents to receive and pass upon, allow or disallow, all applications for scholarships; to contract, increase, decrease, terminate and otherwise regulate all grants for scholarships; and to manage, operate and control all funds appropriated for this purpose.

[Editorial note: Subparagraph 6 was added by an amendment ratified on November 4, 1958.]

7. State departments and agencies of the State government of Georgia shall have the authority to disburse State funds to match federal funds in order to provide qualified employees with educational scholarships and for use in other federal education programs but shall include the condition that personnel to whom the scholarships are extended must, as a prerequisite thereto agree to work for the department or agency granting the scholarships for at least one year for each year spent in study or refund the money received for such scholarships pro rata. The terms and conditions thereof shall be prescribed and regulated by the various departments and agencies granting the scholarships. Provided further that no additional appropriation shall be made by the General Assembly to finance such scholarships, but the same shall be financed from the regular appropriations to the various State Departments and State agencies. It shall be the duty of the various State departments and State agencies to receive and pass upon, allow or disallow all applications for scholarships in accordance with rules and regulations prescribed by them; to contract, increase, decrease, terminate and otherwise regulate all grants for scholarships; and to manage, operate and to control all funds used for this purpose.

[Editorial note: Subparagraph 7 was added in 1958 and amended in 1972.]

8. The State Board of Education shall have the authority to grant to citizens who are interested in becoming teachers and who are bona fide residents of the State of Georgia such scholarships as are necessary for them to complete programs of study in preparation for teaching. The terms and conditions thereof shall be prescribed and regulated by the State Board of Education but shall include the condition that recipients of such scholarships shall, upon the completion of their programs of study, teach in the public schools of Georgia for a period of one year for each $1,000 received, and include the further provision that any person using any such scholarship shall teach in the public schools of Georgia for at least three years in any event.

The General Assembly shall have the authority to appropriate such funds to the State Board of Education as it deems wise and proper to carry out the purposes of this provision.

It shall be the duty of the State Board of Education to receive and pass upon, allow or disallow all applications for scholarships for teachers; to contract, increase, decrease, terminate and otherwise regulate all grants for scholarships; and to manage, operate and control all funds appropriated for this purpose.

[Editorial note: Subparagraph 8 was added by an amendment ratified on Nov. 4, 1958.]

9. There shall be a State Dental Education Board of Georgia, which is authorized to grant loans or scholarships to students who are citizens and residents of the State of Georgia, and who desire to become dentists. The appointment of members of said State Dental Education Board of Georgia, their qualifications, terms of office, powers, duties, functions and authority; and the provision of funds to carry out the purposes provided for herein shall be as enacted and appropriated by the General Assembly of the State of Georgia.

[Editorial note: Subparagraph 9 was added by an amendment ratified on Nov. 3, 1964.]

10. The General Assembly is hereby authorized to provide by law a State Scholarship Commission to be authorized and empowered to activate, inaugurate and conduct a program to provide for the granting of scholarships to students desiring to study courses in the para-medical, professional or educational fields. The General Assembly is hereby authorized to provide for the duties, powers, authority, jurisdiction and composition of any such commission and is authorized to provide for all other matters relative to the purposes provided for herein.

The General Assembly is hereby authorized to provide by law for a program to grant scholarships or other assistance to the children of law enforcement officers, firemen and prison guards, who are permanently disabled or killed in the line of duty, to enable such children to acquire an education beyond the 12th grade, or to enable such children to attend a vocational-technical school. The General Assembly shall be further authorized to provide by law for the terms and conditions for granting such scholarships or other assistance and shall provide that the program established in pursuance of this amendment shall be administered by the State Scholarship Commission or the Higher Education Assistance Corporation, as the General Assembly shall determine. The General Assembly is hereby further authorized to appropriate any funds it deems necessary for the purpose of carrying out the provisions of this amendment.

The General Assembly is hereby authorized and empowered to appropriate any amount of funds it deems necessary for the purposes of implementing any Act which becomes law as authorized by this provision.

[Editorial note: The last three paragraphs were added in 1964 and 1968.]

11. The General Assembly is hereby authorized to appropriate funds to any State department or other State agency for the purpose of being used to obtain funds from the Federal Government for educational scholarships, educational loans and other educational purposes and all such State departments and other State agencies shall be authorized to use the funds so appropriated and the funds received from the Federal Government for the purposes authorized and directed by the Federal Government in making such funds available.

[Editorial note: The paragraph relating to the appropriation of funds to obtain federal funds was added by an amendment ratified Nov. 8, 1966.]

12. The General Assembly is hereby authorized to provide by law for a program of guaranteed student loans and for the payment of interest on such loans, which loans shall be used for the purpose of acquiring an education beyond the twelfth (12th) grade. The General Assembly is authorized to create an authority, a corporation or other entity for the purpose of administering any such law. Such law shall provide the agencies which may participate in any such loan program which may include commercial banks, savings banks, savings and loan associations, life insurance companies, credit unions, and retirement and pension systems. Such law shall provide a maximum rate of interest which may be charged for such loans and shall provide a portion of such interest which will be paid by the State. State funds may be expended for such purposes and the General Assembly is hereby authorized to appropriate money therefor. The General Assembly is also authorized to provide that contributions for the purposes provided herein shall be deductible for State income tax purposes. The General Assembly is also authorized to provide for such tax exemptions as shall be deemed advisable in connection with such program. The General Assembly is hereby authorized to provide for all other matters relative to the purposes provided for herein.

[Editorial note: The provisions relating to guaranteed student loans were added by an amendment of Nov. 3, 1964.]

The General Assembly is hereby authorized to provide by law for the issuance of revenue bonds for the purpose of making direct loans to students in order to allow such students to acquire an education beyond the 12th grade. The amount of such revenue bonds that may be outstanding at any one time, the interest rates, terms and conditions associated with the issuance of such bonds and all other matters relating to the issuance of such bonds shall be as the General Assembly shall provide by law. Such bonds shall be retired by the proceeds derived from the repayment of such student loans plus the interest, which may be such rate or rates as the General Assembly shall determine, on such loans in such manner and under such terms and conditions as the General Assembly shall determine. To the extent necessary to secure the issuance and sale of such bonds, such bonds may be retired from State funds in such manner as the General Assembly shall determine, any other provisions of this Constitution to the contrary notwithstanding.

[Editorial note: This paragraph was added in 1968.]

13. Notwithstanding any other provisions of this Constitution, the General Assembly is hereby authorized to provide by law for the indemnification with respect to death, personal injury or property damage sustained in preventing the commission of a crime against the person or property of another, in apprehending a criminal, or in assisting a peace officer in prevention of a crime or apprehension of a criminal. Such law may provide for the method of payment of such indemnification and all other matters relative to the purposes herein provided. The General Assembly is hereby authorized to appropriate State funds for the payment of such indemnification and for the purpose of implementing any law as authorized by this paragraph.

[Editorial note: The last paragraph, which deals with idemnification, was added by an amendment ratified Nov. 8, 1966.]

14. Notwithstanding any other provisions of this Constitution, whenever the State Board of Vocational Education may be entitled to receive Federal funds made available under the Vocational Rehabilitation Act, 29 United States Code, Chapter 4, or any amendment thereto, said Board shall be authorized to receive and administer such funds in accordance with the terms of the grant, and where the grant so provides, may disburse said funds to non-profit corporations or associations which are engaged solely in the vocational rehabilitation of disabled persons provided, however, that nothing in this paragraph shall be construed to authorize the expenditure of any State funds until the same shall have been appropriated by the General Assembly.

[Editorial note: The last paragraph, which deals with vocational rehabilitation, was added by an amendment of Nov. 8, 1966.]

15. Notwithstanding any other provisions of this Constitution, the Department of Industry and Trade, in order to make Georgia competitive with other states in securing new business, industry and tourism, is hereby authorized to expend available funds for the business meals and incidental expenses of bona

fide industrial prospects and other persons who attend any meeting at the request of the Department to discuss the location or development of new business, industry or tourism within the State. All such expenditures shall be verified by vouchers showing the date, place, purpose and persons for whom such expenditures were made. The State Auditor shall conduct an audit of such expenditures at least every six months.

[Editorial note: This paragraph was added in 1968.]

16. The General Assembly is authorized to provide by law for grants or scholarships to citizens of Georgia who are students attending colleges or universities in this State which are not branches of the University System of Georgia. The General Assembly shall provide the procedures under which such grants or scholarships shall be made and is authorized to provide appropriations for such purposes.

[Editorial note: This paragraph was added in 1970.]

17. Any other provisions of this Constitution to the contrary notwithstanding, the General Assembly is hereby authorized to provide by law, from time to time, for the increase of retirement or pensions benefits of retired persons who retired pursuant to any retirement system, annuity and benefit fund, pension system or any similar system heretofore or hereafter created by law to which the General Assembly appropriates funds. The General Assembly shall be authorized to appropriate funds for the purpose of increasing the retirement or pension benefits of such retired persons.

[Editorial note: This paragraph was added in 1970.]

18. Notwithstanding any other provisions of this Constitution, the General Assembly is hereby authorized to provide by law for a program or programs of loans, scholarships and grants, and the insuring of loans and payment of interest on loans to citizens of this State for educational purposes. The General Assembly is authorized to provide for all matters relative to such programs. Taxes may be levied and public funds expended for such purposes.

[Editorial note: This paragraph was added in 1972.]

19. The General Assembly is hereby authorized to provide by law for tuition grants to qualified students, who are children of certain United States servicemen as hereinafter provided, to enable them to complete programs of study offered in the educational institutions of this State. The tuition grants shall apply to children of servicemen who were bona fide residents of this State at the time of their entry into the Armed Forces and who are certified by the United States Department of Defense or the United States Veterans Administration as missing in action for more than 90 days or captured in line of

duty by a hostile force or forcibly detained or interned in line of duty by a foreign power since 26 March 1964; provided, however, that this shall not include any serviceman who is not in fact missing in action, but is missing because of unlawful actions on his part. The provisions of this Paragraph shall not apply to children born to any serviceman after his missing in action status is clarified or after his release from prison. The provisions of this Paragraph shall not apply to children of any servicemen who were discharged under other than honorable conditions. The provisions of this Paragraph shall not apply to the children of any servicemen who are eligible for federal benefits under the provisions of Chapter 31, Title 38, U.S. Code Annotated (Veterans Vocational Rehabilitation); Chapter 34, Title 38, U.S. Code Annotated (Veterans Educational Assistance); or Chapter 35, Title 38, U.S. Code Annotated (Veterans War Orphans Educational Assistance Act). The recipients of such tuition grants must attend institutions within the University System of Georgia or vocational training institutions administered by the State Board of Education. The educational assistance to children of servicemen under the provisions of this Paragraph shall cover a period not in excess of 36 months (or the equivalent thereof in part-time training). The educational assistance to children of servicemen under the provisions of this Paragraph shall begin on the eighteenth birthday of such children or the successful completion of secondary schooling, whichever occurs first, and end on their twenty-sixth birthday. The term "child" or "children" shall include individuals who are married. The Georgia State Scholarship Commission and the State Board of Education are hereby charged with the administration of this Paragraph and may promulgate necessary rules, regulations and procedures to carry out the purposes of this Paragraph. The General Assembly shall appropriate the necessary funds for said tuition grants.

[Editorial note: This paragraph was added in 1972.]

20. Any other provisions of this Constitution to the contrary notwithstanding, the General Assembly is hereby authorized to provide by law, from time to time, for the increase of retirement or other benefits of retired persons who have retired or who retire in the future pursuant to any retirement system, annuity and benefit fund system, pension system or any similar system, which such system was created by law and such law provided that such system be funded wholly or partly from fines and forfeitures. No formerly retired person shall receive any greater benefits than those benefits provided by law to be received upon retirement by members of the system who have not retired, nor shall any such formerly retired person receive

any increased benefits unless all formerly retired persons entitled to receive such increased benefits participate pro rata therein.

[Editorial note: This paragraph was added in 1972.]

21. Any other provisions of this Constitution to the contrary notwithstanding, the General Assembly is hereby authorized to provide by law, from time to time, for the increase of retirement or pension benefits of retired public schoolteachers who retired pursuant to a retirement or pension system of a county, municipality or local board of education. The General Assembly shall be authorized to expend State funds for such purposes in such manner and pursuant to such terms and conditions as the General Assembly may provide by law.

[Editorial note: This paragraph was added in 1974.]

22. Any other provisions of this Constitution to the contrary notwithstanding, in all cities of this State having a population of more than 300,000, as disclosed by the United States Decennial Census of 1970, or any such future census, the governing authority of any such municipal corporation is hereby authorized to provide, from time to time, for the increase of retirement or pension benefits of persons who have retired from employment with any such municipal corporation and who retired pursuant to any retirement system, annuity and benefit fund, pension system or any similar system heretofore or hereafter created by law to which any such municipal corporation appropriates funds. The governing authority of any such municipal corporation is hereby authorized to appropriate funds for the purpose of increasing the retirement or pension benefits of such retired person.

[Editorial note: This paragraph was added in 1974.]

PARAGRAPH III. *Uniformity; Classification of Property.* All taxes shall be levied and collected under general laws and for public purposes only. All taxation shall be uniform upon the same class of subjects within the territorial limits of the authority levying the tax. Classes of subjects for taxation of property shall consist of tangible property and one or more classes of intangible personal property including money. The General Assembly shall have the power to classify property including money for taxation, and to adopt different rates and different methods for different classes of such property.

Notwithstanding anything to the contrary contained in this paragraph, the General Assembly shall be authorized to enact legislation treating any and all motor vehicles, including trailers, as a separate class from other classes of tangible property for ad valorem property tax purposes, and to adopt different rates, methods or assessment dates for the taxation of such property, and to enact legislation consistent herewith to prevent any person, firm or corporation from escaping payment of their fair share of ad valorem taxes on said motor vehicles.

[Editorial note: The last sentence in Paragraph III was added by an amendment ratified on Nov. 3, 1964.]

PARAGRAPH IV. *Exemptions From Taxation.* The General Assembly may, by law, exempt from taxation all public property; places of religious worship or burial and all property owned by religious groups used only for residential purposes and from which no income is derived; all institutions of purely public charity; all intangible personal property owned by or irrevocably held in trust for the exclusive benefit of religious, educational and charitable institutions, no part of the net profit from the operation of which can inure to the benefit of any private person; all buildings erected for and used as a college, incorporated academy or other seminary of learning, and also all funds or property held or used as endowment by such colleges, incorporated academies or seminaries of learning, provided the same is not invested in real estate; and provided, further, that said exemptions shall only apply to such colleges, incorporated academies or other seminaries of learning as are open to the general public; provided further, that all endowments to institutions established for white people, shall be limited to white people, and all endowments to institutions established for colored people, shall be limited to colored people; the real and personal estate of any public library, and that of any other literary association, used by or connected with such library; all books and philosophical apparatus and all paintings and statuary of any company or association, kept in a public hall and not held as merchandise or for purposes of sale or gain; provided the property so exempted be not used for the purpose of private or corporate profit and income, distributable to shareholders in corporations owning such property or to other owners of such property, and any income from such property is used exclusively for religious, educational and charitable purposes, or for either one or more of such purposes and for the purpose of maintaining and operating such institution; this exemption shall not apply to real estate or buildings other than those used for the operation of such institution and which is rented, leased or otherwise used for the primary purpose of securing an income thereon; and also provided that such donations of property shall not be predicated upon an agreement, contract or otherwise that the donor or donors shall receive or retain any part of the net or gross income of the property. The General Assembly shall further have power to exempt from taxation farm products, including baled cotton grown in this State and remaining in the hands of the producer, but not longer than for the year next after their production.

[Editorial note: The phrase "and all property owned by religious groups and used only for residential purposes and from which no income is derived" was added by an amendment ratified on Nov. 2, 1954.]

The General Assembly is hereby authorized to provide by law that all personal clothing and effects, household furniture, furnishings, equipment, appliances and other personal property used within the home, if not held for sale, rental or other commercial use, shall be exempt from all ad valorem taxation. The General Assembly is further authorized to provide by law that all tools and implements of trade of manual laborers and domestic animals shall be exempt from State, county, municipal and school district ad valorem taxes, in an amount not to exceed $300.00 in actual value.

[Editorial note: This paragraph was added in 1970.]

The homestead of each resident of Georgia actually occupied by the owner as a residence and homestead, and only so long as actually occupied by the owner primarily as such, but not to exceed $2,000.00 of its value, is hereby exempted from all ad valorem taxation for State, county and school purposes, except taxes levied by municipalities for school purposes and except to pay interest on and retire bonded indebtedness, provided, however, should the owner of a dwelling house on a farm, who is already entitled to homestead exemption, participate in the program of rural housing and obtain a new house under contract with the local housing authority, he shall be entitled to receive the same homestead exemption as allowed before making such contract. The General Assembly may from time to time lower said exemption to not less than $1,250.00. The value of all property in excess of the foregoing exemptions shall remain subject to taxation. Said exemptions shall be returned and claimed in such manner as prescribed by the General Assembly. The exemption herein provided for shall not apply to taxes levied by municipalities.

All cooperative, non-profit, membership corporations organized under the laws of this State for the purpose of engaging in rural electrification, as defined in sub-section 1 of Section 3 of the Act approved March 30, 1937, providing for their incorporation, and all of the real and personal property owned or held by such corporations for such purpose, are hereby exempted from all taxation, state, county, municipal, school district and political or territorial subdivisions of the State having the authority to levy taxes. The exemption herein provided for shall expire December 31, 1961.

There shall be exempt from all ad valorem intangible taxes in this State, the common voting stock of a subsidiary corporation not doing business in this State, if at least ninety per cent of such common voting stock is owned by a Georgia corporation with its principal place of business located in this State and was acquired or is held for the purpose of enabling the parent company to carry on some part of its established line of business through such subsidiary.

All laws exempting property from taxation, other than the property herein enumerated, shall be void.

The legislature may exempt from taxation intangible personal property owned by a trust forming a part of a pension, profit sharing or stock bonus plan if such trust is exempt from Federal income tax under Section 165(a) of the Federal Internal Revenue Code. Existing laws exempting such property from taxation are hereby ratified.

[Editorial note: This paragraph was added by an amendment of 1952.]

Each disabled veteran, as hereinafter defined, who is a citizen and resident of Georgia, is hereby granted an exemption of $12,500.00 on his homestead, which he owns and which he actually occupies as a residence and homestead, such exemption being from all ad valorem taxation for State, county, municipal and school purposes. The value of all property in excess of the above exempted amount shall remain subject to taxation. The term "disabled veteran," as used herein, means a disabled American veteran of any war or armed conflict in which any branch of the armed forces of the United States engaged, whether under United States command or otherwise, and who is disabled, as a result of such service in the armed forces, due to loss, or loss of use, of both lower extremities, such as to preclude locomotion without the aid of braces, crutches, canes, or a wheel chair, or blindness in both eyes, having only light perception, plus loss or loss of use of one lower extremity, or due to the loss or loss of use of one lower extremity together with residuals of organic disease or injury which so affect the functions of balance or propulsion as to preclude locomotion without resort to a wheelchair.

[Editorial note: The paragraph on disabled veterans, added in 1958, was amended in 1964, 1968, and 1970.]

Each person who is sixty-five (65) years of age or over is hereby granted an exemption from all State and county ad valorem taxes in the amount of $4,000.00 on a homestead owned and occupied by him as a residence if his net income, together with the net income of his spouse who also occupies and resides at such homestead, as net income is defined by Georgia law, from all sources, except as hereinafter provided, does not exceed $4,000.00 for the immediately preceding taxable year for income tax purposes. For the purposes of this paragraph, net income shall not include income received as retirement, survivor or disability benefits under the Federal Social Security Act or under any other public or private retirement, disability or pension system, except such income which is in excess of the maximum amount authorized to be paid to an individual and his spouse under the Federal Social Security Act, and income from such sources in excess of such maximum amount shall be included as net income for the purposes of this paragraph. The value of the residence in excess of the above exempted amount shall remain subject to taxation. Any such owner shall not receive the benefits of such homestead exemption unless he, or through his agent, files an affidavit with the tax commissioner or tax receiver of the county in which he resides, giving his age and the amount of income which he and his spouse received during the last taxable year for income tax purposes, and such additional information relative to receiving the benefits of such exemption as will enable the tax commissioner or tax receiver to make a determination as to whether such owner is entitled to such exemption. The tax commissioner or tax receiver shall provide affidavit forms for this purpose. Such applications shall be processed in the same manner as other applications for homestead exemption, and the provisions of law applicable to the processing of homestead exemptions, as the same now exists or may hereafter be amended, shall apply thereto. Provided, that after any such owner has filed the proper affidavit, as provided above, and has been allowed the exemption provided herein, it shall not be necessary that he make application and file the said affidavit thereafter for any year and the said exemption shall continue to be allowed to such owner. It shall be the duty of any such owner, however, to notify the tax commissioner or tax receiver in the event he becomes ineligible for any reason for the exemption provided in this paragraph. The General Assembly may provide by law for the proper administration of this exemption including penalties necessary therefor. The increased exemption provided for herein shall apply to all taxable years beginning after December 31, 1974. The ratification of this amendment shall in no way alter, modify, strike or repeal any other amendment to Article VII, Section I, Paragraph IV of the Constitution which may be ratified at the same time as this amendment may be ratified.

[Editorial note: The paragraph on persons 65 years of age was added in 1964 and amended in 1968, 1972, and 1974.]

The General Assembly shall have the authority to provide for the exemption from any and all taxation any facilities which shall be installed or constructed for the primary purpose of eliminating or reducing air or water pollution. The General Assembly is further authorized to provide for the manner in which such exemptions shall be granted and to prescribe the prerequisites which shall be required to be met before any such exemption shall be granted, including the designation of any appropriate state agency or organization to which the General Assembly shall be authorized to delegate any and all powers necessary and appropriate to carry out the purposes and responsibilities of this paragraph.

[Editorial note: This last paragraph, which deals with facilities to reduce air or water pollution, was added by an amendment ratified Nov. 8, 1966.]

The exemptions granted to the homestead within this Paragraph shall extend to and shall apply to those properties, the legal title to which is vested in one or more title holders, if actually occupied by one or more such owners as a residence. In such instances, such exemptions shall be granted to such properties, if claimed in the manner herein provided by one or more of the owners actually residing on such property. Such exemptions shall also extend to those homesteads, the title to which is vested in an administrator, executor or trustee, if one or more of the heirs or *cestui que uses* residing on such property shall claim the exemptions granted by this Paragraph in the manner herein provided.

[Editorial note: This paragraph was added in 1970.]

The General Assembly shall be authorized to exempt from ad valorem taxation property of nonprofit hospitals used in connection with their operation, provided that such hospitals have no stockholders and no income or profit which is distributed to or for the benefit of any private person, and are subject to the laws of Georgia regulating nonprofit or charitable corporations.

[Editorial note: This paragraph was added in 1972.]

Each disabled veteran, as hereinafter defined, who is a citizen and resident of Georgia, is hereby granted an exemption from all ad valorem taxes on the vehicle which he owns and on which he actually places the free HV vehicle license plates he receives from the State of Georgia, such exemption being from all ad valorem taxation for state, county, municipal and school purposes. The term "disabled veteran", as used herein, means any veteran who was discharged under other than dishonorable conditions, and who served on active duty of the Armed Forçes of the United States or on active duty in a reserve component of the United States including the National Guard, and who is receiving or who is entitled to receive a statutory award from the Veterans Administration for:

(1) Loss or permanent loss of use of one or both feet;

(2) Loss or permanent loss of use of one or both hands;

(3) Loss of sight in one or both eyes;

(4) Permanent impairment of vision of both eyes of the following status: Central visual acuity of 20/200 or less in the better eye, with corrective glasses, or central visual acuity of more than 20/200 if there is a field defect in which the peripheral field has contracted to such an extent that the widest diameter of visual field subtends on angular distance no greater than twenty degrees in the better eye.

[Editorial note: This paragraph was added in 1972.]

The homestead of each resident of each independent school district who is 62 years of age or over and who does not have an income from all sources, including the income from all sources of all members of the family residing within said homestead, exceeding $6,000.00 per annum, may be exempt from all ad valorem taxation for educational purposes levied for and in behalf of such school system. No such exemption shall be granted unless an affidavit of the owner of the homestead is filed with the governing authority of his city, or with a person designated by the governing authority of such city, giving his age, the amount of income which he received for the immediately preceding calendar year, the income which the members of his family residing within the homestead received for such period, and such other additional information relative to receiving the benefits of the exemption granted by this paragraph as will enable the governing authority of such city, or the person designated by the governing authority of such city, to make a determination as to whether such owner is entitled to said exemption. The governing authority of the city, or the person designated by the said governing authority, shall provide affidavit forms for this purpose. The exemption granted to the homestead within this paragraph shall extend to and shall apply to those properties, the legal title to which is vested in one or more title holders, if actually occupied by one or more such owners as a residence, and one or more such title holders possesses the qualifications provided for in this paragraph. In such instances, such exemptions shall be granted to such properties, if claimed in the manner herein provided by one or more of the owners actually residing on such property. Such exemptions shall also extend to those homesteads, the title to which is vested in an administrator, executor or trustee, if one or more of the heirs or cestui que uses residing on such property shall possess the qualifications provided for herein and shall claim the exemptions granted by this paragraph in the manner herein provided. The exemption provided for herein shall apply to all taxable years beginning after December 31, 1972.

[Editorial note: This paragraph was added in 1972.]

The homestead of each resident of each county school district who is 62 years of age or over and who does not have an income from all sources, including the income of all members of the family residing within said homestead, exceeding $6,000.00 per annum, may be exempt from all ad valorem taxation for educational purposes levied for and in behalf of such school system, including taxes to retire school bond indebtedness. No such exemption shall be granted unless an affidavit of the owner of the homestead is filed with the Tax Receiver or Tax Commissioner of his county giving his age, the amount of income which he received for the immediately preceding calendar year, the income which the members of his family residing within the homestead received for such period, and such other additional information relative to receiving the benefits of the exemption granted by this paragraph as will enable the Tax Receiver or Tax Commissioner to make a determination as to whether such owner is entitled to said exemption. The Tax Receiver or Tax Commissioner shall provide affidavit forms for this purpose. The exemption granted to the homestead within this paragraph shall extend to and shall apply to those properties, the legal title to which is vested in one or more title holders, if actually occupied by one or more such owners as a residence, and one or more such title holders possesses the qualifications provided for in this paragraph. In such instances, such exemptions shall be granted to such properties, if claimed in the manner herein provided by one or more of the owners actually residing on such property. Such exemptions shall also extend to those homesteads, the title to which is vested in an administrator, executor or trustee, if one or more of the heirs or cestui que uses residing on such property shall possess the qualifications provided for herein and shall claim the exemptions granted by this paragraph in the manner herein provided. The exemption provided for herein shall apply to all taxable years beginning after December 31, 1972.

[Editorial note: This paragraph was added in 1972.]

In order to encourage and enhance overall economic development, increase employment, promote agribusiness, and to provide incentives for the location of new and expanding manufacturing and processing facilities, harvested agricultural products which have a planting-to-harvest cycle of 12 months or less, which are customarily cured and aged for a period in excess of one year after harvesting, and before manufacturing, and which are held in this State for manufacturing or processing purposes, shall be exempt from all ad valorem taxation.

[Editorial note: This paragraph was added in 1974.]

PARAGRAPH V. *Exemptions of Certain Industries Continued.* Existing exemptions under the amendment to the Constitution providing for the exemption of certain industries from taxation appearing in Acts of the General Assembly of 1923, extra session, page 67, ratified November 4, 1924, shall continue of force until the expiration of the term for which granted.

SECTION II

Purposes and Method of Taxation

PARAGRAPH I. *Taxation, How and For What Purposes Exercised.* The powers of taxation over the whole State shall be exercised by the General Assembly for the following purposes only:

1. For the support of the State Government and the public institutions.
2. For educational purposes.
3. To pay the principal and the interest on the public debt, and to provide a sinking fund therefor.
4. To suppress insurrection, to repel invasion, and defend the State in time of war.
5. To make provision for the payment of pensions to ex-Confederate soldiers and to the widows of Confederate soldiers who are unmarried.
6. To construct and maintain State buildings and a system of State highways, airports, and docks.
7. To make provision for the payment of old-age assistance

to aged persons in need, and for the payment of assistance to the needy blind, and to dependent children and other welfare benefits; provided that no person shall be entitled to the assistance herein authorized, who does not qualify for such provisions in every respect, in accordance with enactments of the General Assembly, which may be in force and effect, prescribing the qualifications for beneficiaries hereunder: Provided no indebtedness against the State shall ever be created for the purpose herein stated, in excess of the taxes lawfully levied each fiscal year under Acts of the General Assembly authorized hereunder for such purposes.

7-A. In order to extend to the employees of the State, any department of the State, any State institution or political subdivisions of the State, and to the dependents and survivors of such employees, the basic protection accorded others by the old age and survivors insurance program embodied under the Social Security Act (Act of Congress approved August 14, 1935, 49 Stat. 620, officially cited as the "Social Security Act," as such Act has been and may from time to time be amended), and the Federal Insurance Contributions Act (as set forth in Sub-chapter A of Chapter 9 of the Federal Internal Revenue Code, as such Code has been and may from time to time be amended), the General Assembly is authorized to enact such legislation as may be necessary to insure the coverage to employees of the State, any department of the State, any State institution or political subdivisions of the State, and the dependents and survivors of such employees under said Social Security Act as the same has been or may be amended and the Federal Insurance Contributions Act as the same has been or may be amended; and any provisions of this Constitution notwithstanding the State for and on behalf of itself, its departments, institutions or political subdivisions is hereby authorized to enter into agreements with the Federal Security Administrator or other appropriate official of the United States Government under the provisions of said Social Security Act as the same has been or may hereafter be amended in the manner as provided therein and as provided by the General Assembly. The Teacher Retirement System of Georgia and the Employees Retirement System of Georgia shall have the powers and duties as provided by law existing at the time of the adoption of this provision of the State Constitution together with such further powers and duties as may be hereafter provided by law.

[Editorial note: Subparagraph 7-A, above, was added by an amendment of 1952.]

8. To advertise and promote the agricultural, industrial, historic, recreational and natural resources of the State of Georgia.

9. For public health purposes.

10. Public transportation of passengers for hire is an essential governmental function and a public purpose for which the power of taxation by the State may be exercised and its public funds expended, provided, however, that the State of Georgia shall not provide more than 10 per cent of the total cost, either directly or indirectly. The General Assembly is authorized to provide for the implementation of this provision including the granting of public funds to any public corporation or Authority established by the General Assembly for the performance of the aforesaid function and purpose, or contracting, through appropriate departments or instrumentalities of State government, with any such public corporation or Authority established by the General Assembly for performance of the aforesaid function and purpose.

[Editorial note: Subparagraph 10 was added in 1966.]

11. For school lunch purposes.

[Subpagraph 11 was added in 1968.]

12. To pay the salaries of personnel and to pay for the utilization of school facilities, including school buses, for extracurricular and interscholastic activities, including literary events, music, and athletic programs within individual schools and between schools in the same or in different school systems when such activities are sponsored by local boards of education as an integral part of the total school program.

[Editorial note: Subparagraph 12 was added in 1972.]

PARAGRAPH I-A. *Promotion of agricultural and other products; financing; disposition of funds.* Any other provision of this Constitution to the contrary notwithstanding, the General Assembly may provide for the promotion of the production, marketing, sale, use and utilization, processing and improvement of any one or all of the agricultural products including, but not limited to, registered livestock and livestock products, poultry and poultry products, timber and timber products, fish and sea food, and the products of the farms and forests of this State. The General Assembly may provide for the promotion of such products individually, collectively, or in any combination thereof. The General Assembly may provide that such a program including provisions for quality and/or product control may be instituted, continued or terminated by a specified vote of the producers of the product or products affected participating in a referendum submitting such proposal for their approval. The

General Assembly may create instrumentalities, public corporations, authorities and commissions to administer such programs and may provide a means of financing any such promotion by authorizing such bodies to impose, raise, lower or repeal assessments, fees or other charges upon the sale or processing of the affected products, and to collect the same, after approval by a specified vote of the producers of the affected product in a referendum, and may authorize the acceptance of gifts and donations, and may provide for the disposition of any funds arising under any such program without the necessity of such funds being placed in the State Treasury or being appropriated by the General Assembly. The General Assembly may provide for the supervision of any such program by the Department of Agriculture. The uniformity requirement of this Constitution shall be satisfied by the application of the program upon the affected products.

[Editorial note: Paragraph I-A was added in 1960 and amended in 1968.]

PARAGRAPH II. *Teacher Retirement System – Taxation For.* The powers of taxation may be exercised by the State through the General Assembly and by counties and municipalities, for the purpose of paying pensions and other benefits and costs under a teacher retirement system or systems; provided no indebtedness against the State shall ever be created for the purpose herein stated in excess of the taxes lawfully levied each fiscal year under Acts of the General Assembly authorized hereunder.

PARAGRAPH II-A. The General Assembly is hereby authorized to provide by law for the creation of an actuarially sound, participating retirement system for all employees of public schools who are not covered by the Teachers' Retirement System including, but not limited to, school bus drivers, school lunchroom personnel, school maintenance personnel and school custodial personnel. The General Assembly is further authorized to provide in said Act creating such retirement system, or in any amendatory Acts thereto, for the expenditure of State funds and the funds of county and independent boards of education in support of said retirement system, in such manner as the General Assembly shall determine.

[Editorial note: Paragraph II-A was added in 1968.]

PARAGRAPH III. *Revenue to Be Paid Into General Fund.* All money collected from taxes, fees and assessments for State purposes, as authorized by revenue measures enacted by the General Assembly, shall be paid into the General Fund of the State Treasury and shall be appropriated therefrom as required by this Constitution, for the purposes set out in this Section and for these purposes only.

PARAGRAPH IV. *Tax Returns of Public Utilities.* The General Assembly may provide for a different method and time of returns, assessments, payment and collection of ad valorem taxes, of public utilities, but not a greater basis of value or at a higher rate of taxation than other properties.

PARAGRAPH V. The powers of taxation may be exercised by the State through the General Assembly, and the counties and municipalities, for the purpose of paying pensions and other benefits and costs under a firemen's pension system or systems. The taxes so levied may be collected by such firemen's pension system or systems and disbursed therefrom by authority of the General Assembly for the purposes herein authorized.

[Editorial note: Paragraph V was added by an amendment ratified on November 2, 1954.]

PARAGRAPH VI. Notwithstanding any other provisions of this Constitution, the General Assembly is hereby authorized to provide by law for the granting of State funds to the municipalities of Georgia, in such manner and form and under such procedure as the General Assembly may prescribe. The General Assembly is also authorized, but not directed, to provide the purpose or purposes for which such funds may be expended by the municipalities. The General Assembly is hereby authorized to exercise the power of taxation over the entire State in order to carry out the provisions of this Paragraph.

[Editorial note: Paragraph VI was added by an amendment ratified on November 8, 1960.]

Paragraph VI [A]. The General Assembly shall have the power to create an Industrial Development Commission to make loans, to be secured by second mortgages, to such industrial development agencies as the Industrial Development Commission may select: Provided, that said agencies shall have raised sufficient capital and secured commitments for additional financing, which, in addition to the loan to be extended by said Commission, will adequately insure the completion of said project. The powers of taxation may be exercised through the General Assembly in order to implement and carry out the purposes for which said Commission is to be created.

[Editorial note: Paragraph VI[A] was added by an amendment ratified on November 8, 1960.]

Section III

State Debt

Paragraph I. *Purposes for Which Debt May Be Incurred; Limitations.* Any other provisions of this Constitution to the contrary notwithstanding, the State may incur public debt, as follows:

(a) The State may incur public debt without a limit to repel invasion, suppress insurrection and defend the State in time of War.

(b) The State may incur public debt to supply such temporary deficit as may exist in the State Treasury in any fiscal year because of necessary delay in collecting the taxes of that year but the debt so incurred shall not exceed, in the aggregate, five percent of the total revenue receipts, less refunds, of the State Treasury in the fiscal year immediately preceding the year in which such debt is incurred, and any debt so incurred shall be repaid out of the taxes levied for the fiscal year in which the loan is made. Such debt shall be payable on or before the last day of the fiscal year in which it is incurred and no such debt may be incurred in any fiscal year under the provisions of this subparagraph (b) if there is then outstanding unpaid debt from any previous fiscal year which was incurred under the provisions of this subparagraph (b).

(c) The State may incur public debt of two types for public purposes pursuant to this Paragraph: (1) general obligation debt and (2) guaranteed revenue debt. General obligation debt may be incurred by issuing obligations to acquire, construct, develop, extend, enlarge or improve land, waters, property, highways, buildings, structures, equipment or facilities of the State, its agencies, departments, institutions, and those State Authorities which were created and activated prior to the Amendment adopted November 8, 1960, to Article VII, Section VI, Paragraph I (a) of this Constitution. Guaranteed revenue debt may be incurred by guaranteeing the payment of revenue obligations issued by an instrumentality of the State if such revenue obligations are issued to finance toll bridges, toll roads, any other land public transportation facilities or systems or water or sewage treatment facilities or systems or to make or purchase, or lend or deposit against the security of, loans to citizens of the State for educational purposes. No debt may be incurred under this subparagraph (c) at any time when the highest aggregate annual debt service requirements for the then current year or any subsequent year for outstanding general obligation debt and guaranteed revenue debt, including the proposed debt, and the highest aggregate annual payments for the then current year or any subsequent fiscal year of the State under all contracts then in force to which the provisions of Article VII, Section VI, Paragraph I (a) of this Constitution are applicable, exceed fifteen percent of the total revenue receipts, less refunds, of the State Treasury in the fiscal year immediately preceding the year in which any such debt is to be incurred; provided, however, no guaranteed revenue debt may be incurred to finance water or sewage treatment facilities or systems when the highest aggregate annual debt service requirements for the then current year or any subsequent fiscal year of the State for outstanding or proposed guaranteed revenue debt for water or sewage treatment facilities or systems, exceed one percent of the total revenue receipts, less refunds, of the State Treasury in the fiscal year immediately preceding the year in which any such debt is to be incurred; and provided, further, that the aggregate amount of guaranteed revenue debt incurred to make loans to citizens of the State for educational purposes that may be outstanding at any time shall not exceed $18 million dollars, and the aggregate amount of guaranteed revenue debt incurred to purchase, or to lend or deposit against the security of, loans to citizens of the State for educational purposes that may be outstanding at any time shall not exceed $72 million dollars. For the purposes of this Paragraph, annual debt service requirements shall mean the total principal and interest coming due in any fiscal year of the State; provided, however, with regard to any issue of debt incurred wholly or in part on a term basis, annual debt service requirements shall mean an amount equal to the total principal and interest payments required to retire such issue in full divided by the number of years from its issue date to its maturity date.

General obligation debt may not be incurred until the General Assembly has enacted legislation stating the purposes, in general or specific terms, for which such issue of debt is to be incurred, specifying the maximum principal amount of such issue and appropriating an amount at least sufficient to pay the highest annual debt service requirements for such issue. All such appropriations for debt service purposes shall not lapse for any reason and shall continue in effect until the debt for which such appropriation was authorized shall have been incurred, but the General Assembly may repeal any such appropriation at any time prior to the incurring of such debt. The General Assembly shall raise by taxation each fiscal year, in addition to the sum necessary to make all payments required to be made under contracts entitled to the protection of the second paragraph of Paragraph I (a), Section VI, Article VII of the Constitution, and to pay public expenses, such amounts as are necessary to pay debt service requirements in such fiscal year on all general obligation debt incurred hereunder. The General Assembly shall appropriate to a special trust fund to be designated "State of Georgia General Obligation Debt Sinking Fund" such amounts as are necessary to pay annual debt service requirements on all general obligation debt incurred hereunder. The sinking fund shall be used solely for the retirement of general obligation debt payable therefrom. If the General Assembly shall fail to make any such appropriation or if for any reason the monies in the sinking fund are insufficient to make all payments required with respect to such general obligation debt as and when the same become due, the State Treasurer shall set apart from the first revenues thereafter received, applicable to the general fund of the State, such amounts as are necessary to cure any such deficiency and shall immediately deposit the same into the sinking fund; provided, however, the obligation to make such sinking fund deposits shall be subordinate to the obligation imposed upon the fiscal officers of the State pursuant to the provisions of the second paragraph of Paragraph I (a) of Section VI of Article VII of this Constitution. The State Treasurer may be required to set aside and apply such revenues as aforesaid at the suit of any holder of any general obligation debt incurred hereunder. The monies in the sinking fund shall be as fully invested as is practical, consistent with the requirements to make current principal and interest payments. Any such investments shall be restricted to obligations constituting direct and general obligations of the United States Government or obligations unconditionally guaranteed as to payment of principal and interest by the United States Government, maturing no longer than twelve months from date of purchase.

Guaranteed revenue debt may not be incurred until the

General Assembly has enacted legislation authorizing the guarantee of the specific issue of revenue obligations then proposed, reciting that the General Assembly has determined such obligations will be self-liquidating over the life of the issue (which determination shall be conclusive), specifying the maximum principal amount of such issue and appropriating an amount at least equal to the highest annual debt service requirements for such issue, which appropriation shall be paid upon the issuance of said obligations into a special trust fund to be designated "State of Georgia Guaranteed Revenue Debt Common Reserve Fund" to be held together with all other sums similarly appropriated as a common reserve for any payments which may be required by virtue of any guarantee entered into in connection with any issue of guaranteed revenue obligations. All such appropriations for the benefit of guaranteed revenue debt shall not lapse for any reason and shall continue in effect until the debt for which such appropriation was authorized shall have been incurred, but the General Assembly may repeal any such appropriation at any time prior to the payment of the same into said common reserve fund which shall be held and administered by the State Treasurer. If any payments are required to be made from said fund to meet debt service requirements on guaranteed revenue obligations by virtue of an insufficiency of revenues, the State Treasury shall pay from said common reserve fund the amount necessary to cure such deficiency. The State Treasurer shall then reimburse said fund from the general funds of the State within ten days following the commencement of any fiscal year of the State for any amounts so paid; provided, however, the obligation to make any such reimbursements shall be subordinate to the obligation imposed upon the fiscal officers of the State pursuant to the second paragraph of Paragraph I (a) of Section VI, Article VII of this Constitution and shall also be subordinate to the obligation hereinabove imposed upon the State Treasurer to make sinking fund deposits for the benefit of general obligation debt. The State Treasurer may be required to apply such funds as aforesaid at the suit of any holder of any such guaranteed revenue obligations. The amount to the credit of said common reserve fund shall at all times be at least equal to the aggregate highest annual debt service requirements on all outstanding guaranteed revenue obligations entitled to the benefit of said fund. If at the end of any fiscal year of the State said fund is in excess of the required amount, the State Treasurer shall transfer such excess to the general funds of the State free of said trust. The funds in the said common reserve shall be as fully invested as is practical, consistent with the requirements of guaranteeing the principal and interest payments on the revenue obligations guaranteed by the State. Any such investments shall be restricted to obligations constituting direct and general obligations of the United States Government or obligations unconditionally guaranteed as to the payment of principal and interest by the United States Government, maturing no longer than twelve months from date of purchase.

When any general obligation debt has first been incurred by the delivery of such debt to the purchasers thereof, then and from the date of such delivery, the State and all State institutions, departments and agencies of the State shall be prohibited from entering into any contract (except contracts pertaining to guaranteed revenue debt) with any public agency, public corporation, authority or simily entity if such contract is intended to constitute security for bonds or other obligations issued by any such public agency, public corporation or authority and, from and after the date of such delivery, in the event any contract between the State, or any State institution, department or agency of the State and any public agency, public corporation, authority or similar entity, or any revenues from any such contract, is pledged or assigned as security for the repayment of bonds or other obligations, then and in either such event, the appropriation or expenditure of any funds of the State for the payment of obligations under any such contract shall likewise be prohibited; provided, however, all contracts entered into prior to the date of the first delivery of such general obligation debt shall continue to have the benefit of the protection afforded by the provisions of the second paragraph of Paragraph I (a) of Section VI, Article VII of this Constitution as fully and completely as though this amendment had not been adopted and for as long as any such contract shall remain in force and effect. Furthermore, nothing in this amendment is intended directly or by implication to have any effect upon any provision of any such contract establishing lien rights, priorities regarding revenues or otherwise providing protection to the holders of obligations secured by such contracts.

(d) The State may incur general obligation debt or guaranteed revenue debt to fund or refund any such debt or to fund or refund any obligations issued upon the security of contracts to which the provisions of the second paragraph of Paragraph I (a), Section VI, Article VII of this Constitution are applicable. The issuance of any such debt for the purposes of said funding or refunding shall be subject to the fifteen percent limitation in subparagraph (c) above to the same extent as debt incurred under said subparagraph; provided, however, in making such computation the annual debt service requirements and annual contract payments remaining on the debt or obligations being funded or refunded shall not be taken into account. In the event it is determined by the Georgia State Financing and Investment Commission that it is to the best interest of the State to fund or refund any such public debt or obligation, the same may be accomplished by resolution of the Georgia State Financing and Investment Commission hereinafter created without any action on the part of the General Assembly and any appropriation made or required to be made with respect to the debt being funded or refunded shall immediately attach and inure to the benefit of the obligations to be issued in connection with such funding or refunding to the same extent and with the same effect as though the obligation to be issued had originally been authorized by action of the General Assembly as hereinabove set forth; provided, the debt incurred in connection with any such funding or refunding shall be the same as that originally authorized by the General Assembly (except that general obligation debt may be incurred to fund or refund obligations issued upon the security of contracts to which the provisions of the second paragraph of Paragraph I (a), Section VI, Article VII of this Constitution are applicable and the continuing appropriation required to be made under the said provisions of this Constitution shall immediately attach and inure to the benefit of the obligation to be issued in connection with such funding or refunding with the same force and effect as though said obligations so funded or refunded had originally been issued as a general obligation debt authorized hereunder) and provided further, the term of the funding or refunding issue shall not extend beyond the term of the original debt or obligation and the total interest on the funding or refunding issue shall not exceed the total interest to be paid on such original debt or obligation. The principal amount of any debt issued in connection with such funding or refuiding may exceed the principal amount being funded or refunded to the extent necessary to provide for the payment of any premium thereby incurred.

[Editorial note: Paragraph I was amended in 1972.]

PARAGRAPH II. *Faith and Credit of State Pledged Debt may be Validated.* The full faith, credit and taxing power of the State are hereby pledged to the payment of all public debt incurred under this Article and all such debt and the interest thereon shall be exempt from taxation. Such debt may be validated by judicial proceedings in the manner provided by the General Assembly and such validation shall be incontestable and conclusive.

[Editorial note: Paragraph II was amended in 1972.]

Paragraph III. *Georgia State Financing and Investment Commission; Duties.* There is hereby created the Georgia State Financing and Investment Commission. The Commission shall consist of the Governor, the President of the Senate, the Speaker of the House of Representatives, the State Auditor, the Attorney General, the State Treasurer and the Commissioner of Agriculture. The Commission shall be responsible for the issuance of all public debt incurred hereunder and for the proper application of the proceeds of such debt to the purposes for which it is incurred; provided, however, the proceeds from guaranteed revenue obligations shall be paid to the issuer thereof and such proceeds and the application thereof shall be the responsibility of such issuer. Debt to be incurred at the same time for more than one purpose may be combined in one issue without stating the purposes separately but the proceeds thereof must be allocated, disbursed and used solely in accordance with the original purpose and without exceeding the principal amount authorized for each purpose set forth in the authorization of the General Assembly and to the extent not so used shall be used to purchase and retire public debt. The Commission shall be responsible for the investment of all proceeds to be administered by it. The General Assembly may provide that income earned on any such investments may be used to pay operating expenses of the Commission or placed in a common debt retirement fund and used to purchase and retire any public debt, or any bonds or obligations issued by any public agency, public corporation or authority which are secured by a contract to which the provisions of the second paragraph of Paragraph I (a) of Section VI, Article VII of this Constitution are applicable. The Commission shall be responsible for its own record keeping, reporting and related administrative and clerical functions. The Commission shall have such additional responsibilities, powers and duties as shall be provided by law.

[Editorial note: Paragraph III was amended in 1972.]

Paragraph IV. *State Aid Forbidden.* Except as herein provided, the credit of the State shall not be pledged or loaned to any individual, company, corporation or association and the State shall not become a joint owner or stockholder in or with any individual company, association or corporation.

[Editorial note: Paragraph IV was amended in 1972.]

Paragraph IV-A. *Construction.* Paragraphs I, II, III and IV are adopted for the purpose of providing a new and more effective method of financing the State's needs and their provisions and any law hereafter enacted by the General Assembly in furtherance thereof shall be liberally construed to effect such purpose.

Insofar as any such provisions or any such law may be inconsistent with any other provisions of this Constitution or of any other law, the provisions of such Paragraphs and laws enacted in furtherance thereof shall be controlling; provided, however, the provisions of such Paragraphs shall not be so broadly construed as to cause the same to be unconstitutional and in connection with any such construction such Paragraphs shall be deemed to contain such implied limitations as shall be required to accomplish the foregoing.

[Editorial note: Paragraph IV-A was added in 1972.]

PARAGRAPH V. *Assumption of Debts Forbidden.* The State shall not assume the debt, nor any part thereof, of any county, municipal corporation or political subdivision of the State, unless such debt be contracted to enable the State to repel invasion, suppress insurrection or defend itself in time of war: Provided, however, that the amendment to the Constitution proposed by the General Assembly and set forth in the published Acts of the General Assembly of the year 1931 at page 97, which amendment was ratified on November 8, 1932, and which amendment provided for the assumption by the State, of indebtedness of the several counties of the State, as well as that of the Coastal Highway District, and the assessments made against the counties of said district for the construction and paving of the public roads or highways, including bridges, of the State, under certain conditions and for the issuance of certificates of indebtedness for such indebtedness so assumed, is continued of full force and effect until such indebtedness assumed by the State is paid and such certificates of indebtedness retired.

PARAGRAPH VI. *Profit on Public Money.* The receiving, directly or indirectly, by any officer of State or county, or member or officer of the General Assembly of any interest, profits or perquisites, arising from the use of or loan of public funds in his hands or moneys to be raised through his agency for State or county purposes, shall be deemed a felony, and punishable as may be prescribed by law, a part of which punishment shall be a disqualification from holding office.

PARAGRAPH VII. *Certain Bonds Not to Be Paid.* The General Assembly shall have no authority to appropriate money either directly or indirectly, to pay the whole, or any part, of the principal or interest of the bonds, or other obligations which have been pronounced illegal, null and void by the General Assembly and the Constitutional amendments ratified by a vote of the people on the first day of May, 1877; nor shall the General Assembly have authority to pay any of the obligations created by the State under laws passed during the late War Between the States, nor any of the bonds, notes or obligations made and entered into during the existence of said war, the time for the payment of which was fixed after the ratification of a treaty of peace between the United States and the Confederate States; nor shall the General Assembly pass any law, or the Governor or any other State official, enter into any contract or agreement whereby the State shall be made a party to any suit in any court of this State, or of the United States instituted to test the validity of any such bonds, or obligations.

PARAGRAPH VIII. *Sale of State's Property to Pay Bonded Debt.* The proceeds of the sale of the Western and Atlantic Railroad, and any other property owned by the State, whenever the General Assembly may authorize the sale of the whole or any part thereof, shall be applied to the payment of the bonded debt of the State, and shall not be used for any other purpose whatsoever, so long as the State has any existing bonded debt; provided that the proceeds of the sale of the Western and Atlantic Railroad shall be applied to the payment of the bonds for which said railroad has been mortgaged, in preference to all other bonds.

PARAGRAPH IX. *State Sinking Fund.* The General Assembly shall raise by taxation each year, in addition to the sum required to pay the public expenses, such amounts as are necessary to pay the interest on the public debt and the principal of the public debt maturing in such year and to provide a sinking fund to pay off and retire the bonds of the State which have not been matured. The amount of such annual levy shall be determined after consideration of the amount then held in the sinking fund. The taxes levied for such purposes and the said sinking fund, shall be applied to no other purpose whatever. The funds in the said sinking fund may be invested in the bonds of the State, and also in bonds and securities issued by the Federal Government and subsidiaries of the Federal Government, fully guaranteed by that government. If said bonds are not available for purchase, the funds in the sinking fund may be loaned, with the approval of the Governor, when amply secured by bonds of the State or Federal Government, upon such conditions as may be provided by law.

[Editorial note: Paragraph IX was amended in 1972.]

SECTION IV

PARAGRAPH I. *Power of County Government.* The General Assembly may authorize any county to exercise the power of taxation for any public purpose as authorized by general law or by this Constitution, and unless otherwise provided by this Constitution or by law, no levy need state the particular purposes for which the same was made nor shall any taxes collected be allocated for any particular purpose, unless expressly so provided by the General Assembly or this Constitution.

PARAGRAPH II. *Purposes of Taxation.* In addition to such other powers and authority as may be conferred upon any county by this Constitution or by the General Assembly, counties are hereby authorized to exercise the power of taxation for the following purposes which are hereby declared to be public purposes, and expend funds raised by the exercise of said powers for said purposes and such other public purposes as may be authorized by the General Assembly:

1. Pay the expenses of administration of the county government.

2. Acquire, construct, maintain, improve, or aid in the acquisition, construction, maintenance, or improvement of public buildings, bridges, parks, recreation areas and facilities, libraries, streets, sidewalks, roads, airports, docks, facilities for mass transit system for the transportation of passengers for hire, and other properties for public use; and to acquire any real property or any interest therein in connection with the foregoing.

3. Provide for the operation of the courts, the maintenance and support of prisoners, and the handling of litigation affecting the county.

4. Establish and conduct public health and sanitation programs and provide for the collection and preservation of records and vital statistics.

5. Establish and maintain a county police department.

6. Provide medical or other care and hospitalization for the indigent sick and to support paupers.

7. Pay county agricultural and home demonstration agents and conduct programs utilizing the services of such agents.

8. Establish and conduct programs of welfare benefits and public assistance as may be provided by law.

9. Provide fire protection for forest lands and conserve natural resources.

10. Provide insurance, retirement and pension benefits, coverage under Federal Old Age and Survivors' Insurance programs, hospitalization benefits, and workmens' compensation benefits for its officers and employees, their dependents and survivors, and for public school teachers and personnel, their dependents and survivors: Provided that all such payments for public school

teachers and personnel, their dependents and survivors, shall be paid from education funds.

11. Establish and maintain a recreation system.

12. To provide for paying the principal and interest of any debt of the county and to provide a sinking fund therefor.

13. To provide for reasonable reserves for public improvements as may be fixed by law.

14. To provide for the support and maintenance of public schools, public education, and activities necessary and incidental thereto, including school lunches, as provided in Article VII of this Constitution, upon the assessed value of all taxable property within the county, exclusive of any independent school system therein.

PARAGRAPH III. *Establishment of Taxing Districts.* Except under the authority of a general or local law, a county governing authority may not district a county to provide water, sewerage, garbage, electricity, gas, or fire protection services. Such services shall be authorized only by an act of the General Assembly establishing, or authorizing the establishment of, a special district or districts therefor, and authorizing such county to levy a tax only upon the taxable property in such districts for the purpose of constructing and maintaining facilities therefor, conditioned upon the assent of a majority of the qualified voters of any such proposed district voting in an election for that purpose held as provided by law.

PARAGRAPH IV. *Eminent Domain.* Any county is hereby authorized to exercise the power of eminent domain for any public purpose.

PARAGRAPH V. Nothing herein shall be construed to repeal or modify the provisions of Article VIII, Section XII, Paragraph I of the Constitution of Georgia of 1945, as amended.

PARAGRAPH VI. The powers and authority granted by this amendment shall be cumulative of all powers and authority heretofore granted to counties and shall not operate to repeal any existing local constitutional amendments.

[Editorial note: Section IV was altered by an amendment ratified Nov. 8, 1966.]

SECTION V

PARAGRAPH I. *Taxing Power and Contributions of Counties, Cities and Political Division Restricted.* The General Assembly shall not authorize any county, municipal corporation or political division of this State, through taxation, contribution or otherwise, to become a stockholder in any company, corporation or association, or to appropriate money for, or to loan its credit to any corporation, company, association, institution or individual except for purely charitable purposes. This restriction shall not operate to prevent the support of schools by municipal corporations within their respective limits.

SECTION VI

PARAGRAPH I. *Contracts For Use of Public Facilities.* (a) The State, state institutions, any city, town, municipality or county of this State may contract for any period not exceeding fifty years, with each other or with any public agency, public corporation or authority now or hereafter created for the use by such subdivisions or the residents thereof of any facilities or services of the State, state institutions, any city, town, municipality, county, public agency, public corporation or authority, provided such contracts shall deal with such activities and transactions as such subdivisions are by law authorized to undertake.

Notwithstanding any other provision of any other section of any other article of this Constitution, the General Assembly shall include in each General Appropriations Act in the appropriation payable to each department, agency, or institution of the State, in addition to such other items as may be included in such appropriation, and whether or not any other items are included, sums sufficient to satisfy the payments required to be made in each year under lease contracts now or hereafter entered into pursuant to this Paragraph I(a) by and between such department, agency, or institution of the state and any State authority which has been created and activated at the time of the effective date of this amendment which said lease contracts constitute security for bonds or any other obligations heretofore or hereafter issued by any such authority. In the event for any reason any such appropriation is not made, then the fiscal officers of the State are hereby authorized and directed to set up on their appropriation accounts in each fiscal year as an appropriation the respective amounts required by each such department, agency, or institution of the State to pay the obligations called for under any such lease contract. The amount of the appropriation in each fiscal year to meet such lease contract obligations as authorized hereunder shall be due and payable to each such department, agency, or institution of the State in each fiscal year to be expended for the purpose of paying the lease contract obligation required under the terms and conditions of such lease contracts and said appropriation shall have the same legal status as if the General Assembly had included the amount of the appropriation in a General Appropriations Act.

[Editorial note: The last paragraph above was added by an amendment ratified on November 8, 1960.]

(b) Any city, town, municipality or county of this State is empowered, in connection with any contracts authorized, by the preceding paragraph, to convey to any public agency, public corporation or authority now or hereafter created, existing facilities operated by such city, town, municipality or county for the benefit of residents of such subdivisions, provided the land, buildings and equipment so conveyed shall not be mortgaged or pledged to secure obligations of any such public agency, public corporation or authority and provided such facilities are to be maintained and operated by such public agency, public corporation or authority for the same purposes for which such facilities were operated by such city, town, municipality or county. Nothing in this section shall restrict the pledging of revenues of such facilities by any public agency, public corporation or authority.

(c) Any city, town, municipality or county of this State, or any combination of the same, may contract with any public agency, public corporation or authority for the care, maintenance and hospitalization of its indigent sick, and may as a part of such contract obligate itself to pay for the cost of acquisition, construction, modernization or repairs of necessary buildings and facilities by such public agency, public corporation or authority, and provide for the payment of such services and the cost to such public agency, public corporations or authority of acquisition, construction, modernization or repair of buildings and facilities from revenues realized by such city, town, municipality or county from any taxes authorized by the Constitution of this State or revenues derived from any other sources.

(d) *Special School; Creation; Taxes and Bonds.* The board of education of any county, area school district or independent school system, or any combination thereof, may establish, pursuant to local law enacted by the General Assembly, one or more area schools, including special schools such as vocational trade schools, schools for exceptional children, and schools for adult education, in one or more of such political subdivisions; provided, however, that the establishment and operation of such schools pursuant to such local law, and any subsequent amendments thereof, shall be first approved by a majority of the voters voting thereon in each of the school districts or systems affected thereby in separate referendums held in the manner provided by law. The government, powers and duties of boards of education participating in the establishment or operation of such schools and respecting such schools shall be defined in the local law authorizing the same, and such participating political subdivision shall be authorized to incur bonded indebtedness to require the levy of school tax funds required for the establishment and operation of such schools in such amount and manner as shall be provided in such local law. Schools established pursuant to provisions of this Section shall be operated in conformance with regulations promulgated by the State Board of Education pursuant to provisions of law. The State is hereby authorized to expend funds for the support and maintenance of such schools in such amount and manner as may be provided by law. Special schools, including vocational trade schools, established prior to the adoption of this amendment under former Subparagraph (d) of Article VII, Section VI, Paragraph I of the Constitution shall not be affected by this amendment; any political subdivision which established such a school is hereby authorized to levy taxes for the support of such school regardless of whether it is located within the territorial limits of such subdivision and any such political subdivision is hereby authorized to incur bonded indebtedness for the support of, or acquisition and construction of facilities for such school. Any such bonded indebtedness shall be incurred pursuant to provisions of Article VII, Section VII of this Constitution and the laws of this State relative to incurring other bonded indebtedness. The State is hereby authorized to expend funds for the support of such established schools in such amount and manner as may be provided by law.

[Editorial note: Subparagraph (d) was added by an amendment ratified on November 8, 1960. It was changed by an amendment ratified on Nov. 8, 1966.]

Paragraph III. The governing authority of each county is hereby authorized in its discretion to purchase liability insurance to cover damages on account of bodily injury or death to any person or damage to property of any person arising by reason of ownership, maintenance, operation or use of any motor vehicle by such county, whether as a result of a governmental undertaking or not, and to pay premiums therefor. The governing authority is hereby authorized to levy a tax for such purpose. In the event of purchasing such insurance, the governmental immunity of the county shall be waived to the extent of the amount of insurance so purchased. Neither the county nor the insurer shall be entitled to plead governmental immunity as a defense and may make only such defense as could be made if the insured were a private person. The county shall be liable only for damages suffered while said insurance is in force. No attempt shall be made in the trial of any action brought against the county to suggest the existence of any insurance which covers in whole or in part, any judgment or award which may be rendered in favor of the plaintiff. If the verdict rendered by the jury exceeds the limitation of the insurance, the court shall reduce the amount to a sum equal to the applicable limitations stated in the policy.

[Editorial note: Paragraph III was added by an amendment ratified on November 8, 1960.]

Section VII

Limitation on County and Municipal Debts

Paragraph I. *Debts of Counties and Cities.* The debt hereafter incurred by any county, municipal corporation or political subdivision of this State except as in this Constitution provided for, shall never exceed ten per centum of the assessed value of all the taxable property therein, and no such county, municipality or division shall incur any new debt except for a temporary loan or loans, to supply casual deficiencies of revenue, not to exceed one-fifth of one per centum of the assessed value of the taxable property therein, without the assent of a majority of the qualified voters of the county, municipality or other political subdivision voting in an election for that purpose to be held as prescribed by law; and provided further that all laws, charter provisions and ordinances heretofore passed or enacted providing special registration of the voters of counties, municipal corporations and other political subdivisions of this State to pass upon the issuance, of bonds by such counties, municipal corporations and other political subdivisions of this State are hereby declared to be null and void; and the General Assembly shall hereafter have no power to pass or enact any law providing for such special registration, but the validity of any and all bond issues by such counties, municipal corporations or other political subdivisions made prior to January 1, 1945, shall not be affected hereby; provided, that any county or municipality of this State may accept and use funds granted by the Federal Government, or any agency thereof, to aid in financing the cost of architectural, engineering, economic investigations, studies, surveys, designs, plans, working drawings, specifications, procedures, and other action preliminary to the construction of public works, and where the funds so used for the purposes specified are to be repaid within a period of ten years.

Every county is hereby empowered to create debt, by way of borrowing from private individuals, firms, corporations, or partnerships, as well as from the State, for the purpose of paying the whole or part of the cost of property valuation and equalization programs for ad valorem tax purposes; to contract for the repayment thereof and to issue notes or other like instruments as evidence of the obligation to repay the debt so contracted without being subject to any limit as to amount of such debt so created and without the necessity of approval thereof by the qualified voters of that county; provided nevertheless that the debt shall be payable in one or more equal installments, one of which shall fall due at least each year, but which may fall due each month, the last of which shall mature not more than seven years from the date of creation and shall not bear interest in excess of five (5%) per cent per annum on unpaid principal; and a tax shall be levied on the taxable property of the county as may be needed to repay such debt so created; provided, however, that no county shall be empowered to create debt under the provisions of this paragraph for the purposes of a property valuation and equalization program until such program and all contracts to be entered into pursuant thereto shall have been approved by the State Revenue Commissioner, and until such county shall have entered into an agreement with the State Revenue Commissioner that such program shall be carried out in accordance with such Rules and Regulations pertaining to such programs as may be promulgated by the Commissioner.

All existing local constitutional amendments adopted prior to the ratification of this amendment relating to maximum bond debt limitation shall continue to be of full force and effect and shall not be affected by the ratification of this amendment.

[Editorial note: Paragraph I was amended in 1962 and 1974.]

PARAGRAPH II. *Levy of Taxes to Pay Bonds.* Any county, municipal corporation or political division of this State which shall incur any bonded indebtedness under the provisions of this Constitution, shall at or before the time of so doing, provide for the assessment and collection of an annual tax sufficient in amount to pay the principal and interest of said debt, within thirty years from the date of the incurring of said indebtedness.

PARAGRAPH III. *Additional Debt Authorized When.* In addition to the debt authorized in Paragraph I of this section, to be created by any county, municipal corporation or political subdivision of this State, a debt may be incurred by any county, municipal corporation or political subdivision of this State, in excess of seven per centum of the assessed value of all the taxable property therein, upon the following conditions: Such additional debt, whether incurred at one or more times, shall not exceed in the aggregate, three per centum of the assessed value of all the taxable property in such county, municipality, or political subdivision; such additional debt shall be payable in equal installments within the five years next succeeding the issuance of the evidences of such debt; there shall be levied by the governing authorities of such county, municipality or political subdivision prior to the issuance of such additional debt, a tax upon all of the taxable property within such county, municipality or political subdivision collectable annually, sufficient to pay in full the principal and interest of such additional debt when as due; such tax shall be in addition to and separate from all other taxes levied by such taxing authorities, and the collections from such tax shall be kept separate and shall be held, used and applied solely for the payment of the principal and interest of such additional indebtedness; authority to create such additional indebtedness shall first have been authorized by the General Assembly; the creation of such additional indebtedness shall have been first authorized by a vote of the registered voters of such county, municipality or political subdivision at an election held for such purpose, pursuant to and in accordance with the provisions of this Constitution and of the then existing laws or the creation of a debt by counties, municipal corporations, and political subdivisions of this State, all of which provisions, including those for calling, advertising, holding and determining the result of, such election and the votes necessary to authorize the creation of an indebtedness, are hereby made applicable to an election held for the purpose of authorizing such additional indebtedness.

PARAGRAPH IV. *Temporary Loans Authorized; Conditions.* In addition to the obligations hereinbefore allowed, each county, municipality, political subdivision of the State authorized to levy taxes, and county board of education, is given the authority to make temporary loans between January 1st and December 31st in each year to pay expenses for such year, upon the following conditions: The aggregate amount of all such loans of such county, municipality, political subdivision or county Board of Education outstanding at any one time shall not exceed 75% of the total gross income of such county, municipality, political subdivision or county Board of Education, from taxes collected by such county, municipality, political subdivision or county Board of Education in the last preceding year. Such loans shall be payable on or before December 31st of the calendar year in which such loan is made. No loan may be made in any year under the provisions of this paragraph when there is a loan then unpaid which was made in a prior year under the provisions of this paragraph. Each such loan shall be first authorized by resolution fixing the terms of such loan adopted by a majority vote of the governing body of such county, city, political subdivision or county Board of Education, at a meeting legally held, and such resolution shall appear upon the minutes of such meeting. No such county, municipality, subdivision or county Board of Education shall incur in any one calendar year, an aggregate of such temporary loans and other contracts or obligations for current expenses in excess of the total anticipated revenue of such county, municipality, subdivision, or county Board of Education for such calendar year, or issue in one calendar year notes, warrants or other evidences of such indebtedness in a total amount in excess of such anticipated revenue for such year.

[Editorial note: This subparagraph was changed by an amendment of 1950. It originally read as follows: "In addition to the obligations hereinbefore allowed, each county, municipality and political subdivision of the State authorized to levy taxes, is given the authority to make temporary loans between January 1st and December 31st in each year to pay expenses for such year, upon the following conditions: The aggregate amount of all such loans of such county, municipality or political subdivision outstanding at any one time, shall not exceed seventy-five per centum of the total gross income of such county, municipality or political subdivision, from taxes collected by such county, municipality or political subdivision in the last preceding year. Each such loan shall be payable on or before December 31st of the calendar year in which such loan is made. No loan may be made in any year under the provisions of this paragraph when there is a loan then unpaid which was made in a prior year under the provisions of this paragraph. Each such loan shall be first authorized by resolution fixing the terms of such loan, adopted by a majority vote of the governing body of such county, city or political subdivision, at a meeting legally held, and such resolution shall appear upon the minutes of such meeting. No such county, municipality or subdivision shall incur in any one calendar year, an aggregate of such temporary loans and other contracts or obligations for current expenses in excess of the total anticipated revenue of such county, municipality or subdivision for such calendar year, or issue in one calendar year notes, warrants or other evidences of such indebtedness in a total amount in excess of such anticipated revenue for such year."]

PARAGRAPH V. *Revenue Anticipation Obligations.* Revenue anticipation obligations may be issued by any county, municipal corporation or political subdivision of this State, to provide funds for the purchase or construction, in whole or in part, of any revenue-producing facility which such county, municipal corporation or political subdivision is authorized by the Act of the General Assembly approved March 31, 1937, known as "The Revenue Certificate Laws of 1937," as amended by the Act approved March 14, 1939, to construct and operate, or to provide funds to extend, repair or improve any such existing facility, and to buy, construct, extend, operate and maintain gas or electric generating and distribution systems, together with all necessary appurtenances thereof. Such revenue anticipation obligations shall be payable, as to principal and interest, only from revenue produced by revenue-producing facilities of the issuing political subdivisions, and shall not be deemed debts of, or to create debts against, the issuing political subdivisions within the meaning of this paragraph or any other of this Constitution. This authority shall apply only to revenue anticipation obligations issued to provide funds for the purchase, construction, extension, repair or improvement of such facilities and undertakings as are specifically authorized and enumerated by said Act of 1937, as amended by said Act of 1939; and to buy, construct, extend, operate and maintain gas or electric generating and distribution systems, together with all necessary appurtenances thereof; provided further any revenue certificates issued to buy, construct, extend, operate and maintain gas or electric generating and distribution systems shall, before being undertaken, be authorized by a majority of those voting at an election held for the purpose in the county, municipal corporation or political subdivision affected, and provided further that a majority of the registered voters of such county, municipal corporation or political subdivision affected shall vote in said election, the election for such to be held in the same manner as is used in issuing bonds of such county, municipal corporation or political subdivision and the said elections shall be called and provided for by officers in charge of the fiscal affairs of said county, municipal corporation or political subdivision affected; and no such issuing political subdivision of the State shall exercise the power of taxation for the purpose of paying the principal or interest of any such revenue anticipation obligations or any part thereof.

Provided that after a favorable election has been held as set forth above, if municipalities, counties or other political subdivisions shall purchase, construct, or operate such electric or gas utility plants from the proceeds of said revenue certificates, and extend their services beyond the limits of the county in which the municipality or political subdivision is located, then its services rendered and property located outside said county shall be subject to taxation and regulation as are privately owned and operated utilities.

The General Assembly is authorized to create an instrumentality and department of the State of Georgia to be known as the Brunswick Ports Authority, and to provide for its powers and functions. Act number 314 of the Acts of the General Assembly of 1945 (Ga. L. 1945, p. 1023) as amended by House Bill number 1053 of the General Assembly of 1958 (Ga. L. 1958, p. 82) is hereby ratified and confirmed, so that the said Acts shall have the same force and effect as if they had been enacted subsequent to the ratification of this amendment to the Constitution; provided, however, that nothing herein shall prevent the General Assembly from amending said Acts, so as to add and enlarge powers of the Authority.

[Editorial note: The sentence dealing with the Brunswick Ports Authority was added by an amendment of 1960. Amendments numbered 14 and 15 of 1974, voted on State-wide as "general amendments," created the Covington Parking Authority and the Downtown Savannah Authority. For details, see Georgia Laws 1973, pp. 1506-1522, and Georgia Laws 1974, pp. 1738-1754.]

PARAGRAPH V-A. *Revenue Obligations Authorized.* The development of trade, commerce, industry and employment opportunities is hereby declared to be a public purpose vital to the welfare of the people of this State. The General Assembly may create Development Authorities to promote and further such purposes or may authorize the creation of such Authority by any county or municipal corporation or combinations thereof under such uniform terms and conditions as it may deem necessary. The General Assembly may exempt from taxation Development Authority obligations, properties, activities or income and may authorize the issuance of Revenue Obligations by such Authorities which shall not constitute an indebtedness of the State within the meaning of Section VII of this Article.

The General Assembly may provide for the validation of any Revenue Obligations authorized, and that such validation shall thereafter be incontestable and conclusive.

[Editorial note: Paragraph V-A was added in 1968.]

Paragraph VI. *Refunding Bonds.* The General Assembly is hereby authorized to create a commission and to vest such commission with the power to secure all necessary information and to approve or disapprove the issuance of bonds for the purpose of refunding any bonded indebtedness of any county, municipality or political subdivision of this State issued prior to the adoption of this Constitution, including the authority to approve or disapprove the amount and terms of such refunding bonds, together with such other powers as to the General Assembly may seem proper, but not in conflict with the provisions of the Constitution. Such refunding bonds shall be authorized only where such county, municipality or political subdivision has not the funds available to meet the payment of outstanding bonded indebtedness through failure to levy and collect the required taxes, or through failure to maintain the required sinking fund for such bonds. The General Assembly may approve the issuance of the said refunding bonds under the conditions stated. Such refunding bonds shall not, together with all other oustanding bonded indebtedness, exceed the limits fixed by this Constitution for the maximum amount of bonded indebtedness which may be issued by such county, municipality or political subdivision and shall be otherwise governed by all of the terms and provisions of this Constitution. No bonds shall be issued under this paragraph to refund any bonds issued after the adoption of this Constitution.

Paragraph VII. *Refunding Bonds to Reduce Bonded Indebtedness.* The General Assembly is further authorized to give to the said Commission the power and authority to approve or disapprove the issuance of bonds to refund any outstanding bonded indebtedness of any county, municipality or political subdivision now or hereafter issued, for the purpose of reducing the amount payable, principal or interest, on such bonded indebtedness, and upon the condition that, the issuance of such refunding bonds will reduce the amounts payable upon such outstanding bonds, principal or interest. Such refunding bonds shall replace such outstanding bonded indebtedness. The said Commission shall have the authority to approve or disapprove the terms of any such proposed refunding bonds. The General Assembly may authorize the issuance of such refunding bonds issued for the said purpose, when approved by the said Commission and authorized by the governing authority of such county, municipality or subdivision, without an election by the qualified voters as otherwise required, but in all other respects such refunding bonds shall comply with the provisions of this Constitution.

Section VIII

Paragraph I. *Sinking Funds For Bonds.* All amounts collected from any source for the purpose of paying the principal and interest of any bonded indebtedness of any county, municipality or subdivision and to provide for the retirement of such bonded indebtedness, above the amount needed to pay the prinicpal and interest on such bonded indebtedness due in the year of such collection, shall be placed in a sinking fund to be held and used to pay off the principal and interest of such bonded indebtedness thereafter maturing.

The funds in such sinking fund shall be kept separate and apart from all other moneys of such county, municipality or subdivision, and shall be used for no purpose other than that above stated. The moneys in such sinking fund may be invested and reinvested by the governing authorities of such county, municipality or subdivision or by such other authority as has been created to hold and manage such sinking fund, in the bonds of such county, municipality or subdivision, and in bonds or obligations of the State of Georgia, of the counties and cities thereof and of the government of the United States, of subsidiary corporations of the Federal Government fully guaranteed by such government, and no other. Any person or persons violating the above provisions shall be guilty of malpractice in office and shall also be guilty of misdemeanor, and shall be punished, when convicted, as prescribed by law for the punishment of misdemeanors, until the General Assembly shall make other provisions for the violation of the terms of this paragraph.

Section IX

Appropriation Control

Paragraph I. *Preparation, submission and enactment of General Appropriations Bill.* (a) The Governor shall submit to the General Assembly within five days after its convening in regular session in 1973 and each year thereafter, a budget message and a budget report, accompanied by a draft of a General Appropriations Bill, in such form and manner as may be prescribed by statute, which shall provide for the appropriation of the funds necessary to operate all the various departments and agencies, and to meet the current expenses of the State for the next fiscal year.

(b) The General Assembly shall annually appropriate the funds necessary to operate all the various departments and agencies, and meet the current expenses of the State for the next fiscal year. The fiscal year of the State shall commence on the first day of July of each year and terminate on the thirtieth of June following.

(c) The General Assembly shall by general law provide for the regulation and management of the finance and fiscal administration of the State.

Paragraph II. (a) Each General Appropriation Act, now of force or hereafter adopted with such amendments as are adopted from time to time, shall continue in force and effect for the next fiscal year after adoption and it shall then expire except for the mandatory appropriations required by this Constitution and those required to meet contractual obligations authorized by this Constitution and the continued appropriation of Federal grants.

(b) The General Assembly shall not appropriate funds for any given fiscal year which, in aggregate, exceed a sum equal to the amount of unappropriated surplus expected to have accrued in the State Treasury at the beginning of the fiscal year, together with an amount not greater than the total Treasury receips from existing revenue sources anticipated to be collected in the fiscal year, less refunds, as estimated in the Budget Report and amendments thereto. Supplementary appropriations, if any, shall be made in the manner provided in Article VII, Section IX, Paragraph III of this Constitution, but in no event shall a supplementary appropriations Act continue in force and effect beyond the expiration of the General Appropriations Act in effect when such supplementary appropriations Act was adopted and approved.

(c) All appropriated funds, except for the mandatory appropriations required by this Constitution, remaining unexpended and not contractually obligated at the expiration of such General Appropriations Act, shall lapse.

(d) All federal funds received by the State of Georgia are hereby continually appropriated in the exact amounts and for the purposes authorized and directed by the Federal Government in making the grant.

(e) The State, State institutions, departments and agencies of the State are hereby prohibited from entering into any contract with any public agency, public corporation or authority pursuant to the provisions of Article VII, Section VI, Paragraph I (a), which such contract constitutes security for bonds or other obligations issued by any such public agency, public corporation or authority and the appropriation or expenditure of any funds for the payment of obligations under any such contract, is likewise prohibited at any time when the aggregate annual payments under all such contracts, including the contract or contracts proposed to be entered into, exceed 15% of the total revenue receipts, less refunds, of the State Treasury in the fiscal year immediately preceding the making and entering into of any such contract; provided, however, this provision shall not affect contracts validly entered into prior to its adoption or which conform to this provision at the time the same are hereafter executed. The execution of any such contract is further prohibited until the General Assembly has specifically provided funds in an Appropriations Act for the payment of at least one year's rental under such contract.

[Editorial note: Paragraphs I and II were reworded by amendments of 1962 and 1972.]

PARAGRAPH III. *Other or Supplementary Appropriations.* In addition to the appropriations made by the General Appropriation Act and amendments thereto, the General Assembly may make additional appropriations by Acts, which shall be known as supplementary appropriation Acts, provided no such supplementary appropriation shall be available unless there is an unappropriated surplus in the State Treasury or the revenue necessary to pay such appropriation shall have been provided by a tax laid for such purpose and collected into the General Fund of the State Treasury. Neither House shall pass a Supplementary Appropriation Bill until the General Appropriation Act shall have been finally adopted by both Houses and approved by the Governor.

PARAGRAPH IV. *Appropriations to be for Specific Sums.* (a) Except as hereinafter provided, the appropriation for each department, officer, bureau, board, commission, agency or institution for which appropriation is made shall be for a specific sum of money, and no appropriation shall allocate to any object, the proceeds of any particular tax or fund or a part of percentage thereof.

(b) An amount equal to all money derived from motor fuel taxes received by the State in each of the immediately preceding fiscal years, less the amount of refunds, rebates and collection costs authorized by law, is hereby appropriated for the fiscal year beginning July 1, of each year following, for all activities incident to providing and maintaining an adequate system of public roads and bridges in this State, as authorized by laws enacted by the General Assembly of Georgia; and for grants to counties by law authorizing road construction and maintenance, as provided by law authorizing such grants. Said sum is hereby appropriated for, and shall be available for, the aforesaid purposes regardless of whether the General Assembly enacts a General Appropriations Act and said sum need not be specifically stated in any General Appropriations Act passed by the General Assembly in order to be available for such purposes. However, this shall not preclude the General Assembly from appropriating for such purposes an amount greater than the sum specified above for such purposes. The expenditure of such funds shall be subject to all the rules, regulations and restrictions imposed on the expenditure of appropriations by provisions of the Constitution and laws of this State, unless such provisions are in conflict with the provisions of this paragraph. And provided, however, that the proceeds of the tax hereby appropriated shall not be subject to budgetary reduction. In the event of invasion of this State by land, sea or air, or in case of a major catastrophe so proclaimed by the Governor, said funds may be utilized for defense or relief purposes on the Executive Order of the Governor.

[Editorial note: Subjaragraph (b) was amended in 1960 and in 1972.]

PARAGRAPH V. *Appropriations Void, When.* Any appropriation made in conflict with either of the foregoing provisions shall be void.

SECTION X

PARAGRAPH I. *Existing Amendments Continued of Force.* Amendments to the Constitution of the State of Georgia of 1877 in effect at the date of the ratification by the voters of the State, of this Constitution, shall continue of full force and effect after the ratification of this Constitution, where such amendments are of merely local, and not, general application, including the amendments pertaining to the Coastal Highway District of this State. There is also continued under this provision in force and effect, amendments to the Constitution of 1877 applicable to counties and cities having a population in excess of a number stated in such amendments, amendments applicable to counties having a city wholly or partly therein with a population in excess of, or not less than a number stated in such amendment, and amendments applicable to cities lying in two counties, where such amendments are in force and effect at the time of the ratification of this Constitution. Provided the amendment of Paragraph I of Section II of Article XI of the Constitution of 1877 proposed by Georgia Laws, 1943, page 53, and ratified August 3, 1943, authorizing election by the people of the County Board of Education of Spalding County; prescribing rules of eligibility of members of the Board; providing for election by the Board of the County Superintendent of Schools shall not be continued of force.

ARTICLE VIII

EDUCATION

Section I

Paragraph I. *System of Common Schools; Free Tuition, Separation of Races.* The provision of an adequate education for the citizens shall be a primary obligation of the State of Georgia, the expense of which shall be provided for by taxation. Separate schools shall be provided for the white and colored races.

Section II

Paragraph I. *State Board of Education; Method of Appointment.* There shall be a State Board of Education, composed of one member from each Congressional District in the State, who shall be appointed by the Governor, by and with the advice and consent of the Senate. The Governor shall not be a member of the State Board of Education. The first State Board of Education under this Constitution shall consist of those in office at the time this Constitution is adopted, with the terms provided by law. Thereafter, all succeeding appointments shall be for seven year terms from the expiration of the previous term. Vacancies upon said Board caused by expiration of term of office shall be similarly filled by appointment and confirmation. In case of a vacancy on said Board by death, resignation, or from any other cause other than the expiration of such members' term of office, the Board shall by secret ballot elect his successor, who shall hold office until the end of the next session of the General Assembly, or if the General Assembly be then in session to the end of that session. During such session of the General Assembly the Governor shall appoint the successor member of the Board for the unexpired term and shall submit his name to the Senate for confirmation. All members of the Board shall hold office until their successors are appointed and qualified. The members of the State Board of Education shall be citizens of this State who shall have resided in Georgia continuously for at least five years preceding their appointment. No person employed in a professional capacity by a private or public education institution, or by the State Department of Education, shall be eligible for appointment or to serve on said Board. No person who is or has been connected with or employed by a school book publishing concern shall be eligible to membership on the Board, and if any person shall be so connected or employed after becoming a member of the Board, his place shall immediately become vacant. The said State Board of Education shall have such powers and duties as provided by law and existing at the time of the adoption of this Constitution, together with such further powers and duties as may be hereafter provided by law.

SECTION III

PARAGRAPH I. *State School Superintendent; Election, Term, Etc.* There shall be a State School Superintendent, who shall be the executive officer of the State Board of Education, elected at the same time and in the same manner and for the same term as that of the Governor. The State School Superintendent shall have such qualifications and shall be paid such compensation as may be fixed by law. No member of said Board shall be eligible for election as State School Superintendent during the time for which he shall have been appointed.

SECTION IV

PARAGRAPH I. *University System of Georgia; Board of Regents.* There shall be a Board of Regents of the University System of Georgia, and the government, control, and management of the University System of Georgia and all of its institutions in said system shall be vested in said Board of Regents of the University System of Georgia. Said Board of Regents of the University System of Georgia shall consist of one member from each Congressional District in the State, and five additional members from the State-at-large, appointed by the Governor and confirmed by the Senate. The Governor shall not be a member of the said Board. The first Board of Regents under this Constitution shall consist of those in office at the time this Constitution is adopted, with the terms provided by law. Thereafter all succeeding appointments shall be for seven year terms from the expiration of the previous term. Vacancies upon said Board caused by expiration of term of office shall be similarly filled by appointment and confirmation. In case of a vacancy on said

Board by death, resignation of a member, or from any other cause other than the expiration of such member's term of office, the Board shall by secret ballot elect his successor, who shall hold office until the end of the next session of the General Assembly, or if the General Assembly be then in session to the end of that session. During such session of the General Assembly the Governor shall appoint the successor member of the Board for the unexpired term and shall submit his name to the Senate for confirmation. All members of the Board of Regents shall hold office until their successors are appointed. The said Board of Regents of the University System of Georgia shall have the powers and duties as provided by law existing at the time of the adoption of this Constitution, together with such further powers and duties as may be hereafter provided by law.

SECTION V

PARAGRAPH I. *County System; Board of Education; Election, Term, Etc.* Authority is granted to counties to establish and maintain public schools within their limits. Each county, exclusive of any independent school system now in existence in a county, shall compose one school district and shall be confined to the control and management of a County Board of Education. The Grand Jury of each county shall select from the citizens of their respective counties five freeholders, who shall constitute the County Board of Education. Said members shall be elected for the term of five years except that the first election of Board members under this Constitution shall be for such terms that will provide for the expiration of the term of one member of the County Board of Education each year. In case of a vacancy on said Board by death, resignation of a member, or from any other cause other than the expiration of such member's term of office, the Board shall by secret ballot elect his successor, who shall hold office until the next Grand Jury convenes at which time said Grand Jury shall appoint the successor member of the Board for the unexpired term. The members of the County Board of Education of such county shall be selected from that portion of the county not embraced within the territory of an independent school district.

The General Assembly shall have authority to make provision for local trustees of each school in a county system and confer authority upon them to make recommendations as to budgets and employment of teachers and other authorized employees.

PARAGRAPH II. *Boards of Education; change by referendum* — Notwithstanding provisions contained in Article VIII, Section V,

Paragraph I of this Constitution, or in any local constitutional amendment applicable to any county school district, the number of members of a county board of education, their term of office, residence requirements, compensation, manner of election or appointment, and the method for filling vacancies occurring on said boards, may hereafter be changed by local or special law conditioned upon approval by a majority of the qualified voters of the county school district voting in a referendum thereon. Members of county boards of education shall have such powers and duties and such further qualifications as may be provided by law.

[Editorial note: Paragraph II was added by an amendment ratified Nov. 8, 1966.]

SECTION VI

PARAGRAPH I. *County School Superintendent; Election, Term, Etc.* There shall be a County School Superintendent, who shall be the executive officer of the County Board of Education. He shall be elected by the people and his term of office shall be for four years and run concurrently with other county officers. The qualifications and the salary of the County School Superintendent shall be fixed by law.

PARAGRAPH II. *County school superintendents; change by referendum.* – Notwithstanding provisions contained in Article VIII, Section VI, Paragraph I of this Constitution, or in any local constitutional amendment applicable to any county school superintendent, the term of office of county school superintendents, their residence requirements and the method of their election or appointment may hereafter be changed by local or special laws conditioned upon approval by a majority of the qualified voters of the county school district voting in a referendum thereon. County school superintendents shall have such qualifications, powers, duties and compensation as may be provided by law.

[Editorial note: Paragraph II was added by an amendment ratified Nov. 8, 1966.]

SECTION VII

PARAGRAPH I. *Independent Systems Continued; New Systems Prohibited.* Authority is hereby granted to municipal corporations to maintain existing independent school systems, and support the same as authorized by special or general law, and such existing systems may add thereto colleges. No independent school system shall hereafter be established.

Section VIII

Paragraph I. *Meetings of Boards of Education.* All official meetings of County Boards of Education shall be open to the public.

Section IX

Paragraph I. *Area School Districts; Area Boards of Education; Area School Superintendents.* — The boards of education of any two or more counties, or independent school systems, or any combination thereof, may, by special or local law, provide for consolidation and merger of any two or more county school districts, independent school systems, or any portion or combination thereof, into a single area school district under the control and management of an area board of education. No such consolidation or merger shall become effective until approved by a majority of the voters voting in each of the school districts or school systems affected in a referendum held thereon in each school district or school system being consolidated or merged, provided 51% of the registered voters in each district or system concerned shall vote in such election and provided a majority of said voters voting shall vote in the affirmative. Any area school district so established shall constitute a separate political subdivision of this State, and the school districts or school systems or portions thereof incorporated therein shall stand abolished, and title to all school properties and assets therein shall vest in the area board of education. The number of members of an area board of education, their manner of election or appointment, their terms, residence requirements, qualifications, powers, duties and the method for filling vacancies on said boards shall be as provided by law. There shall be an area school superintendent in each area school district, who shall be the executive officer of the area board of education. The manner of his election or appointment, and his qualifications, term of office, residence requirements, powers, duties and compensation shall be as provided by law. Subsequent to the creation of an area school district, the number and manner of election or appointment of members of the area board of education and method for filling vacancies occurring on said boards, and their terms of office and residence requirements, and the manner of election or appointment of the area school superintendent, and his tenure, and residence requirements, may be changed by local or special law, conditioned upon approval by a majority of the qualified voters in each of the original political subdivisions of the area school district voting in a referendum thereon. Members of area boards of education and area school superintendents shall have such powers, duties, and further qualifications as provide by law.

PARAGRAPH II. *Power of Boards to Contract With Each Other.* Any two or more county boards of education, independent school systems, or area boards of education, or any combination thereof, may contract with each other for the care, education, and transportation of pupils and for such other activities as they may be authorized by law to perform.

[Editorial note: Section IX was altered by an amendment ratified Nov. 8, 1966.]

SECTION X

PARAGRAPH I. *Certain Systems Protected.* Public school systems established prior to the adoption of the Constitution of 1877 shall not be affected by this Constitution.

SECTION XI

PARAGRAPH I. *Grants, Bequests and Donations Permitted.* The State Board of Education and the Regents of the University System of Georgia may accept bequests, donations and grants of land, or other property, for the use of their respective systems of education.

PARAGRAPH II. *Grants, Bequests and Donations to County Boards of Education and Independent School Systems.* County Boards of Education and independent school systems may accept bequests, donations and grants of land, or other property, for the use of their respective systems of education.

SECTION XII

PARAGRAPH I. *Local Taxation for Education.* The fiscal authority of each county shall annually levy a school tax for the support and maintenance of education, not greater than twenty mills per dollar as certified to it by the county board of education, upon the assessed value of all taxable property within the county located outside any independent school system or area school district therein. The independent school system of Chatham County and the City of Savannah being co-extensive with said county, the levy of said tax shall be on all property in said county as recommended by the governing body of said system. The certification to be made by an Area Board of Education to the fiscal authorities of the territories comprising an area school district shall be in such amount and within such limits as may be prescribed by local law applicable thereto, and upon such certification being made it shall be the duty of such fiscal authorities to levy such tax in accordance with such certification, but such levy shall not be greater than twenty mills per dollar upon the assessed value of the taxable property therein. School tax funds shall be expended only for the support and maintenance of public schools, public education, and activities necessary or incidental thereto, including school lunch purposes.

PARAGRAPH II. *Increasing or Removing Tax Rate.* – The twenty mill limitation provided in Paragraph I above may be removed or increased in a county and in territories comprising an area school district under the procedure set out hereinafter. The county or area board of education, in order to instigate the procedure, must pass a resolution recommending that the limitation be removed and upon presentation of such resolution to the ordinary or to the proper authorities of territories comprising an area school district, as the case may be, it shall be their duty, within ten days of receipt of the resolution, to issue the call of an election to determine whether such limitation shall be removed. The election shall be set to be held on a date not less than twenty nor more than thirty days from the date of the issuance of the call and shall have the date and purpose of the election published in the official organ of the county once a week for two weeks preceding the date of the election. If a majority of the electors qualified to vote for members of the General Assembly voting in such election vote in favor of such proposal, there shall be no limitation in such county or in such territories comprising the area school district and the county or area board of education may recommend any number of mills for the purposes set out in Paragraph I above. In lieu of recommending that the limitation be removed entirely, the county or area board of education may recommend that it be increased and shall specify the amount in the resolution. The election provisions for increase shall be the same as for removal and if the proposal is favorably voted upon the county or area board may recommend up to the specified amount. It shall be the duty of the Judge of the Probate Court or the proper authorities, as the case may be, to hold the election, to canvass the returns and declare the results. It shall also be their duty to certify the results to the Secretary of State. The expense of the election shall be borne by the county or by the territories comprising an area school district, as the case may be.

[Editorial note: Section XII was altered by an amendment ratified Nov. 8, 1966.]

SECTION XIII

PARAGRAPH I. *Grants for Education.* Notwithstanding any other provision of this Constitution, the General Assembly may by law provide for grants of State, county or municipal funds to citizens of the State for educational puproses, in discharge of all obligation of the State to provide adequate education for its citizens.

PARAGRAPH II. *Freedom of Association.* Freedom from compulsory association at all levels of public education shall be preserved inviolate. The General Assembly shall by taxation provide funds for an adequate education for the citizens of Georgia.

[Editorial note: Section XIII was added by amendments ratified on Nov. 2, 1954 and Nov. 6, 1962.]

ARTICLE IX

HOMESTEADS AND EXEMPTIONS

SECTION I

PARAGRAPH I. *Amount of Homestead and Exemption.* There is hereby exempt from levy and sale, by virtue of any process whatever under the laws of this State, the property of every head of a family, or guardian, or trustee of a family of minor children, or every aged or infirm person, or person having the care and support of dependent females of any age, who is not the head of a family, realty or personalty, or both, to the value in the aggregate of sixteen hundred dollars; and the General Assembly shall have authority to provide the manner of exempting said property, the sale, alienation and encumbrance thereof, and to provide for the waiver of said exemption by the debtor.

PARAGRAPH II. *Homestead and Exemption Laws Continued.* The laws now of force with respect to homestead and exemptions shall remain in full force until changed by law.

ARTICLE X

MILITIA

SECTION I

PARAGRAPH I. *Organization of Militia.* A well regulated militia being essential to the peace and security of the State, the General Assembly shall have authority to provide by law how the militia of this State shall be organized, officered, trained, armed and equipped; and of whom it shall consist.

PARAGRAPH II. *Volunteers.* The General Assembly shall have power to authorize the formation of volunteer companies, and to provide for their organization into battalions, regiments, brigades, divisions, and corps, with such restrictions as may be prescribed by law, and shall have authority to arm and equip the same.

PARAGRAPH III. *Pay of Militia and Volunteers.* The officers and men of the militia and volunteer forces shall not be entitled to receive any pay, rations, or emoluments, when not in active service by authority of the State.

PARAGRAPH IV. *Discipline of the Militia.* When not in Federal service the discipline of members of the Militia shall be in accordance with the applicable provisions of the Constitution and laws of the United States, Acts of the General Assembly, and directives of the Governor in his capacity as Commander-in-Chief of the Militia. Notwithstanding any other provisions of this Constitution, the General Assembly shall have the authority to provide for trial by courts-martial and nonjudicial punishment of members of the Militia, for the initiation of charges and subsequent procedures thereon, rules of evidence, venue, and all other matters necessary and proper for the maintenance of a well regulated and disciplined Militia.

[Editorial note: Paragraph IV was added by an amendment ratified on November 8, 1960.]

ARTICLE XI

COUNTIES AND MUNICIPAL CORPORATIONS

SECTION I

PARAGRAPH I. *Counties a Corporate Body; Boundaries.* Each county shall be a body corporate with such powers and limitations as may be prescribed by law. All suits by or against a county shall be in the name thereof; and the metes and bounds of the several counties shall remain as now prescribed by law, unless changed as hereinafter provided.

PARAGRAPH II. *Number Limited.* There shall not be more than one hundred and fifty-nine counties in this State.

PARAGRAPH III. *New Counties Permitted, When.* No new county shall be created except by the consolidation or merger of existing counties.

PARAGRAPH IV. The General Assembly shall have power, with the concurrence of a majority of the qualified voters voting thereon in each of the counties affected, to provide for the consolidation of two or more counties into one, or the merger of one or more counties into another, or the division of a county, and the merger of portions thereof into other counties; provided, however, upon the filing with the Judge of the Probate Court of any county of a petition signed by not less than twenty per centum (20%) of the duly qualified voters of such county, seeking such merger, consolidation or division, it shall be the duty of such Judge of the Probate Court to transmit a certified copy of such petition to each Judge of the Probate Court of all other counties affected thereby, and it shall be the duty of the latter to provide for the publication of such petition, omitting therefrom the names affixed to such petition, in the newspaper in which the sheriff's advertisements are published, once a week for a period of six consecutive weeks. If within a period of two years thereafter, a petition is presented to the Judge of the Probate Court or Judges of the Probate Courts of the other county or counties affected, expressing favor or approval of the original petition, signed by not less than twenty per centum (20%) of the duly qualified voters voting therein, it shall thereupon be the duty of the Judges of the Probate Courts of all such countries affected by such petitions, to certify the fact of such petitions to the Governor, whose duty it shall then be to call immediately an election on the same day in each such county, to be held not later than sixty (60) days, and not sooner than thirty (30) days, after the filing of the last petition, publishing notice thereof once a week for two weeks in the newspaper in each county in which sheriff's advertisements are published. Provided, however, that only one such election shall be called by the Governor within any twelve-month period. The Judges of the Probate Courts of each county shall conduct the election, canvass the returns, and certify the results thereof to the Governor, who shall issue his proclamation thereon, and such results shall become effective at such time as may be prescribed by law, but not later than two (2) years following the date of such election, as hereinafter referred to. Provided, however, any election held pursuant to the call of the Governor hereunder shall be null and void unless 51% of the registered voters of the portion or portions of the counties affected shall have voted in said election. The members of the General Assembly from all such counties shall serve out the remainder of their terms for which elected, and at the Session of the General Assembly next following such election, the county site shall be changed by law, without regard to the provisions of Paragraph IX hereof, and the General Assembly shall likewise provide by law for the effective date of such merger, consolidation or division, as the case may be, subject to the above limitation of two years, and shall provide for the election of county officials, where required. The

General Assembly shall have power to further implement this paragraph by law.

[Editorial note: An amendment ratified on Nov. 3, 1964, repealed Paragraph IV and V and substituted in lieu thereof Paragraph IV as quoted above.]

PARAGRAPH VI. *County Government Uniform; Exceptions.* Whatever tribunal, or officers, may be created by the General Assembly for the transaction of county matters, shall be uniform throughout the State, and of the same name, jurisdiction, and remedies, except that the General Assembly may provide for Commissioners of Roads and Revenues in any county, may abolish the office of County Treasurer in any county, may fix the compensation of County Treasurers, and may consolidate the offices of Tax Receiver and Tax Collector in the office of Tax Commissioner, and may fix his compensation, without respect to uniformity.

PARAGRAPH VII. *Consolidation of Governments; Submission to Voters.* The General Assembly may provide by general law optional systems of consolidated county and municipal government, providing for the organization and the powers and duties of its officers. Such optional systems shall become effective when submitted to the qualified voters of such county and approved by a majority of those voting.

PARAGRAPH VIII. *County Lines.* County lines shall not be changed, unless under the operation of a general law for that purpose.

PARAGRAPH IX. *County Sites Changed; Method.* No county site shall be changed or removed, except by a two-thirds vote of the qualified voters of the county, voting at an election held for that purpose and by a majority vote of the General Assembly.

SECTION II

PARAGRAPH I. *County Officers; Election; Term; Removal; Eligibility.* The county officers shall be elected by the qualified voters of their respective counties or districts, and shall hold their office for four years. They shall be removed upon conviction for malpractice in office; and no person shall be eligible for any of the offices referred to in this paragraph unless he shall have been a resident of the county for two years and is a qualified voter.

PARAGRAPH II. *Compensation of County Officers.* County officers may be on a fee basis, salary basis, or fee basis supplemented by salary, in such manner as may be directed by law.

Section III

Paragraph I. In addition to and supplementary of any powers now conferred upon and possessed by any county, municipality, or any combination thereof, any county, any municipality and any combination of any such political subdivisions may exercise the following powers and provide the following services:

(1) Police and fire protection.

(2) Garbage and solid waste collection and disposal.

(3) Public health facilities and services; including hospitals, ambulance, emergency rescue services, and animal control.

(4) Street and road construction and maintenance; including curbs, sidewalks, street lights and devices to control the flow of traffic on streets and roads constructed by counties and municipalities or any combination thereof.

(5) Parks, recreational areas, programs and facilities.

(6) Storm water and sewage collection and disposal systems.

(7) Development, storage, treatment and purification and distribution of water.

(8) Public housing.

(9) Urban Redevelopment Programs.

(10) Public transportation system.

(11) Planning and zoning.

(12) Libraries.

(13) Terminal and dock facilities and parking facilities.

(14) Building, housing, plumbing, and electrical codes.

(15) Air Pollution Control;

Provided, however, that no City or County may exercise any such powers or provide any such service herein listed inside the boundaries of any other local governments except by contract with the City or County affected unless otherwise provided by any local or special law and no existing local or special laws or provision of this Constitution is intended to be hereby repealed.

Each county and municipality, and any combination thereof, shall have the authority to enact ordinances and to contract with each other in pursuance of this Paragraph and for the purpose of carrying out and effectuating the powers herein conferred upon such political subdivisions and in order to provide such services. Any county, municipality, and any combination thereof, or the General Assembly, may provide for the creation of special districts within which the above services, or any portion thereof, shall be provided, and to determine and fix reasonable charges and fees for such services. In addition, the powers of taxation and assessment may be exercised by any county, municipality or any combination thereof, or within any such district, for the above powers and in order to provide such services.

[Editorial note: Section III was added in 1972.]

Section IV

Paragraph I. *Douglasville-Douglas County Stadium Authority.*

[Editorial note: For details, see Georgia Laws 1974, pp. 1781-1796, ratified as a "general amendment" to the Constitution in 1974.]

ARTICLE XII

THE LAWS OF GENERAL OPERATION IN FORCE IN THIS STATE

SECTION I

PARAGRAPH I. *Supreme Law.* The laws of general operation in this State are, first: As the Supreme law: The Constitution of the United States, the laws of the United States in pursuance thereof and all treaties made under the authority of the United States.

PARAGRAPH II. *Second in Authority.* Second: As next in authority thereto: This Constitution.

PARAGRAPH III. *Third in Authority.* Third: In subordination to the foregoing: All laws now of force in this State, not inconsistent with this Constitution shall remain of force until the same are modified or repealed by the General Assembly.

PARAGRAPH IV. *Local and Private Acts.* Local and private acts passed for the benefit of counties, cities, towns, corporations and private persons, not inconsistent with the Supreme law, nor with this Constitution and which have not expired nor been repealed, shall have the force of Statute law, subject to judicial decision as to their validity when passed, and to any limitations imposed by their own terms.

PARAGRAPH V. *Proceedings of Courts Confirmed.* All judgments, decrees, orders, and other proceedings, of the several courts of this State, heretofore made within the limits of their several jurisdictions, are hereby ratified and affirmed, subject only to reversal by motion for a new trial, appeal, bill of review or other proceedings, in conformity with the law of force when they were made.

PARAGRAPH VI. *Existing Officers.* The officers of the Government now existing shall continue in the exercise of their several functions until their successors are duly elected or appointed and qualified. But nothing herein is to apply to any officer, whose office may be abolished by this Constitution.

ARTICLE XIII

AMENDMENTS TO THE CONSTITUTION

SECTION I

PARAGRAPH I. *Proposals to amend the Constitution; new Constitution; submission to people.* A new Constitution may be proposed by the General Assembly or by a constitutional convention. The proposal by the General Assembly to provide for a new Constitution or to amend this Constitution shall originate as a resolution in either the Senate or the House of Representatives and, if approved by two-thirds of the members elected to each branch of the General Assembly in a roll call vote, such proposal shall be entered on the Journals of each branch with the "Ayes" and "Nays" taken thereon. Any proposal to amend this Constitution or any proposal for a new Constitution may be amended or repealed by the same General Assembly which adopted such proposal by the affirmative vote of two-thirds of the members elected to each branch of the General Assembly in a roll call vote entered on their respective Journals, if such action is taken at least two months prior to the date of the election at which such proposal is to be submitted.

The Governor, the Attorney General, and the Secretary of State shall meet and determine whether a proposed amendment is general, and if not general, shall determine what political subdivision or subdivisions are directly affected by such proposed amendment. If a proposed amendment is general, it shall be published, as provided by law, in full, once each week for three consecutive weeks immediately preceding the date of the election at which such proposed amendment is to be submitted, in one newspaper of general circulation in each Congressional District of the State. If such proposed amendment is not general, it shall be published, as provided by law, in full, once each week for three consecutive weeks immediately preceding the date of the election at which such proposed amendment is to be submitted, in one newspaper of general circulation in each county in which the directly affected political subdivision or subdivisions are located. In the event no such newspaper is located in such county, a newspaper in an adjoining county shall be used. A proposal for a new Constitution shall be published in the same manner as proposed general amendments.

Any proposed amendment which is general or a proposal for a new Constitution shall be submitted to the people of the entire State at the next general election which is held in the even-numbered years, and if ratified by a majority of the electors qualified to vote for members of the General Assembly voting thereon, such amendment shall become a part of this Constitution or shall become the new Constitution, as the case may be. A proposed amendment which is not general shall be submitted at the next general election which is held in the even-numbered years, but shall only be submitted to the people of the political subdivision or subdivisions directly affected. The votes of the electors in each political subdivision affected shall be counted separately in determining whether such proposed amendment is ratified, and it must be ratified by a majority of the electors qualified to vote for members of the General Assembly voting thereon in each such political subdivision before it shall become a part of this Constitution. The General Assembly, in the resolution, shall state the language to be used in submitting the proposed amendment or proposal for a new Constitution. When more than one amendment is submitted at the same time, they shall be so submitted as to enable the electors to vote on each amendment separately, but this shall not apply to a proposal for a new Constitution.

[Editorial note: Paragraph I was altered by amendments of 1956 and 1968.]

PARAGRAPH II. *Convention, How Called.* No convention of the people shall be called by the General Assembly to revise, amend or change this Constitution, unless by the concurrence of two-thirds of all members of each house of the General Assembly. The representation in said convention shall be based on population as near as practicable. This Constitution shall not be revised, amended, or changed by the Convention until the proposed revision, amendment, or change has been submitted and ratified by the people in the manner provide for submission and ratification of amendments proposed by the General Assembly.

PARAGRAPH III. *Veto Not Permitted.* The Governor shall not have the right to veto any proposal by the General Assembly to provide a new Constitution or to amend this Constitution.

PARAGRAPH IV. *Effective Date of Amendments.* Unless the amendment itself shall provide otherwise, an amendment to this Constitution shall become effective on the first day of January following its ratification.

[Editorial note: Paragraph IV was added in 1970.]

ARTICLE XIV
MERIT SYSTEM

SECTION I

PARAGRAPH I. *State Personnel Board.* A non-salaried State Personnel Board comprised of three citizens of this State, of known interest in the improvement of public administration, shall administer a State Merit System under which state personnel shall be selected on a basis of merit, fitness, and efficiency according to law. The members of the State Personnel Board shall be appointed by the Governor with the advice of the Senate. The first members shall be appointed for terms of three, five and seven years, respectively, the terms to be designated by the Governor. All subsequent appointments shall be for a period of seven years, except unexpired terms. No State official or employee shall be a member of the State Personnel Board.

PARAGRAPH II. *Retirement System. Appropriation.* The General Assembly is authorized to establish an actuarially sound retirement system for employees under a merit system. Adequate appropriations shall be provided for the operation of a merit system and the State Personnel Board.

ARTICLE XV
HOME RULE

SECTION I

PARAGRAPH I. The General Assembly is authorized to provide by law for the self-government of municipalities and to that end is hereby expressly given the authority to delegate its powers so that matters pertaining to municipalities upon which, prior to the ratification of this amendment, it was necessary for the General Assembly to act, may be dealt with without the necessity of action by the General Assembly. Any powers granted as provide herein shall be exercised subject only to statutes of general application pertaining to municipalities.

[Editorial note: By an amendment ratified on November 2, 1954, the original home rule provision of the Constitution was stricken in its entirety and replaced by the above provision.]

SECTION II

PARAGRAPH I. *Home Rule for Counties.* (a) The governing authority of each county shall have legislative power to adopt clearly reasonable ordinances, resolutions or regulations relating to its property, affairs and local government for which no provision has been made by general law and which is not inconsistent with this Constitution, or any local law applicable thereto. Any such local law shall remain in force and effect until amended or repealed as provided in Subparagraph (b). This, however, shall not restrict the authority of the General Assembly by general law to further define this power or to broaden, limit or otherwise regulate the exercise thereof. The General Assembly shall not pass any local law to repeal, modify or supersede any action taken by a county governing authority under this Section except as authorized under Subparagraph (c) hereof.

(b) Except as provided in Subparagraph (c), a county may, as an incident of its home rule power, amend or repeal the local acts applicable to its governing authority by following either of the procedures hereinafter set forth:

1. Such local acts may be amended or repealed by a resolution or ordinance duly adopted at two regular consecutive meetings of the county governing authority not less than seven nor more than sixty days apart. A notice containing a synopsis of the proposed amendment or repeal shall be published in the official county organ once a week for three weeks within a period of sixty days immediately preceding its final adoption. Such notice shall state that a copy of the proposed amendment or repeal is on file in the office of the clerk of the superior court of the county for the purpose of examination and inspection by the public. The Clerk of the Superior Court shall furnish anyone, upon written request, a copy of the proposed amendment or repeal. No amendment or repeal hereunder shall be valid to change or repeal an amendment adopted pursuant to a referendum as provided in 2 of this Subparagraph or to change or repeal a local act of the General Assembly ratified in a referendum by the electors of such county unless at least twelve months have elapsed after such referendum. No amendment hereunder shall be valid if inconsistent with any provision of this Constitution or if provision has been made therefore by general law.

2. Amendments to or repeals of such local acts or ordinances, resolutions or regulations adopted pursuant to Subparagraph (a) hereof may be initiated by a petition filed with the Judge of the Probate Court of the county containing in cases of counties with a population of five thousand or less, the signatures of at least twenty-five per centum of the electors registered to vote in the last general election; in cases of counties with a population of more than five thousand but not more than fifty thousand, at least twenty per centum of the electors registered to vote in the last general election; and in cases of a county with a population of more than fifty thousand, at least ten per centum of the electors registered to vote in the last general election, which petition shall specifically set forth the exact language of the

proposed amendment or repeal. The Judge of the Probate Court shall determine the validity of such petition within 60 days of its being filed with the Judge of the Probate Court. In the event the Judge of the Probate Court determines that such petition is valid, it shall be his duty to issue the call for an election for the purpose of submitting such amendment or repeal to the registered electors of the county for their approval or rejection. Such call shall be issued not less than ten nor more than sixty days after the date of the filing of the petition. He shall set the date of such election for a day not less than sixty nor more than ninety days after the date of such filing. The Judge of the Probate Court shall cause a notice of the date of said election to be published in the official organ of the county once a week for three weeks immediately preceding such date. Said notice shall also contain a synopsis of the proposed amendment or repeal and shall state that a copy thereof is on file in the office of the Judge of the Probate Court of the county for the purpose of examination and inspection by the public. The Judge of the Probate Court shall furnish anyone, upon written request, a copy of the proposed amendment or repeal. If more than one-half of the votes cast on such question are for approval of the amendment or repeal, it shall become of full force and effect, otherwise it shall be void and of no force and effect. The expense of such election shall be borne by the county and it shall be the duty of the Judge of Probate Court to hold and conduct such election. Such election shall be held under the same laws and rules and regulations as govern special elections, except as otherwise provided herein. It shall be the duty of the Judge of the Probate Court to canvass the returns and declare and certify the result of the election. It shall be his further duty to certify the result thereof to the Secretary of State in accordance with the provisions of Paragraph 4 of this Section. A referendum on any such amendment or repeal shall not be held more often than once each year. No amendment hereunder shall be valid if inconsistent with any provision of this Constitution or if provision has been made therefore by general law.

In the event that the Judge of the Probate Court determines that such petition was not valid, he shall cause to be published in explicit detail the reasons why such petition is not valid: Provided, however, that in any proceeding in which the validity of the petition is at issue, the tribunal considering such issue shall not be limited by the reasons assigned. Such publication shall be in the official organ of the county in the week immediately following the date on which such petition is declared to be not valid.

(c) The power granted to counties in Subparagraphs

(a) and (b) above shall not be construed to extend to the following matters or any other matters which the General Assembly by general law has preempted or may hereafter preempt, but such matters shall be the subject of general law, or the subject of local acts of the General Assembly to the extent that the enactment of such local acts is otherwise permitted under this Constitution:

1. Action affecting any elective county office, the salaries thereof, or the personnel thereof, except the personnel subject to the jurisdiction of the county governing authority.

2. Action affecting the composition, form, procedure for election or appointment, compensation, and expenses and allowances in the nature of compensation, of the county governing authority.

3. Action defining any criminal offense or providing for criminal punishment.

4. Action adopting any form of taxation beyond that authorized by law or by this Constitution.

5. Action expanding the power of regulation over any business activity regulated by the Public Service Commission beyond that authorized by local or general law or by this Constitution.

6. Action affecting the exercise of the power of eminent domain.

7. Action affecting any court or the personnel thereof.

8. Action affecting any public school system.

(d) The power granted in Subparagraphs (a) and (b) of this Paragraph shall not include the power to take any action affecting the private or civil law governing private or civil relationships, except as is incident to the exercise of an independent governmental power.

(e) Nothing in this Paragraph shall affect the provisions of Paragraphs 2 and 3 of this Section.

PARAGRAPH II. *Salary of County Employees; How Fixed.* The governing authority of each county is authorized to fix the salary, compensation and expenses of those employed by such governing authority and to establish and maintain retirement or pension systems, insurance, workmen's compensation, and hospitalization benefits for said employees.

PARAGRAPH III. *County Planning and Zoning.* The governing authority of each county is empowered to enact for unincorporated areas of the county appropriate planning and zoning ordinances for public safety, historic, health, business, residential, and recreational purposes. Such governing authority is hereby authorized to establish planning and zoning commissions separately or in conjunction with any combination of other counties and municipalities of this State and adjoining states. The General Assembly is hereby authorized to provide by law for such joint planning and zoning commissions and provide the powers and duties thereof. Such governing authority is hereby authorized to participate in the costs of such planning commission.

PARAGRAPH IV. *Filing and Publication of Laws.* No amendment or revision of any local act made pursuant to Paragraph 1 of this Section shall become effective until a copy of such amendment or revision, a copy of the required notice of publication, and an affidavit of a duly authorized representative of the newspaper in which such notice was published to the effect that said notice has been published as provided in said Paragraph, has been filed with the Secretary of State. The Secretary of State shall provide for the publication and distribution of all such amendments and revisions at least annually.

PARAGRAPH V. The powers granted by this amendment shall be cumulative of all powers heretofore granted to counties by the Constitution of Georgia of 1945 and amendments thereto. and this amendment shall not operate to repeal any existing local constitutional amendments.

[Editorial note: All of Section II was added by an amendment ratified Nov. 8 1966.]

ARTICLE XVI

SLUM CLEARANCE AND REDEVELOPMENT

The General Assembly may provide by law that any city or town, or any housing authority now or hereafter established, or any county may undertake and carry out slum clearance and redevelopment work, including the acquisition and clearance of areas which are predominantly slum or blighted areas, the preparation of such areas for re-use, and the sale or other disposition of such areas to private enterprise for private uses or to public bodies for public uses. Any such work shall constitute a governmental function undertaken for public purposes, and the powers of taxation and eminent domain may be exercised and public funds expended in furtherance thereof.

[Editorial note: This article was added by an amendment ratified on November 2, 1954.]

The General Assembly may establish procedures whereby any municipal corporation having a population of more than 400,000 according to the last or any future United States Decennial Census may carry out and enforce the removal or demolition or closing of buildings or structures, and clearing of premises, not of necessity a part of any slum or blighted area, at public expense, after an administrative determination that a building or structure is unfit for human habitation, or is unfit for commercial, industrial or business occupancy or use and is economically unrepairable, under standards for such determination as prescribed by the General Assembly, and which may provide for commencement of an administrative proceeding in rem provided the owner and person having an interest in the real property involved are given notice and an opportunity to appear and be heard on the question of unfitness or unrepairability of the building or structure at issue. All expenses of such removal or demolition, or closing and clearing of premises and all costs of any such proceeding may be included in the amount of the lien against the property on which the building or structure is located. All such proceedings and work shall constitute and are hereby declared to be a governmental function undertaken for public purposes, and the powers of taxation and eminent domain may be exercised and public funds expended in furtherance thereof.

[Editorial note: The paragraph on municipalities over 400,000 was added in 1974.]

ARTICLE XVII

PUBLIC TRANSPORTATION OF PASSENGERS FOR HIRE

SECTION I

Public Transportation of Passengers for Hire in the Metropolitan Area of Atlanta

PARAGRAPH I. The acquisition, establishment, operation or administration of a system of public transportation of passengers for hire within the metropolitan area of the City of Atlanta and the Counties of Fulton, DeKalb, Cobb, Clayton and Gwinett, is an essential governmental function and a public purpose for which the powers of taxation and eminent domain may be exercised and public funds of said counties and municipality expended.

PARAGRAPH II. The General Assembly may create a public corporation or authority as an instrumentality of the City of Atlanta and the Counties of Fulton, DeKalb, Cobb, Clayton and Gwinnett, or any one or any combination thereof, to perform the aforesaid function, to have the power of eminent domain, the power to borrow money and issue obligations payable from its revenues, and such other powers as may be necessary or convenient for the accomplishment of the aforesaid function and purpose.

PARAGRAPH III. The General Assembly may provide that such public corporation or authority, as an instrumentality of the participating counties and municipality, its property, acts, activities, income and obligations and the interest thereon, shall be exempt from any tax obligations and from regulation by any agency or commission of the State.

PARAGRAPH IV. The General Assembly may authorize the City of Atlanta, and the Counties of Fulton, DeKalb, Cobb, Clayton and Gwinnett to contract with such public corporation or authority for the performance of the aforesaid function and purpose; to pay for the public transportation services and facilities contracted for, including the payment of the principal and interest on any obligations issued by such public corporation or authority in order to acquire the necessary facilities and property therefor and in connection therewith to establish and maintain reasonable reserves; to levy taxes to the extent necessary to fulfill the obligation incurred in such contracts; and to convey to such public corporation or authority property or facilities, or render services, which may be useful to the establishment, operation or administration of a public transportation system within the aforesaid metropolitan area; provided that no county shall have the power to levy any tax on any subject of taxation situated within the territorial limits of any incorporated municipality which has a contract with said public corporation or authority and is itself levying a tax for that purpose.

PARAGRAPH V. The provisions of this article shall be liberally construed to effectuate its purpose and shall not be limited or restricted by any existing provision of or amendment to this Constitution, or any general or special law heretofore enacted, and the authority granted by this Article to the General Assembly may be exercised by general, special or local laws without regard to uniformity.

[Editorial note: Article XVII was added in 1964.]

TABLE OF AMENDMENTS

	Number Proposed		Number Ratified		Number Rejected	
Year	General	Special	General	Special	General	Special
1946	1	0	0	0	1	0
1948	0	17	0	15	0	2
1950	4	33	2	26	2	7
1952	10	36	9	31	1	5
1954	7	40	7	28	0	12
1956	12	46	12	36	0	10
1958	16	56	5	38	11	18
1960	19	68	14	50	5	18
1962	16	121	10	99	6	23
1964	14	103	12	76	2	27
1966	19	93	17	63	2	30
1968	23	106	19	88	4	18
1970	15	48	6	29	9	19
1972	24	70	22	53	2	17
1974	16	63	12	52	4	11
Total	196	900	147	684	49	217

Total number of amendments to 1975: 831

NOTE: For a brief analysis of these amendments in chronological order, see *Local Amendments to the Constitutions of 1877 and 1945.* Atlanta: Office of Legislative Counsel, 1961. See also "Constitutional Amendments," *Georgia State Bar Journal*, February, 1969, pp. 331-345.

Questions on the Constitution of Georgia

PART I

History and Fundamental Principals

1. Give a general account of the constitution history of Georgia, including the dates of the adoption of new constitutions.
2. Explain fully the meaning of "constitutional government," including a distinction between constitutional law and statutory law.
3. Explain the principle of "the separation of powers" and "checks and balances," including illustrations.
4. Write an essay on the method used in framing the Constitution of 1945, showing how this method differed from the the conventional method of framing constitutions, and evaluating the merits of the procedure.
5. Write a critical essay on the Constitution of Georgia, pointing out its strengths and weaknesses and proposing such changes as you consider desirable.

PART II

The Constitution As An Objective Document

I. *Bill of Rights*

1. What purpose is served by a bill of rights?
2. List several provisions of the Bill of Rights and comment upon their meaning.
3. Explain the meaning of the following terms: (1) due process of law, (2) double jeopardy, (3) writ of *habeas corpus*, (4) treason, (5) corruption of blood, (6) lobbying, (7) *ex post facto laws*, (8) bill of attainder, (9) judicial review, (10) libel.
4. Does the Constitution provide for judicial review? Explain.

II. *Article II*

1. Who can vote in Georgia? Explain the procedure for registration.

III. *Article III*

1. How many members are there in the General Assembly?

2. What is the basis of the apportionment of representation in the House? in the Senate?
3. What is the term of representatives? Of senators?
4. How often are sessions of the General Assembly held, and how long does a session last?
5. State the provisions made for special sessions of the General Assembly.
6. Give the qualifications of both representatives and senators.
7. Describe the process of impeachment.
8. Discuss the privileges of members of the General Assembly.
9. What limitation is placed upon the provisions of the general appropriation bill? When does a general appropriation act expire?
10. Can members of the General Assembly be appointed to executive offices?
11. What difference is there between the vote necessary to pass a bill in the General Assembly of Georgia and the vote necessary to pass a bill in Congress?
12. Summarize the limitations on local legislation.
13. What is the compensation of members of the General Assembly? Can the General Assembly change the compensation of its own members? Of other State officials?

IV. *Article IV*

1. Give the composition and function of the Public Service Commission.
2. What is the significance of the provision that the renewal or amendment of a charter will make it subject to the provisions of the Constitution?
3. What provisions are stated for the protection of policy holders of insurance companies?
4. Explain the terms "eminent domain" and "police power".
5. Can the General Assembly make the property of a wife liable for the debts of her husband?

V. *Article V*

1. List the executive officers named in the Constitution and comment upon the function of each.
2. Name the executive boards established by the Constitution and give the composition and function of each.
3. Are the powers of the executive boards named in the Constitution subject to the control of the General Assembly?
4. How is the Governor elected?

5. What is the term of the Governor? Is he eligible to succeed himself? What is his salary?
6. Discuss the succession to the governorship.
7. Discuss the following aspects of the Governor's power: (1) appointments, (2) removal, (3) veto (including the "pocket veto"), (4)pardons.

VI. *Article VI*

1. In what courts are the judicial powers of the State vested? Give the composition and jurisdiction of each.

VII. *Article VII*

1. Is the paragraph entitled "Taxation, a sovereign right" of any importance?
2. Summarize the limitations on the purposes and amount of taxation by both the State and its political subdivisions.
3. Summarize the limitations on debts that may be incurred by the State or by its political subdivisions.

VIII. *Article VIII*

1. Give the composition of each of the following: (1) State Board of Education, (2) Board of Regents, (3) County Board of Education.

IX. *Article IX*

1. Summarize the provisions and explain the meaning of Article IX, "Homesteads and Exemptions."

X. *Article X.*

1. Is there any provision of importance in Article X, "The Militia"?

XI. *Article XI*

1. Explain the legal status of a county.
2. How many counties are there in Georgia? How could this number be reduced?
3. List the county officers named in the Constitution and comment upon the function of each. How are they chosen? For what term? How are they paid?

XII. *Article XII*

1. What are the laws of general operation in Georgia? In case of conflict, which law prevails?

XIII. *Article XIII*

1. How can the Constitution be amended? Is this process too easy? (Give reasons for your answer.)
2. How could a new constitution be framed for Georgia?

XIV. *Article XIV*

1. State the provisions of Article XIV and explain whether you think they will be effective in giving Georgia a true merit system.

XV. *Article XV*

1. Do you consider the "Home Rule" provision as now stated in the Constitution as surplusage? (Explain your answer.)

XVI. *Article XVI*

1. Why was the "Slum Clearance" article adopted and what does it state?

BIBLIOGRAPHY

Chart of Georgia State Government, revised periodically and published by the Institute of Government, University of Georgia, Athens, Ga.

The Code of Georgia, available in multi-volume annotated edition, and a one volume unannotated edition, revised frequently and sold by the Harrison Company, Atlanta, Ga.

Coulter, E. Merton, *Georgia, A Short History*. Chapel Hill: University of North Carolina Press, 1947.

Georgia Statistical Abstract, revised frequently and published by the Bureau of Business Research, University of Georgia, Athens, Ga.

Georgia Election Code, revised frequently and distributed by the office of the Secretary of State, State Capitol, Atlanta, Ga.

Georgia Official Directory of State and County Officers, revised frequently and distributed by the Secretary of State.

Georgia Official and Statistical Register, revised biennially and published by the Department of Archives and History, Atlanta, Ga.

Gibson, Frank and T. L. Hammock, *Forms of City Government in Georgia*. Institute of Government, University of Georgia, 1957.

Saye, Albert B., *A Constitutional History of Georgia*. Athens: University of Georgia Press, 1970.

Sentell, R. Perry, *Handbook for Legislators*. Athens: Institute of Government, 1974.

Turnbull, Augustus B., *Selected Bibliography on Georgia Government*. Athens: Institute of Government, 1968.